INTERNATIONAL SOCIAL WORK: THEMES AND PERSPECTIVES

To Paul, Kevin and Claire – you have provided stimulus and support (and sometimes distractions!) throughout my working life, not least in the endeavours which have resulted in this book. Thank you.

International Social Work: Themes and Perspectives

Karen Lyons

Ashgate
ARENA

Aldershot • Burlington USA • Singapore • Sydney

Published by
Ashgate Publishing Limited
Gower House
Croft Road
Aldershot
Hants GU11 3HR
England

Ashgate Publishing Company
131 Main Street
Burlington, VT 05401-5600 USA

Ashgate website:http://www.ashgate.com

Reprinted 2000

British Library Cataloguing in Publication Data
Lyons, Karen
　International social work : themes and perspectives
　1. Social service
　I. Title
　361.3'2

Library of Congress Cataloging-in-Publication Data
Lyons, K. H. (Karen Hamilton), 1944–
　International social work : themes and perspectives / Karen Lyons.
　　p.　cm.
　Includes bibliographical references.
　ISBN 1-85742-389-5 (hc.)
　1. Social service–Cross-cultural studies.　2. Social service–
International cooperation.　3. International agencies.　I. Title.
　HV41.L98　1998
　361.2'6–dc21   98-35470
                                                                          CIP

ISBN 1 85742 389 5

Typeset by Manton Typesetters, 5–7 Eastfield Road, Louth, Lincs, LN11 7AJ, UK.

Printed and bound in Great Britain by Biddles Limited,
Guildford and King's Lynn.

Contents

Preface

From my earliest studies in geography and involvement as an undergraduate in international workcamps and a World Student Christian Federation conference, I have been fascinated by the commonalities and diversity in the human condition, and by the responses to issues which confront individual societies and cross national borders. An early choice to pursue qualifications in social welfare and then social work rather than international relations rooted me in the UK, and in fact in the East End of London.

A family tradition of migration gave me some feeling for the impact of population mobility on individuals and groups, which was heightened by my initial professional experience in school social work and by links with others in that field in Europe and the US. As an academic in the 1980s, I was involved in curriculum developments relating both to the recognition of racism and other forms of discrimination in the UK (and acutely felt in East London) and to the increasing regionalisation being brought about by European policies and impacting on higher education through exchange schemes.

It was the bringing together of these two strands which motivated the establishment in the early 1990s of a one-year programme about international social work. As part of this programme, students undertake a three-month project outside the UK, in a country and on a topic of their own choosing. The course not only required me to develop specific teaching material but has also resulted in the presentation by students of a wealth of comparative data and perspectives on welfare systems, social work and their experiences (as 'temporary outsiders') across a range of societies.

Meanwhile, periodic opportunities to participate, in various capacities, in national, regional and international activities have enabled me to establish professional relationships with others in the field and in academic work across five continents. Many colleagues have been similarly engaged in the development of regional and international exchange, knowledge, policies and practice while others have enriched my understanding of more local problems and approaches.

My debts therefore are many and diffuse (in time and space) and the singling out of individuals for thanks would be invidious. Periodic intentions to undertake a systematic analysis of the (boxes of) notes accumulated from my own travels and later of student assignments, which might have resulted in individual acknowledgements, have proved quite impractical! In any case recent years have seen a growth in literature which is central or adjacent to the themes of this book, some of which is formally referenced in the pages which follow. Additionally, in an age of mass communications, information about changing concerns and events is disseminated by items in the press, media and Internet, not to mention official reports and agency literature.

This book represents, therefore, the bringing together from many sources of ideas about issues which I think are pertinent to the development of international social work, and aims to encourage the greater recognition of globalisation as relevant to the concerns and work of social professionals in myriad roles and places. I have avoided use of the word 'millennium' in this text but clearly there are significant uncertainties for many in the world at this time, which, however, will not be resolved by the passing from one century to another (according to the Western calendar). The challenges to social professionals involved in researching, designing and implementing welfare programmes, in demonstrating the way economic, political and technological decisions impact on vulnerable people and in educating others, for these tasks will continue to be considerable. I believe that increased understanding of global forces and opportunities for international exchange and action will assist in these processes.

In conclusion then, I acknowledge the incalculable contribution of past and present students at the University of East London and of the many colleagues at home and abroad, who have consciously or unwittingly informed my thinking and influenced my perceptions about comparative and international social work. At a more prosaic level, thanks are due to Kevin Lyons for technical assistance with the production of this text from one who has recognised the need for social professionals to be IT literate but who is still learning in this field – as in many others!

Karen Lyons
London, June 1998

Introduction: defining the area

This book aims to advance ideas about the nature of international social work and to provide theoretical and illustrative material as a basis for developing its practice. It argues that even an activity apparently so intimately linked to the socio-economic characteristics and culture (or cultures) of a given country must recognise the impact of globalisation and of regional policies on the welfare of citizens in diverse societies. Additionally, there is a place for social work activity which is more explicitly cross-national or international in its form. While leaders in the field have historically been aware of social work developments elsewhere and have often been active at an international level, recent rapid globalisation has impacted on social welfare as much as on other aspects of daily life, and now requires all social workers to place their local activities in a wider frame, or, in some cases, to operate outside or across political boundaries.

This opening chapter examines some of the concepts and contextual factors which underpin the development of international social work, and reviews briefly some of the commonalities and international aspects of the historical origins of social work, before discussing the purpose and nature of social work as a local and global profession. The concluding section summarises the rationale for 'internationalising' social work and outlines the content of the remaining chapters.

The book is aimed both at those new to the idea of international social work and those who may already be engaged in this pursuit in some way. It necessarily focuses on selected themes and issues to the exclusion of others, and in this sense it is introductory rather than comprehensive in its coverage, identifying specific areas as a basis for developing research and practice knowledge. The book does not aim to provide a comparative view of social work as a world-wide but nationally based activity, although there are many comparative examples in the text, and use has been made of some of the existing literature, much of which uses comparative methodology or perspectives to analyse social welfare and social work.

Similarly this book is not intended to provide a world view of social work or a prescription for international social work from an exclusively British (or even European) perspective. However, the writer's own nationality, language and access to literature and other resources, inevitably influence the assumptions made and examples used. So far as possible, assumptions are articulated and examples are drawn from across five continents, as described in the literature, press or agency material or as gleaned from experience and exchange in a range of countries and at regional and international level.

The global context and social change

Social work has traditionally been seen as a local, 'culture-bound' activity (Lorenz 1994; Payne 1991), specific to a given time and place; clearly there is an essential relationship between much social work practice and the nature, needs and requirements of the society in which the activity takes place. But in the concluding decades of the twentieth century, even countries which had previously been regarded as isolated or independent, homogeneous and stable, have been subject increasingly to external, international economic forces; and many have experienced rapid social change and increased diversity internally. Such changes have posed challenges to social policy and welfare provision, with direct implications for the organisation and practice of social work and community development.

Changes have occurred at a global level in relation to political, ideological, economic, technological and environmental conditions, the effects of which have penetrated every society. Increased economic and political interdependence has been reflected in the growth in number, size and influence of cross-national networks and organisations, ranging from multinational industrial and commercial corporations to international and regional political groupings. Alongside, or sometimes in opposition to, these powerful bodies, non-governmental organisations (hereafter NGOs) and voluntary associations represent sectional interests, often concerned with environmental or welfare issues.

Among the political changes, the virtual end of colonialism (in political form), the collapse of communism in the former Soviet Union (hereafter FSU) and Central/East European countries, and the formal ending of apartheid in South Africa, for instance, pose new challenges and opportunities for particular countries, including changes in their external relationships. Elsewhere, the increased role of the European Union has entailed shifts in the power of the local and national states, relative to each other and to the rest of the world. In some regions, for example Central Africa and the Balkan states, the world has seen a 'tribalisation' of politics and an increased emphasis on nationality, religion, race, ethnicity and/or culture as sources of collective and individual identity, entailing, in some cases, the revision of political boundaries and systems, and/or the displacement of huge populations (White et al. 1997).

While the change from communism to independent states with free market economies represented major political and ideological change in large areas of eastern Europe and central Asia and altered fundamentally the nature of international relations, other ideological shifts have been more varied in their influence. Feminism has been an important thread in recent thinking and this and other movements concerned with the rights of minorities have had significant impact at legislative level in some societies. However, in many parts of the world, the vulnerable or inferior position of women, racial or ethnic minority groups, or others deemed 'different', has changed little (Van Wormer 1997). The rhetoric of 'valuing difference' adopted by some of the world's global corporations has yet to impact on many societies and populations.

Elsewhere ideology is closely related to religion, and age-old tensions between people of different religious belief (or of factions within particular religions) are related to ongoing conflicts, for example in the Middle East, the Asian subcontinent and Northern Ireland. Even when not associated with overt conflict, religious convictions influence the course of elections and policy developments in countries as diverse as the United States of America (hereafter the US) and Turkey; religious beliefs affect the attitudes of host societies to minority communities in many countries of the world. The possibility of global strife related to political differences, apparent in the Cold War period, has been replaced by a struggle for dominance, related, in part at least, to religious ideology (Esposito 1992; Ehteshami 1997). While the rise of Islamic fundamentalism is sometimes seen by 'the West' as the source of such problems, the consequences of other forms of religious or sectarian bigotry are evident in many societies.

In the economic sphere the growth of multinational companies, or more recently global corporations (Axford 1995), has already been mentioned, and some would see their influence, coupled with the increasing pressure on all governments to be economically competitive, as the basis of global changes in the labour market. These changes have included increased unemployment, under-employment, job insecurity and deterioration in wages and working conditions in countries regarded as wealthy and advanced, with a concomitant increase in the gap between the 'haves' and the 'have-nots' in all societies, and pressures on states or voluntary organisations to provide for those outside the workforce.

At a global level the differential pace of industrialisation and economic growth, while making some countries attractive as a source of 'cheap labour', also invites the intervention of external bodies such as the World Bank or of NGOs offering 'aid' programmes to counteract the worst effects of poverty, and/or to ensure political stability. Additionally, economic change in one country or region has repercussions across the world, as the recession among the Asian 'tiger economies' demonstrated in 1997/98.

Technological developments, particularly in the form of (mass) air transport, electronics, telecommunications and information technology have given rise to rapid or instantaneous communication possibilities and have made the world a smaller place for many. However, such advances have also contributed to the deepening socio-economic divisions, since the opportunities for individuals to participate in the 'information society', and related job prospects and international exchange, are heavily dependent on educational and economic status, both within and between different countries and continents.

Finally, the problems of environmental pollution and climate change and the need for sustainable development have been raised, initially mainly by NGOs, and are making their way onto international political agendas, again with varying attention at national levels (Vogler 1997). The extent to which all humankind is dependent on clean air and water, and on adequate food, shelter and power supplies, the risks to these commodities in some of the current policies and practices, and the interconnectedness of economic/industrial activity and consumption patterns in different parts of the world, are being increasingly recognised as having implications for social work (Hoff and McNutt 1994).

It is in this context of change at international level that national governments seek to promote the welfare, or at least to maintain the harmony and productivity, of their populations, and that social work in some form or other is given a mandate, in most cases, to provide care or control for vulnerable or deviant individuals and groups. But before proceeding to a summary of the international dimensions of the origins and roles of social work, some of the assumptions underpinning this text are further discussed in relation to the concept of *globalisation*.

According to Richards (1997) the term 'globalisation', the buzz word of the 1990s, was first coined by Modelski, an international affairs specialist, in the early 1970s to describe 'the process by which previously discrete societies come into contact with and influence each other' (p.19): another writer attributed the seminal work to Wallerstein (1974), 'who argued that the expansion of the capitalist world economy has given rise to a single "world system"'(Trevillion 1997:1). Richards (1997) described how the term has now taken on a range of meanings, dependent on the standpoint of the user. To a geographer it implies the compression of time and place incurred in rapid and frequent movements of people and information; to a cultural anthropologist it signifies the world-wide spread of McDonald's and Coke, and the dominance of the English/American language; while to the economist it signals the triumph of free trade and the development of global corporations and markets.

The significant point about globalisation is the extent to which various processes are interrelated and interact on each other, but, as Richards (1997) suggests, the economic aspects of globalisation have had the most impact, to the point where nation-states and national economies are rendered almost powerless. While some see evidence of increasing regionalisation as a countervailing trend to the effects of globalisation (Smith 1997), there is considerable debate about the role of the state and governments in the new global order, and the extent to which government policies, including minimum wage levels and cuts in public spending, are justified on the grounds of global competitiveness.

In similar vein, Axford (1995) has described globalisation as 'a multidimensional process, [which should be] analysed by making connections between the personal and the global, even where that requires abjuring conventional levels of analysis' (p.ix) and he cites Robertson's (1992) definition of globalisation as 'the process by which the world is being made into a single place with systemic qualities' (Axford 1995:5). Like Robertson, he links the economic and political processes evident in globalisation to culture change; and sees globalisation as a dynamic state, 'fluid' and 'contingent ... [upon the] interactions within and between societal and inter-societal systems' (p.8).

Such language is not unfamiliar to social workers acquainted with systems theory or interactional analysis, for whom Wright Mills' (1959) evocative linking of 'private troubles' and 'public issues' has long had resonance; and it suggests that an increased understanding of the social consequences of globalisation is not only essential for national, regional and world-wide policy-making bodies, but also an important stage in the development of international social work. Perhaps to the social worker globalisation is evident in the poor socio-economic status and attendant health and housing problems of immigrant families; or the ethical dilemmas presented by cross-national adoptions or child abductions; or the challenges to traditional communities posed by international companies pursuing logging activities; or the ready availability and use of drugs by disaffected youth on urban estates; or child prostitution in response to both local economic need and demand from tourists. But on a more theoretical level, it has been argued that social work was a product of 'the first wave of globalisation' and is now (in Europe) going through a transition from 'the old globalism of social engineering [to] the new globalism of networks and markets' and that the future shape of social work 'in the new discourses of welfare' is unclear (Trevillion 1997:7–8).

Origins of social work at national and international level

The evolution of social work as a distinct activity has been closely related to the development of state intervention and provision in the broad field of *social welfare*, a term used here to include policies related to health, education, housing and income support measures as well as community development or more narrowly defined social services. Social work often developed initially in relation to these other types of welfare provision, as well as having independent roots in the voluntary sector. In Europe and North America, social work had its origins in the late nineteenth century in the processes of industrialisation and urbanisation, with their resultant poverty and poor health and living conditions of large numbers of people. Elsewhere it has developed during the twentieth century at varying pace, but often in response to similar processes and resultant social problems.

While a more sophisticated comparative analysis of the history of social work would reveal differences in the timing and form of particular developments, the common threads of altruistic 'charity work' and attempts to make more humane some of the institutions of social control, such as workhouses, prisons and asylums, are recognisable across a number of countries. Similarly there is evidence of the involvement or close association of social workers in early 'research' into the circumstances of particular population groups, and of their role in *social action*, that is, attempting to address the structural causes of problems through policy change. Thus, social work can be seen as having three strands broadly corresponding to the care, control and change functions still apparent in various forms of social work (Suin de Boutemard 1990; Lorenz 1994; Van Wormer 1997).

In terms of 'methodology' or focus, different social work approaches have been identified, particularly a field-based casework tradition (exemplified, for instance, in the work of the Charity Organisation Society in both Britain and the US); group and community work approaches (as evident in the Settlement movement in Europe and the US), and also 'child rescue' services, variously based on residential provision, or on fostering or adoption arrangements, including in this century policies of 'exporting children' to the former colonies, such as Canada and Australia. More recently there has been a shift away from 'paternalistic' and 'expert' approaches, consequent upon wider social movements originating in the 1960s, towards practice underpinned by the concepts of concientization and empowerment. This was illustrated in the rise, mainly in the 1970s, of 'radical social work' or community social work in Europe and the US, sometimes informed by feminist and/or black perspectives; and also in the more widespread community development and social action approaches which have evolved in Latin American countries, such as Brazil (O'Gorman 1992).

In a recent consideration of the history of social work within the European context, Lorenz (1994) usefully identified the different philosophical underpinnings of early social work evident in many European countries, and identified these as related to Christian, philanthropic, feminist and socialist ideals. Other religions have also provided the basis of social welfare provision elsewhere, usually prior to the development of state provision and more formalised types of social work. To some extent these motivations were identified in an earlier account of the role of women in the evolution of social work in the UK (Walton 1975); throughout the world, social work has been closely associated with a move of women from the domestic sphere into voluntary work or employment in a field seen as compatible with their 'nature' and traditional roles, or in Suin de Boutemard's phrase, 'motherliness as a profession' (1990:263).

Indeed most of the early leaders of social work and social work education were women in Europe and North America, and to some extent this tradition has continued in the later development of social work elsewhere, for instance in some of the South American countries. Van Wormer (1997), in an account of the development of social work in the US, singled out Mary Stewart (Britain), Jane Addams and Mary Richmond (the US), and Alice Salomon (Germany) as among those who shared ideas and laid the bases of social work provision and education in the late nineteenth century and early twentieth century; and noted that Salomon and a later leader, Eileen Younghusband, were active in the League of Nations and United Nations, respectively.

Linked to the emergence of social work as a paid activity was the development of education and training for social work, also taking place in Europe and the US around the turn of the twentieth century. Apart from the significant role which women played in the establishment of social work education, often in women-only schools outside the university system, Lorenz among others has also drawn attention to the tradition of social pedagogy associated with an educative and normative approach long established in the German university system and also found in surrounding countries (Lorenz 1994).

This approach can be contrasted with the more medically influenced and pathologising approach, widespread in the UK and much of the English-speaking world. For instance, some of the former British colonies, such as South Africa, initially had a system of social work education and provision more closely modelled on British lines, and unsuited to the needs of the indigenous population subsisting in rural areas or crowded in urban squatter camps. Elsewhere, the development of social work in South America owes more to the former approach, having been influenced more recently by the work of Brazilian educator, Paulo Friere (1972).

Colonisation was only one route spreading ideas about social work, and in the 1930s and 1940s the migration of many, mainly Jewish, exiles from Fascism in Europe included individuals who subsequently continued to develop ideas and activities in the social work field in their adopted countries (Lorenz 1994). A further wave of migration in the post-war period promoted the additional spread of ideas and saw a significant growth of international and regional organisations and associations, including in the field of social work.

In terms of the organisation of social work and welfare, a pattern can be detected in Europe and North America where provision initially by the voluntary sector has been replaced in part by state-funded and approved services, with more recent evolution, in some cases, 'back' to an emphasis on service provision by the voluntary or independent sector, in the face of a widespread shift to the right in political and economic policy, at national and global levels. Here the term *voluntary* is used throughout to identify agencies, often initially small and locally based, in the 'not-for-profit' sector, which subsequently often employed trained social workers, while the term *independent* is a broader term which might include agencies in the *private*, that is, commercial, sector. Use of the term 'NGO' is generally restricted to large organisations which are national, regional or international in scope.

This pattern of provision has been replicated in countries where state welfare systems are less developed and/or poorly resourced and where social work is a newer profession. In many parts of Africa, Asia and Latin America, the role of voluntary agencies and NGOs has been significant in attempts to counteract the effects of poverty and in change efforts, while the private sector may cater for the psycho-social and broader welfare needs of those who can pay. In some countries, the place of employment has provided a different or additional basis for welfare provision, as in Japan (Matsubara 1992), and the growth of social work in the occupational field has also occurred in some European countries (for example, the Netherlands and Spain) and in the US.

Core values and roles in social work

At the end of the twentieth century, social work is a diverse, and often contested, activity, taking many different organisational and methodological forms, contingent upon the political ideology, economic position and cultural assumptions of the host society. But for all this, members of the International Federation of Social Workers (hereafter IFSW) in a working party of the United Nations in 1994 were able to agree a 'global definition':

> Social work originates variously from humanitarian and democratic ideals. It focuses on meeting human need and developing human potential and resources. Social work is a profession whose purpose is to bring about social changes in society in general and in its individual forms of development. (Centre for Human Rights 1994:4).

In 1998 an IFSW task force is reviewing this definition, but the organisation clearly recognises a 'core identity ... [and] professionality that we can identify as ... social work' (IFSW Newsletter 3/97–1/98:2). The IFSW has also developed the theme of the social work role in relation to human rights and social justice, and referred to concepts which were important in the early development of some social work activity and which have increasing relevance to the developing role and activities of the profession, including at international level (IFSW 1997).

The first concept is *peace*, which Burt (1994) describes as 'a necessary condition for prosperity and social progress' at both domestic and international levels. The effects of war on individuals and communities were portrayed globally by the media in the break-up of the former Yugoslavia in the early 1990s and later in the civil strife of Rwanda; these effects continue to be felt in the needs of refugees from other conflicts, with significant implications for social work (Pugh 1997).

The second concept is the *environment*, since again the consequences of the exploitation and despoiling of the environment, both for particular communities and globally, have been increasingly brought to public attention through the activities of NGOs and media reports (Vogler 1997). While early social workers responded to the damaging effects of the local environment on particular populations, there is some growing recognition of the need for understanding and intervention in relation to regional and international aspects of environmental protection and improvement in a holistic approach to social work (Rogge and Darkwa 1996).

It is suggested, therefore, that local political, socio-economic and cultural differences notwithstanding, there are core values and roles which differentiate social work – or a broader range of activities in what are being termed in Europe 'the social professions' (Otto and Lorenz 1998) – from other professional roles and activities in the welfare field. World-wide, social workers are concerned with the effects of poverty, hunger, illness or disability, homelessness, environmental damage, inequality, injustice or violence; in fact with issues related to the 'quality of life' (Burt 1994) of individuals, groups or communities. Burt went on to suggest that quality of life is a function both of economic prosperity *and* of social integration (p.4), and it is in relation to the latter that social workers have a role, with others, at national and international levels.

The term *social exclusion* has gained currency in the European Union in the 1990s, conveying the social, cultural and political marginalisation, in addition to the economic disadvantage, which those who are absolutely or relatively poor in a society have always experienced (Jordon 1996). As mentioned, some social workers in South America have long seen their role in relation to the disenfranchised. This therefore indicates another concept which has relevance in the ensuing discussion, that of *citizenship*, with its attendant assumptions that, in all societies, people should have (equitable) civil, political and social rights, with opportunities for all of inclusion and participation. In promoting the idea of international social work, Rees (1996) suggested that we need to think in terms of 'international citizenship', discussed further as global citizenship in the concluding chapter. This idea has also been elaborated by Lister (1998) and linked to the concept of *human rights*, also returned to later.

However, in relation to economic considerations, various writers have pointed out that the development of social welfare, and of social work, are not simply a function of the wealth of a nation, but also of the political choices about how that wealth is spent and shared, and which, if any, welfare policies are promoted, even within countries. For instance, the Indian economist Sen (1991) illustrated how the literacy and live births rates were comparable with a rich nation in one Indian state, Kerala, despite a low per capita income, while the Punjab had experienced more economic growth, but had lower levels of literacy and higher infant mortality rates, facts attributed to the politics and culture of these states, rather than to actual levels of economic growth.

Other comparative studies (for example, Cochrane and Clarke 1993) of welfare policies in Europe and various countries in the English-speaking world have also illustrated not only how different philosophies and cultures produced different welfare arrangements, but also how recent changes in ideology have promoted similar trends in reduced (state) welfare provision, with consequent effects on the expectations placed on social workers. As noted in an analysis of the state of welfare and social work in the US, deteriorating labour market conditions, associated with economic and industrial changes, and cuts in public spending, have combined to result in increased demand for services at a time of reduction in those very services (Van Wormer 1997); the 'leaner, meaner' organisations evident in the industrial and commercial sphere are paralleled or replicated at national level, not just in the US, but in a wide range of countries generally regarded as 'wealthy'.

Thus social work roles can be described as concerned with amelioration of social problems, and support and empowerment for the individuals, families, groups and communities affected by them; with advocacy and negotiation about policies and practices (including those of mezzo-systems, such as schools or hospitals); and sometimes with intervention aimed at reconciliation between individuals or groups. This is not to deny the authority role of social workers in various situations, but to argue for a clearer and unifying focus on the distinctive (though not unique) responsibility of social work to defend and promote the human and civil rights of usually the least powerful individuals and groups in society, in the pursuit of social justice.

Returning to a consideration of social work theory and approaches, it has already been noted that these are diverse, and that different traditions have promoted intervention at micro, mezzo or macro levels, sometimes seen as corresponding to casework or therapeutic interventions, and sometimes to the educative mode or to the community work or social action end of the spectrum. Elliot has suggested that social work's 'diffuse professional identity [is] due in no small measure to its inability to reconcile these different elements theoretically', and has put forward ideas for 'an integrative model of social work practice' which would 'bring together the knowledge, skills and values underlying casework with those espoused in the social development approach' (Elliot 1993:21).

Individual casework has been strongly represented in the development of Western social work and in many cases is seen as separate from the social pedagogic/educative and social action and community development approaches referred to earlier. The *social development* approach has been articulated more recently, for example by Midgley. He defined it as 'a process of promoting people's welfare in conjunction with a dynamic process of economic development' (1995:8), and saw it as relevant to practice in both the advanced industrial and less advanced countries. Another American academic has discussed the levels and definitions of social *and economic* development practice and illustrated how this approach can be applied at national, regional and international levels. In the last case, 'world building' is concerned with interventions which contribute to 'world peace, increased social justice, the universal satisfaction of basic human needs and the protection of the planet's fragile ecosystem' (Estes 1997:49).

Both approaches concerned with social development and that described as the ecosystems model, have in common a concern with sustainable development. Van Wormer summarised the *ecosystems* approach as involving 'the application of ecology (the study of the relationship between organisms and their environment) and the general systems theory to promote individual and social welfare' (1997:29). Thus individuals and society are seen to be in dynamic interaction: 'the ecosystems framework does not dichotomise social phenomena but rather perceives reality in terms of reciprocity and interactionism', and social work has a unique role 'in its intervention at both individual and environmental levels, often at the point of their intersection' (p.198).

Finally, partly under the influence of feminism and black perspectives, there has been a renewed recognition that the 'personal is political' (and vice versa), and that social work is not a value-neutral activity. Thus, as the twentieth century draws to a close, social work is being (re)defined by some as having a social action role and a concern with (a more widely defined) environment, foreshadowed in the activities of many early social workers and practised more recently, in more democratic or radical ways, by social workers in less economically developed areas of the world. This offers exciting opportunities for professional exchange and international intervention in the global context.

Internationalising social work

The preceding discussion has aimed to provide some initial basis and rationale for promoting international social work. It seems clear that this is a nebulous concept, with elements of cross-national comparison, and application of international perspectives to local practice, as well as participation in policy and practice activities which are more overtly cross-national or supranational in character. The existence of international social work in the form of cross-national casework is not new (as demonstrated by the establishment of the International Social Services in 1924), nor is the acknowledgement of the value of international exchange (as illustrated in the formation in the same period of an international professional association) but internationalisation has been given an added impetus by the increased recognition of the relevance of globalisation to the welfare sector, and to the roles and tasks of social workers, whatever their arena or level of practice.

Two particular factors, changes within societies (including in many countries, an increasingly heterogeneous population), and the opportunity or need for more exchange and cross-national activity, have raised awareness of the commonality of some basic human needs and problems, and of the cultural differences which influence their expression and the forms of societal and social work responses. These in turn have promoted an increased appreciation of the value of international perspectives, reflected in Van Wormer's phrase, 'the capacity of ... differences to make us look with fresh eyes on that which we thought we knew and understood' (1997:229), and also reflected in another recent American text (Ramathan and Link forthcoming).

In Europe many social workers have had their views and vision of what constitutes social work challenged and enriched by involvement in activities within the context of European Union programmes, including in some cases, those extending to Central Europe and the FSU. Social workers in North and South America have participated in exchanges and East–West dialogue has also been promoted, not least through the flow of people and ideas in the 'Pacific Rim' region, linking Asian influences with ideas derived from settlers of European origin in Australia and New Zealand. Africa has been the scene of significant intervention through the activities of international relief agencies (as well as Western-dominated financial bodies), and the Middle East has been the focus of international political and humanitarian concern.

Chapter 1 explores the role of social work education in promoting the profession and in developing the area of international social work. Recent comparative work and acknowledgement of the consequences of globalisation suggest that, while social work has commonly drawn on the disciplines of psychology and sociology and required a clear understanding of (national) social administrative and legislative provisions, a fuller understanding of some aspects of economics, social anthropology and political science are also required for developing theory and practice in this field.

The book then moves on to a consideration of the contexts within which social work operates, moving from international to national and familial levels. The form and activities of some of the political, economic and welfare organisations operating at regional and international level, which have often provided the basis for social work exchange and activity, or are otherwise relevant to social work concerns, and described here as constituting the international welfare scene, are discussed in Chapter 2.

Chapters 3 and 4 analyse the two major frameworks in relation to which social work everywhere operates, at macro level the state, and at micro level the family. The first of these looks at the extent to which social work is a state approved, sponsored or regulated activity, or the ways in which social work can be seen as being in opposition to the state, and the variations in relationships between the state and social work organised under other auspices. In relation to the family, differences in assumptions about the place of the family and of its individual members in caring for dependants are related to an examination of cultural influences on gender roles, and the implications for the organisation of welfare and practice of social work.

The book then presents an analysis of three major themes which have international and cross-national ramifications, as well as specific consequences for social work provision and practice. The first of these (Chapter 5) concerns *poverty*, which, as this introduction has indicated, was recognised as an initial spur to the development of social work and continues to require examination and action on the part of the social professions, at many levels. The second theme (Chapter 6), which is not unrelated, concerns the causes and effects of migration, and the particular challenges it poses to those engaged in social work with refugees and immigrant communities.

Chapter 7 introduces an area of concern which is less conventionally included in many Western texts about social work, but which is not unfamiliar to social workers in some areas of the globe or in particular NGOs. It discusses the causes and effects of disasters, particularly those which have international dimensions.

Finally, Chapter 8, in referring to some of the previous themes and developing some ideas further, puts forward some concluding thoughts about the need for more internationally informed and located activity by the social professions. It suggests some ways in which international social work can be further developed as both offering important perspectives on the local practice of the social professions and as a specific field of activity.

1 Educating for the social professions – an international perspective

Introduction

Education for the social professions has 'emerged' in different forms at different times in different places, related to the shift from social and community work as voluntary activities or adjuncts to other professions, to an occupation for which education and agreement about principles and standards of practice are deemed necessary. Ideas about the forms of knowledge required, the nature and assessment of practice skills, and even sometimes the value base, vary widely and the content and form of the educational process can be seen as dynamic and sometimes contentious. However, some commonalities can be discerned.

There is an essentially interactive relationship between the nature of social work education and the organisation and practice of social work: education for the social professions has an important function both in preparing people for the realities of practice, and in helping them to question and shape those realities. Social work education plays an important role in the processes of defining and progressing the development of the profession, through research and knowledge creation, and of establishing and maintaining professional standards and credibility.

From its inception, there has been some appreciation of the value of sharing ideas and experience across national boundaries and, as illustrated in the next chapter, opportunities for exchange and international activity have partly been formalised through the establishment of international professional bodies, as well as through the development of other 'schools-based' cross-national and regional networks.

This chapter identifies a range of characteristics of education for the social professions which can be compared and some of the debates about the nature of its knowledge, values and skills base; it also examines some of the aspects and implications of 'internationalising' this process.

Social work education: some characteristics in comparative focus

There have been periodic studies about the form and extent of social work education, globally or in particular regions (for example UN 1964; Brauns and Kramer 1986; Council of Europe 1995); and some recent texts about comparative social work and welfare services have included reference to it at national level (Hokenstad et al. 1992). At national level or comparatively, social work education can be described according to a number of characteristics, including its origins and philosophical underpinnings, its current location and organisation, the length of training and level at which awards are offered, its entry criteria and student characteristics, its regulation, its teaching and assessment methods and its theoretical and practical content. These characteristics are used to structure the following discussion, with the exception of pedagogy and content which are examined in the next section.

With regard to *origins*, mention has already been made in the Introduction of the different roots of social work in traditions, drawing on the 'medical model' or on 'educational' and/or 'collective' approaches. These laid the basis for continuing debates about the boundaries and theoretical content of social work, apparent in national training arrangements and in different emphases in course content, partly related to place but also changing over time. A distinction between social services/casework-based courses and ones oriented to social development were evidenced in an international survey a generation ago (UN 1964); more recently 'Europeanisation' and exchange programmes at a regional level have illustrated both similarities and differences between social work and social pedagogy (Lorenz 1994), leading to the use of the term 'social professions' as an 'inclusive' device (Otto and Lorenz 1998).

The establishment of education programmes (whatever their theoretical orientation) throughout the world has spanned a century, from the earliest examples in the US and Europe to the most recent examples over the past decade in the East. The (early) establishment of social work in some countries – for example, Chile and South Africa both had schools established in the 1920s (Hokenstad et al. 1992) – tended to reflect the predominant thinking of colonial powers about the population to be served and the nature of social work, and thus the form that education should take, rather than enabling the establishment of indigenous forms of social provision and training programmes. Elsewhere, the establishment of educational programmes has taken place in the second half of the twentieth century and between 1950 and 1965 the UN, through its Economic and Social Affairs Department, undertook four international surveys of provision, characteristics and trends in training for social work which could be identified almost world-wide. A notable omission during that period was any reference to eastern Europe, but by the time of the last survey reference was made to the development of new schools in Africa and the Middle East.

The reports provided an important historical, global and comparative perspective on the development of social policies and welfare services in the mid-twentieth century with special reference to the form and content of educational programmes. The fourth report commented on 'an increased awareness that economic and social development are interdependent' (UN 1964:107); and noted a significant expansion of educational provision for social workers, and also in Latin America and Asia, for auxiliary workers (p.111), reflecting growing recognition, in the early 1960s, of social needs, in the face of a lack of higher education opportunities and trained personnel. In some countries the influence of colonial thinking and educational models apparently began to shift as political power changed hands (UN 1964), but periodic concerns have been expressed since about the ongoing effects of cultural imperialism (Midgley 1983). Guzzetta (1996) recently criticised the continuing dominance of North American models, related to economic power and provision of literature, and this danger has also been identified in relation to the re-establishment, sometimes through partnership schemes, of social work education in the FSU and Central Europe (Cemlyn 1995).

Since the 1980s and particularly through the 1990s, there has been increased attention given to globalisation and regional policies, and opportunities for reciprocal learning between the advanced industrial and less developed countries or within particular regions (Europe being a case in point). This has led to renewed debate about the nature of social work and relevant educational models, both in the European context (Cannan et al. 1992; Lorenz 1994) and in the North American literature (Van Wormer 1997; Ramathan and Link forthcoming) with some renewed interest in comparative surveys, including about the extent of teaching about cultural diversity and international social work (Falk and Nagy 1997).

Up to the 1990s there had been a lack of a substantial, international survey and analysis of social work education provisions and developments of the kind previously undertaken by the UN; however the IFSW undertook a comparative survey of social work training and employment perspectives in the European Union (Cocozza 1990), and the Council of Europe funded a more in-depth study of the initial and further training of social workers across a wider area (27 countries from Ireland to Romania and from Iceland to Greece) in the mid-1990s (Council of Europe 1995). Meanwhile the International Association of Schools of Social Work (hereafter IASSW) in 1996 initiated a Global Census. More dispersed evidence (including in membership applications from newly established national associations to the IFSW) has identified a rapid growth (often re-establishment) in the number of schools and countries providing education for the social professions in Central Europe and FSU (Doel and Shardlow 1996; Connelly and Stubbs 1997), as well as in China (Ngai 1996), during the past decade.

With regard to *location* and *organisation*, as the term 'education for the social professions' implies, an overriding characteristic of the activity is its location in higher education, with the purpose of providing and developing knowledge, values and practice skills appropriate to a professional field. It can thus be seen as both a specialist area of activity relative to the wider field of social work, and a particular subject area in the academic context. This dichotomy, together with the nature of societal expectations or requirements of the social professions, can produce tensions in its national development and practice, some of which are inherent in all forms of professional education (Lyons 1997; Currey et al. 1993).

While education and training programmes have invariably been located at the tertiary level, they are not necessarily sited in the university sector. The establishment of schools of social work, sometimes under the auspices of the Church and/or reserved for women, and outside the university system, was previously evident in many European countries (Lorenz 1994). These have mostly now been integrated into more broadly based institutions (for instance, in Spain and Sweden), though still not necessarily having university status. For example Greek social work education is based in the Technological Education Institutes (TEIs), and Dutch departments are in the Highschools (*Hogeschoolen*). The picture becomes even more confused in some European countries, such as Germany where some training for social pedagogy has long had a place in the universities, while the post-war development of social work training has taken place in the *Fachochschulen*.

Elsewhere, for example in the US, educational programmes may be found in both universities and other higher education institutions; in the UK social work education shifted from a long held position in the universities to a predominance in the polytechnic sector in the 1970s and 1980s, and back to a majority base in the university sector in the early 1990s when the polytechnics gained university status. Location of training opportunities (according to type of higher education institution) may have implications for research capability and/or for continuing professional development and qualification opportunities beyond first degree level, and sometimes for the posts which qualified workers may hold on graduation or subsequently.

Meanwhile, in other countries (India, Australia), social work education was initially and is still based in universities, though often in a range of different departments (for instance social administration, psychology, education, sociology). World-wide there is a very mixed picture as to the extent to which social work constitutes an independent department, or is associated with other subjects in a more diverse department or school. This may have implications for the resources available to the subject area and is clearly related to debates about its academic standing, and the relative influence of other disciplines on course content and the wider social work agenda (Hartman 1989).

The *length* of social work education and the academic *level* of the qualifying award are also features which show significant variation, ranging from widespread development of two-year Master's degrees in Social Work (MSW) in North America (following non-professional undergraduate degrees), through degree-level courses of three to five years' duration in most European countries, to a minimum of two-year non-graduate courses in the UK. However, there is also a widespread trend towards the development of three- or four-year undergraduate programmes, already the norm in Australia and some Asian and African countries, and now increasing in the US and UK.

The level and length of training may have implications for the type of work available: this is invariably the case in the US, but not necessarily so in the UK, where the same professional award is offered at *three* different academic levels, with the largest proportion of students taking non-graduate diplomas. Length of course and the academic level of the professional award may also have implications for status, and thus the nature of relationships with other professional groups, and the credibility of social work representation in interdisciplinary work or in policy matters.

Of greater relevance in the international context are questions about *comparability* of qualifications across national and regional boundaries. The anomalous position of the UK in the run-up to the creation of the Single European Market in 1992 was a matter of concern to British social work educators as reflected in meetings and conferences at the time, and in the literature (Barr 1990; Harris and Lavan 1992). A European Directive on mutual recognition of professional education qualifications (EEC 1989) effectively put British social work outside the framework of 'three year courses, at higher education level, with regulated use of the title of social worker', requirements which other EU countries already met or have actively addressed since (for example, Ireland), and which, with a change in government in 1997, was still a matter for periodic lobbying in the UK.

Turning now to the entry criteria and characteristics of students, apart from the obvious differences in entry requirements of those applying for courses at post-graduate level, some similarities are observable. Social work is still predominantly a 'women's profession', in terms of the high proportion of female students entering (and completing) training programmes universally, but there is slightly more variation in age, with a tendency to recruit 'mature' students (over 25 years) to non-graduate courses in the UK, and also to courses in countries which have developed part-time training opportunities (for example, Denmark and Switzerland), but most students proceeding to undergraduate social work degrees do so directly from school at 18 or 19 years of age. This means that the entry criteria are directly related to previous academic performance (for example, in Greece and Germany), with little or no selection according to 'suitability' for an occupation which some might consider 'vocational'.

Elsewhere, some weight is given to previous work or voluntary experience and an attempt is made to assess how realistic and motivated students are for the chosen course. Selection procedures may also be informed by local or national 'open access' policies, though in many places people from ethnic minorities or with disabilities, for instance, are under-represented in higher education, including on social work courses. The UK central body responsible for approving courses and determining content and direction of social work education, the Central Council for Education and Training in Social Work (CCETSW, a quasi-autonomous governmental body), has attempted to address a number of these issues, including setting (overall) figures for intake to programmes (matching supply to demand); requiring overt policies and practice in relation to equal opportunities and anti-discrimination; and undertaking follow-up studies to monitor the take-up of employment opportunities. (At the time of writing in 1998, major changes are being proposed for the regulation of social work and social work education in the UK and the exact nature of the changes anticipated from the year 2000 remains to be clarified.)

The US also has a well-established course accreditation system which shares some similar concerns. However, the structure of the American Council for Social Work Education differs significantly from the UK model, in that the Council is substantially comprised and controlled by social work educators, without the wide range of government-nominated or agreed members of the UK Council. Accrediting bodies in other countries range from government ministries to the universities themselves, with a general trend towards greater public accountability in higher education and social work, and the development of various monitoring and audit exercises aimed at cost effectiveness and quality control (Becher 1994).

While social work education clearly has a vital role in establishing the basis for ethical, informed and skilful practice, and for awarding qualifications which signify readiness to practice, the actual *regulation* of social work as an occupation – with the registration of social workers, expectations about continuing professional development and disciplinary powers – is usually in the hands of the profession itself (through the professional associations), or is regulated by the local or national state. Sometimes, as in the case of the South African Council for Social Work, a statutory body is 'charged with the regulation of social work and the training of social workers' (Mazibuko et al. 1992:121). But social work is not a universally regulated activity and, as discussions in the late 1990s about the setting up of a General Council in either Social Work or Social Care or Social Services in the UK illustrate, the remit and range of occupational groups which might be covered by such a body is far from clear-cut.

Knowledge, skills and values for social professions

Just as there are some similarities and differences observable in relation to the characteristics discussed above, earlier comparative studies and some of the recent literature suggest some commonalities but also distinctive characteristics in the ethos and content of education for the social professions as illustrated in its pedagogical approaches, college curricula, including the teaching of principles, values or ethics; and the requirements for practice which feature in all programmes.

Pedagogical approaches here refer to the teaching, learning and assessment methods prevalent in relation to social work education in any one country. These in part reflect the norms and assumptions of a particular society about higher education (including the scale of provision), about how students learn and about the nature of relationships between staff and students. In some places, this results in a fairly didactic approach to teaching, and formal/traditional assessment methods, which may not be best suited to the integration of personal values and professional skills with academic knowledge which the establishment of professional identity, with a capacity for continuous evaluation and learning, requires.

Elsewhere, social work has demonstrated innovative approaches to experiential learning, case- and problem-based learning, the use of audio-visual technology, development of indigenous material and formative assessments, including use of self and peer assessment. The 'massification' of higher education in some societies and the dispersed nature of population in others, together with the substantial developments in information and communications technology (ICT), have prompted some growth of open and distance learning opportunities in this field (for example, in Australia), as in other subjects. Even on college-based courses, the increasing availability of personal computers, relevant software, and growth of e-mail and the Internet, offer new opportunities for learning and assessment in many countries, while the very apparent resource constraints in less developed countries (including lack of technological equipment) throw these advantages into sharp relief.

Whatever the norms and expectations of a given society with regard to higher education practices, and the level of resourcing available, the need to both develop learning opportunities and assessment styles compatible with the goals of social work education; and ensure academic rigour while also allowing for creativity and the integration of personal and professional development pose a constant challenge to social work educators.

Turning from issues about how best a professional subject can be taught, learned and assessed, the questions of what needs to be learned and what should be taught in the form of college and field-based curricula also reveal both some commonalities and divergence. With regard to the relationship between curriculum content, including social work theory and methods, and societal needs, tensions continue in many places, ranging from the pressure to prepare students for particular forms of practice in the statutory sector in the UK, to the need for training for social development work in rural areas in South Africa or India, relative to courses which still favour case-based approaches (Bose 1992). The lack of an agreed theoretical paradigm has been cited by some as a source of 'weakness' of the subject area, as well as of conflict between its proponents. Elliott (1993) suggested that it is necessary to develop an 'integrative framework' which could encompass the 'casework' – 'social development' approaches, sometimes presented as dichotomous – while others have argued for an inclusive paradigm in which Western thinking does not predominate (Sacco 1996).

Others have written about the contested nature of social work knowledge and the tensions between its academic and practice forms. These are commonly reflected in the theory–practice dichotomy, or in status distinctions between subject-based teaching and skills teaching in educational institutions (Sheppard 1995), or in the relationships between 'faculty' and field supervisors or practice teachers. Hugman (1996) has linked development of the subject in changed global and local circumstances, particularly as represented in the concept and realities of social and cultural diversity, to the continuing need of the subject to define its professional identity and distinctive knowledge base.

To some extent, ideas about the appropriate knowledge, skills and value bases are represented at local level in the curricula of programmes, both as they are delivered within higher education institutions and through the practice/agency placements. On the basis of an earlier exploration of course material from selected European countries (Cannan et al. 1992), augmented by perusal of a small number of course documents from programmes outside Europe (Australia, Papua New Guinea, Singapore, South Africa, the US) and reference to the limited comparative literature in this field, some common elements can be identified in college curricula and with regard to placements.

College curricula include social science teaching, sometimes as distinct contributions from sociology and psychology, but sometimes in more integrated forms concerned with human development and family life-cycle in the context of social structures and issues. Curricula also focus on law and social administration or policy, perhaps linked to the organisational settings within which social work takes place, and social work theory and methods, often utilising the individual/family/group and community frameworks as well as reference to stages of intervention. With regard to skills, there is usually an expectation that these will be developed in the context of practice placements, although there may also be college-based skills training in anticipation of or alongside field placements.

Social research methods are commonly taught on degree or post-graduate level courses, sometimes with some expectation that students will undertake an assessed project, while other courses such as social planning, or deriving from anthropology, economics, criminology or health studies are more likely to be in evidence in some countries' programmes than others. A recent cross-national study about the teaching of information technology in the European Union suggested variations and a gap between what (social work) schools were teaching relative to the increased use of information technology in agencies (Grebel and Steyaert 1995). There seems to be a tendency to offer initial generic or core training with some specialism in the later stages of programmes. These might be related to setting (for example, school social work in some states of the US, or industrial social work in South Africa), or approaches (for example, management information systems in Singapore, or conflict resolution in South Africa), or, frequently, client group.

Social work values and ethics may be taught either as an integral aspect of case-based teaching, or as discreet programmes, and are sometimes linked to teaching and learning about cultural difference and/or structural and personal aspects of power and oppression. As well as the existence of national codes of ethics in some countries, there has also been the more recent development of a range of international codes, which are sometimes used as a starting point or framework for this teaching. These include: the UN Convention on the Rights of the Child; the *Human Rights and Social*

Work manual developed by the IFSW with its themes of right to life, personal freedom and liberty, equality and non-discrimination/empowerment, legal and social justice, solidarity/fraternity, social responsibility, peace and non-violence, and sustainable environment (Centre for Human Rights 1994), and a revised Policy Paper, *The Ethics of Social Work*, also produced by IFSW (1994), an international declaration to be adapted to different cultural and social settings). Link (forthcoming) has undertaken an analysis of social work values and ethics from a global perspective, which illustrates well the different assumptions on which ethical practice may be based; along with others, she has also identified the goals of social justice and human rights as affording the social professions a shared value base.

Practice placements (also known as fieldwork or internships) are a universal feature of educational programmes, and while regarded as essential and generally very much appreciated by students, securing the number and quality of placements is often problematic. Concerns about their quantity and quality (including availability of suitably experienced, if not trained, supervisors or practice teachers) are not new, having been noted by the earlier mentioned UN report on training (1964). The types of agencies and projects in which students are based is considerable, demonstrating diversity in terms of what is considered appropriate, but the variation also illustrates innovative responses to resource shortages in countries as different as Papua New Guinea, Russia and the UK.

The length of placements, stage in the course and form (whether block or concurrent) also vary, but virtually all require some input and assessment by a supervisor or practice teacher. The norms with regard to training of such personnel, and expectations about learning contracts and assessment reports vary considerably, even within the European region, as illustrated in the exchange of students on ERASMUS placements. Doel and Shardlow (1996) provided an international perspective on the place of practice learning in education for the social professions which drew out a number of common themes from the literature (Rogers 1996) and from the national examples presented.

Finally, the role of educators in advancing the knowledge base of the field of social work through research and in promoting continuing professional and service developments, perhaps through post-qualifying courses or consultancy activities, should be noted. Such activities are sometimes a source of tension in the face of competition for resources both within the field and between subject areas – the role of cross-national consultancy, in particular, is one which requires a sensitive approach and critical evaluation (Cemlyn 1995). The issue of research in the subject area is part of the wider debate about the nature of professional knowledge and the aims and requirements of higher education. If social work education is to justify its place in higher education it must meet its expectations with regard to the creation of knowledge, while also debating which forms of research (and consultancy) are compatible with the overall goals of the profession and how findings can be disseminated in ways which inform the practice of social work.

In this connection, schools may act as the focus for national or regional initiatives to share knowledge and improve communications between social workers through the publication of journals and other material. Examples include the University of Papua New Guinea which produces a periodic *PNG Social Development Newsletter* circulated to individuals and agencies nationally, and the launch of a new, regionally focused journal, *Social Work: Africa* produced by the University of the Transkei (1998). The latter is an important initiative in view of a lack of active national and pan-African professional bodies which might otherwise sponsor such a journal, as was the case in the launch of another new publication, the *Japanese Journal of Social Services* (in 1997).

'Internationalising' social work education

Moving on from some of the national and comparative characteristics and concerns of social work education, the latter part of the twentieth century has seen clear moves to establish international or comparative perspectives in social work education and, in a few cases, to offer students the opportunity to participate in studies relating to international social work as an optional or required part of their programme. Questions arise about form, rationale and opportunities in relation to any curriculum innovation, and international dimensions or a more specific specialism called international social work is no exception. What social work educators might mean by this term, the arguments for its development and examples of its manifestation are discussed in this section.

A number of attempts have been made to consider what the term 'international social work' means, usually in the context of studies which identify perspectives or discrete courses in global or international social work, or espouse such goals. These mainly date from the 1980s (Boehm 1980; Sanders and Pederson 1984; Healy 1986) with a rise in their number in the 1990s (Estes 1992; Devore and Seale 1993; Elliott et al. 1994; Healy 1996; Ramathan and Link forthcoming; Falk and Nagy 1997). Growing interest has also been evident in the rise in the number of papers on this theme presented at conferences in Washington (1992), Amsterdam (1994), Calgary (1995) and Hong Kong (1996). This is apart from literature related more specifically to cross-cultural work, the experience of students overseas, or the expansion of cross-national activity at the European level.

Estes (1992), taking peace and social justice as the unifying concepts underpinning international social work, identified three levels of 'internationalisation' – selective, concentrated and fully integrated – as well as a range of resources for internationalising the curricula for specialised fields of practice or with particular populations. (He also suggested other topics in the (US) undergraduate curricula which might form a relevant basis for subsequent studies in international social work including human rights, privatisation and deforestation, and concluded with a section on opportunities for careers in international social work.)

Falk and Nagy (1997) described a survey carried out in 1995/96 of 800 schools of social work in Europe, North America and Australia (covering 20 different countries, and with a 50 per cent response rate) and noted the difficulty in defining terms: specifically, what is international social work and what is cross-cultural work? The following is a summary of their classification of international social work knowledge and activities (derived from respondents' views):

1. International events and social forces that generate the problems faced by the world's peoples
2. The implications of the increasing interdependence of nations
3. The role of international governments and NGOs
4. The increasing influence of multinationals and global financial organisations
5. Comparative social policies, structures, values and cultural assumptions
6. Practice approaches, programmes and methods used in other cultures
7. The range of international practice opportunities
8. Struggles for a more just world and support for human rights
9. Working with immigrants and refugees in one's own country
10. Educational exchanges for educators, students and practitioners
11. International consultation projects
12. International seminars and conferences.

These items were identified as being contained in international social work programmes or infused into other courses, and are listed here since they accord well with the perspectives and activities developed by the author and reflected in this text.

In terms of the aims of international social work, the study revealed that most respondents were more concerned to introduce a global perspective, rather than to prepare students for careers in cross-national or international social work. This seems realistic in view of an earlier study which suggested that, despite some apparent congruence between the knowledge, skills and values required for various posts advertised as offering overseas opportunities with international NGOs, only a very small proportion of American social work graduates might be interested (Rosenthal 1990). This also accords with the experience of the author over three cohorts of students graduating from an International Social Work Studies Degree (about 40 students), none of whom chose to work in an international agency or abroad initially, but a minority of whom considered this might be a serious option in the future.

But the rationale for internationalising social work education is not mainly about future work possibilities: it is related more to broadening the knowledge and attitudinal base by which future practice (wherever it may take place) will be informed. As Link and Peters expressed it (in the context of an evaluation of a Mexican–US school exchange) 'focusing only on our familiar domestic environments puts false limits on our sense of what can be' (cited in Van Wormer 1997:213). Elsewhere, arising from the experience gained as a result of European ERASMUS exchange schemes, others have referred to the extent to which exposure to different cultures, social systems and forms of practice prompts a critical and deeper understanding of local situations and possibilities (Coleman 1996). It is further suggested that there are many instances now where an appropriate response to 'local problems' can only be developed through an appreciation of the effects of global forces and interdependence.

So how effectively is social work education adjusting to global changes, and preparing for the millennium? To some extent internationalisation, or at least regionalisation, has been given some impetus by the establishment of wider policy initiatives (aimed at harmonisation) and funding arrangements which enabled staff and student exchange programmes or student placements abroad. Much of the recent cross-national and intercultural learning in Europe, for example, developed from the ERASMUS and TEMPUS programmes, covering European Union, and Central and East European countries respectively until 1997. At this point new arrangements commenced under SOCRATES which favoured institutional rather than subject area arrangements and resulted in a decrease in funding for intensive multilateral seminars. However, a consortium of professional organisations (ECSPRESS), co-ordinated by the European Centre for Community Education (ECCE), secured funding for development of a thematic network to evaluate and develop further work in the area of the social professions (Lorenz 1998).

In other cases, efforts have also been made to obtain resources from a more diverse range of funding bodies to enable individual exchanges by faculty and/or students, or to arrange small-scale group study visits or seminars, or joint research programmes. Some of the arrangements between North American schools and their counterparts, particularly in South America, have been mentioned by Van Wormer (1997), and a number of articles have appeared in the social work literature over the past decade analysing the experiences and learning gained in this field of work in Europe.

While such events are only one aspect of a possible programme of internationalisation, and are invariably limited to a minority of staff and students in terms of participation, they often provide the stimulus for more general moves towards the introduction of international or regional perspectives in the curriculum. This was evident in responses by schools to a survey undertaken in connection with the (national) evaluation of the impact of the ERASMUS scheme in the UK (Lyons 1996b). It is thus even more regrettable that some schools and countries are relatively excluded from the opportunities for exchange and joint work, constrained by lack of resources (including in ICT), sometimes coupled with geographical isolation or barriers associated with language or political ideology.

The ERASMUS evaluation exercise and other studies identified a variety of models for joint curriculum development and exchange opportunities, a number of which were illustrated in presentations at the 1996 IASSW/ IFSW World Congress. While some programmes are clearly based on formal partnership arrangements between two or more institutions in different countries, for instance, the UK and Denmark (Horncastle and Brobeck 1995), and are based on direct reciprocity, alternative models are based on more fluid relationships, and underpinned by the notion of serial reciprocity. They are likely to rely more heavily on student initiative in seeking international learning opportunities in the context of programmes which may or may not include internationalisation as a clear goal informing structure and content (Lyons 1996a).

Some of the characteristics of students who study abroad and the implications of hosting them have been explored in the literature (Clarkson 1990; Cetingok and Hirayama 1990; Leung et al. 1995). Elsewhere, Lyons and Ramanathan (forthcoming) have discussed some of the issues to be considered in developing 'global placements'. These include the purpose and form of such 'placements' (which do not necessarily constitute assessed practice placements in the conventional sense) and the resources available and required. Other issues include the personal as well as professional learning agendas of students, practical considerations to do with travel, accommodation, health care and security; as well as the opportunities for preparation, support mechanisms while away, and 'debriefing' on return. Some case examples are included which highlight some of the rewards and stresses of such 'placements', and the possible element of culture shock which students may experience, even when preparation has been undertaken.

In other respects, the advent of e-mail and the Internet has opened up new possibilities for (instantaneous) international exchange of ideas and information – the international network established by the (British) National Institute of Social Work (NISW) is one such example; a considerable range of websites in the broad fields of welfare policy/social issues/health and social care/social development gives access to individuals to pursue their own lines of inquiry and interest. Information technology also gives much larger groups of students the opportunity to have comparative dimensions and cross-national communications built into their learning and assessment, an opportunity already realised by some schools of social work in Australia, Europe and the US.

Some concluding thoughts

Social work education is both a medium for internationalising social work and provides examples of ways in which ideas and practices can be shared cross-nationally and globally. One of the dangers in advocating such an approach is the continuation of cultural imperialism noted initially by Midgley (1983) but by others since, and there is a wider concern that Europeanisation and current moves to internationalise the curriculum perpetuate the advantages and dominance of some people and countries at the expense of others. This is a serious concern, and one that needs to be constantly addressed. However, increasing numbers of social work educators espouse the cause of multilateral relationships, and acknowledge that multidirectional flows of knowledge and reciprocity are important dimensions of these initiatives.

Additionally, international social work education is seen as offering the possibility of developing new paradigms of intervention and enhancing understanding of cultural difference and structural oppression. In some instances, it has been a source of practical or moral support to educators and practitioners, validating their efforts or providing renewed energy and direction to educational programmes. Development of international programmes and perspectives does not provide ready-made or automatically transferable solutions to any of the serious and urgent problems facing societies and social workers at the turn of the twenty-first century, indeed in some respects it offers new challenges, but it is an essential response to the realities of global politics and economics as they affect all societies, as discussed in the next and subsequent chapters.

2 The international social work scene

Introduction

This chapter is concerned with the range of organisations and associations which provide the context and the focus for social work activity at cross-national and international level. It describes the origins and roles of organisations which are not extensively analysed in the social work literature, but which have a significant bearing on either the socio-economic circumstances of the subjects of social welfare provision, the form in which such provision is made, or the opportunities for social workers of international employment or association.

The chapter is divided into three sections focusing primarily on the roles of governmental or quasi-governmental global economic bodies, of the United Nations and international NGOs in the field of humanitarian aid and social welfare provision, and of international associations representing social workers. Between them these entities can be seen as providing both the context and the infrastructure for social policy formation, service provision and professional exchange, globally. The concluding section relates the discussion to ideas about networks and networking as a method of intervention.

Global economic organisations

While the organisations discussed in this section may not have 'provision of social welfare' in their remit, they nevertheless influence the socio-economic and other conditions under which large parts of the world's population exists, and their interventions have a bearing on the well-being of specific populations. Their goals and activities are therefore relevant to social workers concerned about the effects of policies formulated at international level and implemented in relation to particular countries or communities. It is an irony of the times that, notwithstanding an apparently widespread concern with democratic and accountable government, largely unelected, supranational bodies have come to have increasing influence over the fortunes of all the world's citizens, as the power of the nation state is challenged (Axford 1995). Among these regional and international bodies are the global corporations already mentioned, but, while they have undoubted impact at political levels, they are not further discussed here.

The UN is now seen as a key player in the arena of international relations, but other organisations, more overtly concerned with the functioning of the global or regional economies, play a very significant role in determining the conditions of countries and regions, and maintaining a balance of power which broadly favours the global capitalist enterprise. Just as war was identified in a previous generation as providing a stimulus to (social) policy development at national level (Titmus 1974), so some of the organisations which now wield so much regional and global power had their origins in post-war settlements, concerned with peace, democracy, economic order and human well-being. A recent text by Cho (1997) provides a systematic commentary on the growth and development of trade, aid and interdependence, including trade theories and reforms, and the role of multinationals, 'aid' agencies and institutions such as the General Agreement on Trade and Tariffs (GATT), and the implications of technology transfer in this field.

Meanwhile Hewitt (1992) summarised the origins of the International Monetary Fund (hereafter IMF), the World Bank, the UN and GATT in the discussions which took place at Bretton Woods in the US in 1944, and related these to ideas and policies aimed at development. This conference of 44 nations, dominated by the US (to which virtually all countries were in debt by the end of the war), was concerned to secure the post-war economic, political and social order. It proposed the move from nation-centred economic behaviour to internationally co-ordinated finance and trade, and established the International Bank for Reconstruction and Development (later called the World Bank) as the source of long-term investment finance and the IMF as the source of short-term finance.

The United Nations was to be the organisation through which 'international decisions were taken and ... political and military stability was maintained' and GATT would 'regulate international trade and stabilise world commodity prices' (Hewitt 1992:222). While all these organisations were seen as having a role in relation to post-war reconstruction and assisting the socio-economic development of the less developed countries (LDCs) (and much later, of the Central European and FSU countries in the post-Communist era), the balance of power, and thus determination of priorities and programmes, have always been firmly in the hands of Western, capitalist states.

Development of another economic organisation, the Organisation for Economic Co-operation and Development (OECD) in 1961, with its membership drawn from 25 advanced industrial countries (AICs) and dominated by the Group of 10 (initially G7, comprising Canada, France, Italy, Japan, Germany, the UK and the US, with the addition of Austria, Netherlands and Sweden in 1996, and Switzerland as an observer), has further tipped the balance in favour of AICs, and prompted the establishment of 'the Group of 77 – a UN based grouping of "developing" states' which seeks to reach a common position on a range of issues, including the environment (Vogler 1997:230).

Of interest to social scientists, including social workers, has been the establishment of a Social Data Bank by the OECD which has enabled cross-national comparisons across a range of social indicators, for example, patterns of income distribution or public expenditure on welfare or defence. From this it is possible to identify broad social trends and issues, although, as Cochrane and Clarke (1993) warn, such statistics are submitted by national governments and their reliability or strict comparability may be open to question. One such example would be the basis for the classification of people as unemployed, which underwent significant and numerous changes in the UK in the 1980s and 1990s.

It was in this economic context that a paradigm of development was established whereby a Western-influenced conception of 'modernity' was to be reached through economic growth and breaking with traditional ways; living standards universally would rise, as in western Europe and North America in the 1950s and 1960s. There would be sufficient welfare services for the diminishing numbers of those in need and the development of social work along Western lines would be fostered throughout the world. Significant industrialisation did indeed occur in some of the LDCs and welfare services in other countries also expanded; Guzzetta (1996) has powerfully described how the 'American model' of social work was established internationally.

But the oil crisis of the mid-1970s foreshadowed a disillusionment with modernity, including state welfare systems, and by the end of the 1980s, the Western world had moved on to the uncertainties of the post-modern condition, including increased pluralism and residualism in welfare provision in wealthier countries (Cochrane and Clarke 1993), and a decrease in aid for social development elsewhere (Halloran Lumsdaine 1993). A Canadian social work academic with substantial experience in South America offered a personal overview of these global changes, and discussed their implications for changing paradigms of development and relationships between both governmental and voluntary organisations and between the countries of the North and South (Campfens 1996).

Meanwhile in post-war China and the FSU, a substantial part of the world's population was organised according to communist political and economic principles (Kilmister 1992), giving rise to a different conception and organisation of welfare. Even in countries previously closely related to West European traditions, social work was deemed an unnecessary activity; and religion as a personal or communal spiritual practice or basis for welfare was discouraged, if not banned. Just as the ending of the Cold War, symbolised in the dismantling of the Berlin Wall in 1989, marked a significant change in political ideology and economic goals internally, so it witnessed the (re)development of new forms of welfare and social work in many countries of Central Europe, Central Asia and China.

The demise of communism prompted the IMF to turn its attention from predominant intervention in LDCs to the 'transition economies' of Central and eastern Europe and Central Asia, including the establishment of a specialist department, 'Europe II' (a reference to the 'Marshall Plan'-era when significant efforts of the newly formed institutions were directed at the post-war reconstruction of western Europe). Its task was to assist economies adjusting to the changes from centrally planned systems and the collapse of internal trade patterns to market-oriented systems.

The emphasis on budgetary discipline and macroeconomic stability associated with short- and long-term loans from the IMF and World Bank, together with rapidly rising unemployment, poverty and crime has, as elsewhere, prompted the implementation of unpopular policies, though at least one economic commentator has questioned how far these are the result of IMF (and World Bank) policies, or whether these institutions, in seeking to maintain financial probity and economic stability, become a convenient scapegoat for national governments and for critical interest groups (Milner 1994). (The same writer noted that the membership of the World Bank and IMF increased from 155 in 1991 to 178 by 1994, with the most rapid rise in the 1991/92 period.)

Elsewhere the establishment of the forerunners of the European Union (EU) (the European Coal and Steel Community in 1951 and the European Economic Community in 1957, also formulated as an antidote to war) can be seen as one example of a *regional* body with economic and political goals, which were subsequently extended to include a social dimension (Cannan et al. 1992). There are also other, newer regional bodies, which as yet have more exclusively economic functions. Some discussion of the origins, roles and impact of these, including the North American Free Trade Association (NAFTA) and the Asia-Pacific Economic Co-operation forum (APEC) can be found elsewhere (Van Wormer 1997; White et al. 1997).

Axford (1995) has noted that GATT was showing signs of strain relative to the emergence of (regional) trading blocs, including the EU, and its role has been strengthened by the establishment of the World Trade Organisation (WTO) since 1994 (the 'Uruguay Round' of talks). Apart from extending the coverage of the organisation, for instance, to include intellectual property protection, the new organisation is based on a 'one nation, one vote system' which may give less economically powerful countries a more significant voice, relative to a weighted voting system favouring richer countries and common in other economic institutions (Russell 1997).

Meanwhile, also in the mid-1990s, a British economist called for a review of these various international bodies, suggesting that they had outlived their original purpose and should be replaced by an economic secretariat and 'cabinet' under the aegis of the UN. In predicting that 'uncontrolled speculation [threatened] to destabilise the whole world economy', he suggested that the IMF should do more to co-ordinate central banks' actions to maintain agreed exchange rates in the face of speculative pressure and proposed that 'we need a world economic strategy in which the net flow of productive capital is directed towards the most pressing needs of the developing and ex-communist world' (Grieve Smith 1994:5).

With regard to the social consequences of economic and monetary policies promoted by the IMF and World Bank, Van Wormer (1997) has described how, for instance, Latin American countries have been forced to reduce their national debt as a condition for receiving aid, leading to retrenchment in expenditure in areas of health, social housing and education. Such measures in response to IMF requirements, including an enforced rise in the costs of staples, bear most heavily on the poorest sections of society with consequences which were experienced by the author in Peru in 1990 in the form of 'empty pots' marches by women, increased pressures on soup kitchens in the squatter camps around Lima, and the declaration of a state of emergency, with a rise in the military presence and tension on the streets. Desperate responses were also evident in 1998 in media and press reports of rioting and looting in Indonesia in the face of austerity measures provoked by the economic crises in Asia.

A report in the British press in 1994 gave an example of the potential of the World Bank in socio-economic development, but also of its limits. It funded a study about the economy and employment needs of Mozambique, as a result of which the numbers and salary levels of civil servants were 'capped' while specific (re)training projects were encouraged (but not directly funded). One such project was a short-term programme by an

Italian NGO providing employment training for (about 600) soldiers discharged from the army. This was undertaken in the face of pressing need for development of a skills base and economic self-sufficiency (appropriate to the needs of a largely rural population), but its efforts were only a drop in the ocean relative to the high levels of unemployment and social need in a country disrupted by war and enforced migration (Brittain 1994).

In the face of increasing criticisms that the World Bank's interventions, particularly in the form of structural adjustment programmes (SAPs), are not in tune with the needs of the countries seeking help, and that economic measures have (unintended) social consequences, there are some indications that the World Bank may be becoming more responsive. One such indication is its agreement to conduct joint, participatory, country-level reviews of the effects of SAPs in ten countries (the first identified were Bangladesh, Ecuador, El Salvador, Mali, Uganda and Zimbabwe). Field investigations are to be carried out by teams of representatives from the World Bank and interested NGOs (which had formed themselves into a network, the Structural Adjustment Participatory Review Initiative Network, SAPRIN) (IFSW Update 1/97)

Some commentators more directly engaged in development work have called for accountability in economic matters and reiterated that austerity measures forced on poor countries in order to ensure debt repayments are destructive and not justified. Danaher (1997) argued that the World Bank gets some of its money from its member governments, which also effectively underwrite risk involved in long-term investment by those who purchase World Bank bonds. Since some of these bonds are purchased by 'public institutions, such as Pension Funds', he urges social workers to target these institutions with a view to them ceasing to invest in World Bank bonds, and sees this as a way of bringing pressure to bear on how and where capital is invested.

It therefore seems possible that there may be some change in the remits, resources, form or relationships of global economic institutions, but there is clearly an increasing need for greater awareness by all social workers of global economic and monetary policies and of efforts to influence the directions of such policies.

The UN, NGOs and social welfare

Turning now to the global welfare scene, this is represented substantially through the policies and provisions of the UN, as agreed through its member states, and through the activities of a myriad of NGOs with an international remit or perspective in their work. Some of these bodies have their origins in 'the Church' or other religious institutions, and, with limited exceptions, the role of religious groups in striving for social justice or as providers of welfare is discussed more directly in relation to the state (Chapter 3).

The United Nations had its origins in the League of Nations, established 'to preserve peace and security', by a multilateral treaty after the First World War. Sixty-three members joined the League but its 'aspirations were dashed' by the onset of the Second World War (Axford 1995:85–7). The United Nations organisation, established following this, has been described as an international forum in which all member states (nominally) have an equal voice, and which provides a 'vision of a new world order based upon a meeting of governments and ... a supranational presence in world affairs championing human rights' (Held 1995:88). However, Held critiques the organisation as 'susceptible to the agendas of the most powerful states' and as having failed 'to generate a new principle of organisation in the international order ... or to generate new democratic mechanism of political co-ordination and change'. Among a diverse public it can be criticised as both too beholden to the wishes of its richest members (not least the US, for instance in its policy towards Iraq in the late 1990s), and as an organisation which threatens the sovereignty of even the most powerful states.

Notwithstanding such concerns, in a 1995 'fiftieth-anniversary' press advertisement issued by the UK United Nations Association (and seeking public subscriptions), its supporters claimed the prevention of at least 150 wars through UN intervention and also referred to its 'struggle against drugs, pollution and abuse of human rights'. It is through the work of its constituent bodies, including the Children's Fund (UNICEF); the Educational, Scientific and Cultural Organisation (UNESCO); the High Commission for Refugees (UNHCR); its Development and Environment Programmes (UNDP and UNEP); the International Labour Office (ILO, building on the work of an earlier organisation established in 1919); and the World Health Organisation (WHO) that it is most likely to be familiar to those in the social professions.

From the framing of the Universal Declaration of Human Rights in 1948, through the International Covenant of Civil and Political Rights (1966) to the Convention on the Rights of the Child in 1989, the UN has provided a benchmark against which the behaviour of states towards their own citizens and others can be judged. Through a series of International Conferences in the 1990s – for instance on the Environment and Development (1992), Populations and Development (1994) and Women (1995) – it has sought to raise the profile of issues of global social concern and to influence the policy agendas of nation states. The costs of such an organisation (met by the member states in proportion to GNP, and sometimes the source of critical questioning) are estimated at $8 billion, of which about half is spent on humanitarian relief and peacekeeping operations (Held 1995:88).

Specific examples of the activities of the UN, gleaned from promotional literature and reports, which have relevance to the work of the social professions, can be seen in the development of policies and projects to combat the HIV/AIDS pandemic (since the 1980s), and the establishment of a joint Project (1996/7) with the World Psychiatric Association on the Psychiatry of the Elderly by WHO; country-based and interregional Projects aimed at poverty alleviation and building LDCs' capacities for sustainable human development, including the advancement of women, by the UNDP (1996); the participation of UNICEF in the campaigns against land-mines and child labour, its immunisation programmes and work with children orphaned by war (1997); or in the production of policy statements and guidelines on subjects as diverse as suicide (1996) and environmental concerns (1997).

Finally, given the central role of employment in individual and collective welfare, the regular inquiries and data produced by the ILO about the nature and future of work, including in the LDCs, and more specific studies, for instance about sexual harassment in the work place (1996), or the employment of children (1997), are an important resource for professionals concerned about needs and practice in the welfare field.

Turning to the NGOs, while smaller in scale and often more 'local' in impact, these are nevertheless an important source of information and provision in relation to particular aspects of social need and welfare development, and are likely to be the site of voluntary or paid employment for some social and community development workers. The significant growth in the number of voluntary organisations world-wide (not only those with an international remit, but including those concerned with social development and welfare) has been described by a number of writers (McGrew 1992; Yadama 1997). In describing the growth and range of NGOs in the context of European networks, Harvey (1992) noted that there were about 900 NGOs having accredited status with the UN at the beginning of the decade (but did not suggest what proportion of these might be 'service organisations' or whether with a regional or international remit).

Organisations such as OXFAM, Voluntary Service Overseas (VSO), Help the Aged, Y Care, Save the Children Fund, or the Canadian University Service Overseas (CUSO) have varied origins and remits but can be said to share similar objectives concerned with social development and the improved well-being of individuals and communities. They can be seen as a means of voluntary sharing of resources between richer and poorer countries, originally between North and South but also in the 1990s between West and East.

As such, they can be viewed with suspicion as 'do-gooding', and/or continuing a form of paternalism and cultural imperialism widespread in a previous colonial era, and/or promoting dependency in the communities or countries where work is based. Similarly, views on their fund-raising activities in the 'donor countries' range from apathy (donor fatigue) to a concern about how the money is spent, either on the administrative machinery of the organisation or overseas. Yet in the 1990s, increasing numbers of NGOs have recognised the need to tread warily in establishing projects on 'foreign turf' and to be guided by principles which respect the wishes of national governments. They seek the active participation of local communities in defining needs and ways and means of meeting them and aim to foster developments which will have multiplier effects and/or be self-sustaining.

Campfens has suggested that some of these organisations have indeed undergone significant paradigm shifts in their principles and practices in the late 1980s/1990s, moving from paternalism to power sharing, from individually based short-term programmes to longer-term community-based ones, and having a multidirectional flow in their relationships rather than a unidirectional one (Campfens 1996:217). He cites the example of OXFAM, established as a relief agency (from Britain to Greece in 1942) which subsequently spread its bases to other (mainly English-speaking) countries and has shifted its focus from relief to local development work in the 1960s. It can be seen as having shifted again to the development of trade projects in the 1990s and now has activities in about seventy countries, including projects for street children in India, provision of materials for construction of shelters in Afghanistan, and promoting skills and livelihoods through Fair Trade schemes (Oxfam reports and promotional literature 1996).

Other organisations with their origins in relief work have maintained a more specific focus on response to emergencies and disasters, or longer-term schemes in relation to refugees or prisoners of war. However, organisations such as the Red Cross (established 1863) and its Muslim equivalent, Red Crescent, or Médicins sans Frontières will only intervene if requested to do so and/or if assured of the co-operation of the ruling power and protection of their staff. Meanwhile, organisations such as Greenpeace or Amnesty International may be less concerned (or able) to secure the co-operation of governments, but have equally to consider the safety of their own staff or volunteers in undertaking environmental campaigning work or bringing to light individual or collective cases of human rights abuses.

Finally, there are a few examples of international agencies with 'casework' responsibilities. The best known of these is International Social Services (ISS). This was founded in 1924 on the basis of work with refugees initiated by the Young Women's Christian Association, and now has its headquarters in Geneva, with a small number of national offices. This organisation undertakes a range of work with people who might otherwise come to the attention of local social work agencies (for instance because of mental health or family problems) but where their circumstances also require some cross-national intervention, and also continues to work with refugees (ISS agency literature; Cox 1986; Chow and Ho 1996).

A more recent example of cross-national development in the casework field concerns the establishment of quite small-scale ventures to trace the origins or destinies of children sent for fostering or adoption overseas, although this work is sometimes undertaken by experienced workers on a private basis or under the auspices of national child welfare agencies, including those under whose auspices children were previously sent abroad (personal communication). This is separate from an established, cross-national tracing service offered by the Salvation Army, which (from its establishment as a religious organisation in the UK in 1865 and development of an international presence since the 1880s) continues a long tradition of social service in over 100 countries world-wide, including assistance to international relief teams (Annual Report 1995).

International social work associations

International social work associations have existed since the establishment of the International Permanent Secretariat of Social Workers in Paris in 1928. This was the forerunner of the three major organisations in the field discussed here, although the smooth evolution of the original body to the current organisations was disrupted by the Second World War. The organisations are the International Federation of Social Workers (IFSW), the International Association of Schools of Social Work (IASSW), and the International Council on Social Welfare (ICSW).

Notwithstanding their actual or potential roles and relevance to developing international perspectives and practice, there is relatively little reference to these associations in the literature, and the following discussion is partly based on 'internal' material and on the author's own experience. Before describing the form and activities of the individual associations, there are wider considerations about the nature and functioning of 'associations' which must inform any analysis of organisations of this type.

While many would see these organisations as having an important part to play in developing international perspectives and initiatives, as voluntary, membership-based associations, they are all, to some extent, concerned with the promotion of the social professions themselves, and as such they are not without their critics. However, as with the voluntary organisations, national associations and the schools which comprise their membership, the international bodies claim to relate their existence, not only to members 'needs' and interests, but also to the maintenance of professional standards of practice, and the development of policies and provisions in support of individual, group and societal well-being.

The extent to which such organisations progress such goals or else simply operate as a 'talking shop' for privileged cliques or perpetuate a form of continuing cultural imperialism, represents a constant challenge, as does the maintaining of viable finances (which recognise the widely differing means of their constituencies), relative to realising more democratic, inclusive and altruistic aspirations. The working languages of the three associations are English, French and Spanish, and while these enable many people who wish to participate to do so, there are clear continuities in the traditional power of the West, and particularly the Anglo-American world, to dominate international activities, in language if not in other respects. The organisations discussed here have all experienced occasional crises related to one or more of these tensions, and attention to the difficulties inherent in membership associations are a requirement for officers and members alike.

Similarly, questions can be asked about the 'representativeness' of such organisations, since they rarely achieve total coverage of all the people or organisations who might be eligible to join – or may indeed include associations whose own membership base is but a proportion of all the social workers, schools or voluntary agencies in a given country. An example of this occurs in relation to the membership of IFSW, where membership of the American association (NASW) stands at about a quarter of the possible number (Van Wormer 1997:190), while that of Britain (BASW) is estimated at less than one-tenth, and that of Denmark (DS) is nearly 100 per cent (Cannan et al. 1992:59). The international bodies have also to accept, to some extent, the definitions, priorities and differentials of their members at national level, requiring a degree of compromise and pragmatism in their cross-country work and strategic decision making.

Such reservations and critiques notwithstanding, a basic or enhanced knowledge about these organisations can be useful to social workers expecting to engage in international social work or to apply international perspectives in their national practice. IFSW was established in 1956 at an International Conference on Social Welfare (in Munich), following an earlier International Conference on Social Work (in Paris) in 1950, and preparatory work in the early 1950s. 1993 saw a change in a long-established secretariat (effectively comprising the activities of a salaried Secretary General) and a move in the organisational base from Geneva to Oslo.

As the title suggests, it is a federal organisation based on membership by 68 national associations of social workers, representing 435,000 individuals (out of an estimated 1 million world-wide), and scattered around every region of the world, listed alphabetically from Albania to Zimbabwe, in an information sheet issued by the association (IFSW Update 1/98). The principle of national membership by a single association has been long established, but this has sometimes been a source of difficulty, for instance, where there are two (or more) national associations, serving different (competing) interest groups, or where there have been too few social workers, faced with resource and communication difficulties or a lack of 'leadership capacity', related to the stage of the development of the profession in some countries.

However, the 1990s has seen a healthy expansion of the IFSW, related to a rise in the number of national associations applying for membership. Some of those joining the Federation recently have done so on the basis of the formation of new national associations (China, 1992; Malta, 1995; Macedonia, 1998) or arising from the (re)establishment of associations, for instance in Central Europe and the FSU (Czech Republic, 1995; Latvia, Belarus, 1996), or from the agreements reached between national associations about amalgamation or establishment of co-ordinating mechanisms (Germany, Denmark, 1996; Japan, 1998). Some of these developments have been assisted by the establishment of a Twinning Fund in 1995 and by specific 'twinning' arrangements between well-established and emerging associations, for instance between Denmark and Zimbabwe (IFSW Update 3/97); and/or by the active support of the Secretary General or Regional Executive members.

Additionally, an important initiative in the early 1990s developed the participation and subscription base with a new category of individual and corporate membership, the 'Friends of IFSW' (31 in 1992, to over 600 in 54 countries by 1997 (IFSW Update 5/97)). This policy and improved communications (partly related to the effective use of new technology for the production and circulation of a periodic newsletter to all members and of brief 'Updates' to a wider constituency) has resulted in the impression of an organisation responding dynamically to the pace and scope of change in the global scene over the past decade.

There have also been conscious efforts to develop the operation of the Federation democratically, with the main decision-making body being the General Assembly, where a one nation, one vote system operates, and with attention to the balance of membership of the Executive Committee, including the existence of five vice presidents (one for each region, broadly corresponding to continents). The siting of events such as executive meetings and international symposia, have also been planned to take into account the need both to spread the costs, work, and opportunities for participation; and to avoid too close an association with any one country or region.

The promotion of social work and the support of national associations are clearly stated among the four aims of the Federation, and partly realised through the structures described above, but also supported by the work of various task groups and committees. These include a Permanent Committee on Ethics, established in 1994, following work to produce a new document based on two earlier papers concerned with a Code of Ethics, and Ethical Principles (IFSW 1994).

A third aim is to facilitate contact and communications between social workers, as reflected in the regular organisation of an international conference, biennially since 1974 (Nairobi), as well as through intervening regional events. The IFSW is also one of the sponsoring organisations of the journal *International Social Work* (established in 1957 in collaboration with IASSW and ICSW) and produces other publications and reports. These include a range of Policy Papers, either developed or revised during the 1990s, some concerned with the needs of and interventions with particular 'client groups' (such as Children and Youth, the Elderly (sic), Rural Communities) and some with more generic themes (Migration, Peace and Disarmament, Protection of Personal Information). Some material has been jointly prepared with other organisations, such as a study on social work and AIDS with WHO, and the previously mentioned manual about human rights and social work with the UN Centre for Human Rights.

These collaborations partly reflect the Federation's last aim, that is, to represent the views of social workers at international level, and to work cooperatively with bodies with related concerns. Thus the Federation has special consultative status with the Economic and Social Council of the UN and with UNICEF, and is on the Special List of NGOs referred to by the ILO, as well as having official recognition with some regional bodies, including the Council of Europe and the EU.

The Federation also links with Amnesty International through a group (established in 1988) constituting the Human Rights Commission which has responsibility to liaise with other relevant bodies, to make representations in cases where social workers' rights have been denied or threatened and to publicise concerns and promote human rights education. There has been no diminution in the need for the enquiries and activities of this group in the past decade, and Resolutions supported by the General Council in the mid-1990s suggested that such concerns were not limited to the particular activities of a minority committee (for example, one expressing concern about the implications of 'sexual tourism' for children in 1994; and another calling for human rights and democracy in Burma in 1996).

The shifting concerns of the IFSW, and similar needs to democratise and modernise its operations, can be observed in relation to the International Association of the Schools of Social Work (IASSW). This might be seen as having similar goals, at least at the meta-level, though it obviously serves a distinct and smaller constituency, drawing its membership from the (higher education) institutions around the world in which social workers are trained, specifically through 'school' membership, but also, for longer than IFSW, on an individual basis, with voting rights since 1995 (IASSW 1995). An open letter from the new President in February 1997 announced a membership of 450 schools and about 500 individual academics in over 70 countries. Its Board membership includes some places for representatives from national associations of schools of social work (including new ones in the Russian Federation and China) through which links between the schools and the IASSW are partly maintained, and 'members at large'.

In an introduction to a Directory of *all* sites of social work education (about 1700 schools in 100 different countries) the then President of the Association described IASSW as 'the sole organisation through which programmes of social work and social work educators strive collectively at the international level to promote the scientific, humane and systematic preparation of social workers'. The Association is concerned to advance development and innovation 'in methods of social work action and practice' including in international social work, and to support schools and national bodies striving to this end; its activities include research and consultancy initiatives (IASSW 1995:ii–iii).

As mentioned previously, the association undertakes collaborative activities with IFSW and ICSW in the form of the journal and biennial conferences, the latter activity also having taken place independently on a biennial basis in the period 1950–74. The organisation similarly has consultative status with the UN, UNICEF, UNESCO and regional bodies such as the Council of Europe and the Organisation of African Unity (OAU). It also produces a periodic newsletter (from which some of this information is derived) and other publications and has recently taken responsibility for making available papers from the biennial international conferences. It recently launched a new World Census Project (1996–2000), under the direction of the previous President, aimed at establishing an improved knowledge of the state of social work and social work education around the world, through data collection from 'the schools'; and aims also to produce a thesaurus of social work terms in use, following another project (1996–98).

Like the IFSW, the IASSW is governed by a General Assembly meeting biennially, with voting rights on the basis of national organisations. Its executive mechanism takes the form of a large Board of Directors (with over 30 elected or nominated seats), and since the mid-1990s, following a serious financial crisis in 1993, the association dispensed with the services of a paid secretariat in Vienna, and took on a more dispersed form with more responsibilities falling on an honorary secretariat drawn from the Board members. Its income is mainly derived from membership subscriptions, conference fees and sale of publications (with additional resourcing from a variety of sources for specified projects).

It is in this changed resource climate that the IASSW has seen the continuation of some regional initiatives, for instance through projects and conferences in the Asia-Pacific region, the demise of a regional African grouping (although there are some activities at sub-regional level), and the launch of a new European Association of Schools of Social Work (EASSW) at the World Congress in Hong Kong in 1996. This organisation combined with the IFSW and the Irish Association of Social Workers (IASW) to stage a successful initial regional conference in 1997. The role of such conferences, not only in progressing the aims of international dialogue and identification of common concerns, but also in stimulating the identification and sharing of new theoretical, research and practice developments, is important in advancing the knowledge base and critical function of the profession.

Finally, the International Council on Social Welfare (ICSW) 'describes itself as "a non-governmental agency committed to social development" ... [as such] ... it is a bridge between voluntary and governmental sectors from the grass roots level to the international level, and an agent for their mutual co-operation and co-ordination ... It sees its role as defining social needs and finding measures to respond to them, and to promoting the voluntary sector' (Harvey 1992:151). Membership is open to voluntary organisations concerned with social welfare policy and provision, and it now has members in more than 70 countries. It operates through national committees and regional and international executive bodies. Through its ten European members has a place on the Platform of European Social NGOs (established in 1995 to provide a forum for comment on EU social policy).

Following the completion of a period in office of the previous Secretary General, a new Executive Director was appointed in 1998 and plans were announced to expand its operations from the existing headquarters in Canada to two new 'global offices' in western Europe and East Asia by the year 2000 (IFSW Update 1/98), suggesting some change in ethos and aspirations approaching the millennium. Among its other activities, it organises regional and international conferences, open to a wider constituency, and the international symposia, offered on a biennial basis, are usually located in the same venues and on similar dates to those organised by the IFSW and IASSW, the focus of such meetings being on broad social themes, such as 'social rights and social exclusion', or 'peace and justice'.

Conclusions: international organisations and networking

The preceding material has described a range of international governmental and non-governmental organisations which can be seen as forming part of a complex web of actual and potential *networks*, in which actors in the social professions have a role. In this context a network has been described as 'an international association, union, federation or grouping of organisations, experts or individuals to share information and [devise] a common course of action on a problem or issue' (Harvey 1992:xii), who also suggested that networks can be differentiated according to how closed or open they are to membership and sharing of resources. Harvey and others have also indicated that, alongside the growth mentioned in the number and scope of NGOs, the 1980s and 1990s have seen a significant growth in the number of networks involving individuals and organisations at formal and informal levels.

The concepts of networks (as entities), and of networking as an activity (liaising and working with other individuals and organisations, developing knowledge of the range of human and other resources), are familiar to social workers world-wide, but have a range of meanings related to the traditions in which they have trained and their different fields of practice. Thus, for many workers operating at an individual, family or small group level, networks usually imply the social networks of relationships of individuals and families which, in the case of social work intervention, need to be strengthened or established (Payne 1991).

Taking a structural perspective and giving an increased emphasis to the concept of empowerment clarifies the need to promote community networks and their interaction with the formal organisations in society (Rees 1991); this is consistent with the ecosystems approach mentioned briefly in the introductory chapter. This frame of reference has more frequently been held and acted upon by some social pedagogues and by those engaged in community and social development roles.

Literature in the field of women's studies or based on feminist perspectives has identified the potential of networks to be democratic and empowering, giving access to emotional as well as practical support, and this may be a characteristic of the ethos of the international professional associations described above. But a study of women's policy networks and the European Union suggested that gender-based power differentials continued to operate, in terms of women accessing some (formal) networks and the resources available through them (Sperling and Bretherton 1996), and this finding would resonate with the experience of ethnic minority or other marginalised groups, such as people with disabilities (Powell and Lovelock 1997).

Such findings are relevant to social work at international or regional level, both because of the gender make-up of the social professions and because of the relatively weak position of the profession in economic and status terms. However, just as advocacy and negotiation for change at local and national level are part of the role of all social workers, so it is the responsibility of social professionals operating at cross-national and international levels to identify regional and global aspects of social need and injustice and offer suggestions for their causes and 'cure'. Collective organisations such as the member associations described above may provide an important mechanism for identifying and carrying forward policy and practice agendas, particularly if bridges are built with organisations which have related concerns and goals (including some of those mentioned in the second section of this chapter). Joint attempts can then be made to influence the more established, formal and powerful institutions and networks of the sort described in the first section. Effective networking needs to be based on a knowledge of the range and nature of organisations, including at international level, which are directly involved in, or impact upon, the welfare scene.

3 The state, welfare and social work

Introduction

The state forms the national context for, and an influence upon, the formation of individual identity and collective societal aspirations. The political and sometimes religious ideology of individual states informs expectations of citizens, and ideology and economic circumstances determine the extent and form of welfare provision. The latter in turn has a bearing on the place of social work in individual societies, from the extremes of compliant agents of the state to people engaged in struggle against the state.

But states are not static, homogenous or autonomous entities, and many contemporary problems are the result of the arbitrary or conflictual historical conditions under which national boundaries were established, and the subsequent treatment of minority (or disempowered) groups within those boundaries. Just as the behaviour of some individuals or families can be experienced as problematic within particular communities and societies, so, in the global context, the behaviour of some states can be viewed as 'dangerous' to internal populations or threatening to neighbours or to world security.

Thus, a discussion about international social work requires some appreciation of the current debates about statehood, including reference to nationality and citizenship; about the role of the state in welfare, including relationships with the voluntary, private and informal sectors, and about the relationships between the state and the social professions. With the exception of the informal sector (mainly discussed in Chapter 4) these are discussed in this chapter, taking examples from around the world to illustrate some of the points, and concluding with a brief consideration of the implications of intra- and international conflict for international social work.

The state, nationality, citizenship and ethnicity

Webber identified *states* as having the following generally accepted characteristics 'a territory, a sovereign government and a subject population' (1997:24); to which, he suggested, some would add other requisite features including, 'a common culture and sense of national identity (or, in its more xenophobic formulation, the possession of an exclusive ethnicity), a minimum level of political stability and order, and a modicum of social and economic welfare' (p.25). He summarised the 'remarkable growth in the number of states, from around fifty in 1945 to more than 180 in 1996' (p.24), identifying specific phases of state formation in the twentieth century (after both world wars, in the 1960s with the ending of colonial rule, and again in the 1990s with the break-up of the Soviet Union).

However, in relation to the number and characteristics of states, Webber mentioned the very limited size of some states (for example, Monaco) relative to the vast size or huge population of other states (citing Russia and China at these extremes). He also suggested that other countries, while having formal external recognition, lack the internal characteristics which constitute statehood. Such cases have been described as 'quasi-states' (p.31), lacking the internal capacity to govern effectively, as demonstrated by economic underdevelopment and political instability, and 'failed states', which are 'entities totally deficient in internal order' and unable to function as members of the international community (p.36).

The purpose of the state was classified by Frost (1991) as being to promote international order, secure its own survival, protect its chosen form of political rule and defend the dominant class interests and economic arrangements. Webber (1997) acknowledged the important role of states in pursuing these goals, but he and others have identified significant changes in the global order, including the rise of supranational bodies (some of which have already been mentioned), which call into question the previously assumed pre-eminence of states (or of selected powerful ones) in determining global political and economic stability and direction. However, he concluded that international governance assumes the existence of states and no alternative forms of organisation have been advanced; or as Held said, 'the age of the nation state is by no means exhausted' (1995:92).

One of the recent challenges to individual societies and to the international community has been the extent to which states have internal autonomy, or the conditions under which some external authority may be agreed or imposed (Held 1995; Axford 1995). Thus, the 'threat' to the sovereignty of the national Parliament relative to the increasing remit and legislative powers of the European Union has been a source of political and personal difference in the UK and other member states, such as Denmark. In the more directly economic sphere, the influence of the IMF and the World Bank on national policies and priorities, for instance in Peru and Indonesia, was mentioned in Chapter 2.

Much debate in the 1990s has centred on the extent to which UN institutions, particularly the peace-keeping (military) forces directed by the Security Council, should intervene in 'domestic' affairs in countries such as Iraq (attempts to control the spread/use of chemical weapons) or Croatia (concern about treatment of the Albanian minority by the Serb government). Berridge (1992) has suggested that there are three grounds on which the policy of non-intervention might be over-ridden, namely in self-defence, on humanitarian grounds, or in the case of civil war. But in each case, the specifics of a particular situation requires judgements about rights and risks, and few interventions are readily agreed or supported by all members of the international community.

There are two implications of the foregoing points for the role of the social professions (possibly at international level), both of which relate to the underpinning values of social justice and human rights. The first concerns the plight of people subject to atrocities and/or forced into exile by civil or international conflict, and the position of refugees, in particular, is considered in the context of a later discussion about migration. The second is the position of minorities within (nation-)states, whose human and civil rights may be infringed or not protected by the state. This can be linked to a brief discussion of the concepts of nationality, citizenship and ethnicity.

At a very basic level, *nationality* has been defined as 'the fact of belonging to a particular nation' (*The Shorter Oxford English Dictionary* 1983), and *citizenship* 'determines who belongs to a national community and [how] it distributes resources to members of the community' (Runnymede Trust 1998:1). The notion of 'citizenship' is thus related to nationality: technically, citizenship 'is a legal construct which encapsulates a political status. [It gives the individual] full political membership of the state and [requires] their allegiance to it' (Runnymede Trust 1998:1). Citizenship may be acquired through birth, through parentage or through a process of naturalisation. It establishes certain rights and responsibilities and contributes to individual sense of identity and 'belonging' to the wider society.

But recent concerns have focused on two issues. The first is the extent to which some individuals or groups may be denied citizenship, for instance in the case of some asylum seekers, and through the introduction of more restrictive legislation aimed at limiting immigration from former colonial territories (as in the UK), or through restrictive definitions of nationality, for example as affects second-generation family members of Turkish 'guest workers' long settled in Germany. The second is the limitation of the concept itself. Thus, in 1990 a British Commission on Citizenship identified citizenship as having three main elements – civil, political and social rights – but it has been suggested that there is a fourth important category, that of cultural rights, which have particular significance for ethnic minorities in any given state, and which are currently not generally acknowledged (Runnymede Trust 1998:2).

In some countries and regions, there has been evidence in the policy agenda of growing appreciation of cultural diversity within societies, and of concern about increased socio-economic divisions which can often be traced on racial and ethnic lines, with concomitant marginalisation or alienation of minority groups. The US, with its particular history of colonisation and slavery, and subsequent immigration (often associated with flight from economic and political persecution) has been the scene of a series of movements concerned with civil rights for different sectors of the population, not least related to race, and now has a well-developed legislative basis for anti-discriminatory policies and practice, although considerable socio-economic divisions on racial lines persist (Van Wormer 1997). Other writers have examined the links between economic disadvantage, political discrimination and the racial or ethnic identity of particular minorities in a wider range of countries in an edited text by Ratcliffe (1996).

On the other side of the Atlantic, the European Union has funded programmes during the 1990s aimed at combating *social exclusion*, that is, the interactive effects of poverty, discrimination, and lack of social rights experienced by minorities who are not seen or heard in particular societies. These moves have been taken up more recently by the UK government through the establishment of a (cross-departmental) Social Exclusion Unit. Among one of the strategies suggested is the promotion of 'active citizenship': this concept and the tensions inherent in the universalism implied by notions of citizenship and recognition of difference have been discussed by Lister (1998). The notion of active citizenship can also be related to the recent espousal of *communitarianism*. This philosophy, emanating from the US, aims to promote responsibility and participation of *all* citizens in the democratic process of building a 'good society', and to move away from the polarised positions of welfare liberalism and economic individualism (Etzione 1993).

But the problems of establishing or promoting the civil rights and active participation of minorities in multicultural and multiracial societies may be of a different order from those of maintaining the rights and security of a particular minority in a more homogenous society, and the growing recognition in some places of the need to foster cultural pluralism can be set alongside increased *nationalism*, in other countries. This can be defined as an extreme form of patriotism, giving rise to xenophobic ideas and discriminatory or persecutory behaviour (Guibernau 1995). This feeds in to the political climate in which laws are enacted and enforced, and, in some cases, undermines attempts to protect or promote the welfare and security of minority groups (whether recently arrived or of long standing), or even informs official policies. Some of the past and present manifestations of this phenomenon in Europe, and the particular implications for the social professions have recently been examined by Lorenz (1994) and, in relation to the youth work field, by Hazenkamp and Popple (1996).

Ryan (1997), in recognising frequent disjunctures between the political borders of the state and the cultural boundaries of national groups (1997:157), suggested that, in the redrawing of political boundaries in the post-First World War period, there was some recognition of the need to protect the rights of minorities (distinguished by language, religion or other cultural features), as promoted originally by the League of Nations. However, he suggested that subsequently concerns about minority rights were overshadowed by the ideological struggle between the 'first' (capitalist) and 'second' (communist) worlds in the 'Cold War' era, and have resurfaced in the form now described as *ethnic conflict*, particularly in the last decade of the twentieth century. Such conflict is related to the denial of 'citizenship' and/or violation of human rights, experienced by some minority groups, identified on the basis of ethnicity.

Smith (1991) defined *ethnicity* as people who have a sense of shared origins and history, related to a specific territory, and giving rise to a common culture. Ideas about ethnicity and culture can be contrasted with the modern idea of the state, when political boundaries have so often cut across the territory occupied by a particular ethnic group, or when population dispersal and resettlement (for whatever reason), has led to the establishment of more heterogeneous populations within state borders, making individuals or groups vulnerable to national or local stereotyping, discrimination or attack.

Thus, ethnicity may be the basis for civil war or unrest aimed at separation or at improving the legal and socio-economic position of particular groups already established or wishing to remain within the country (the position of the Kurds in Turkey or the Irianjayans in Indonesia can be cited as examples). The extent to which such conflicts or movements command international attention varies considerably, not least according to the level and visibility of violence or denial of human rights, but also related to the strategic location of the site of conflict and the allegiances of the parties involved. Further, judgements are made about the extent to which an 'offending state' professes allegiance to the democratic ideals and institutions of the West, or demonstrates different ideological convictions: such judgements also have a bearing on whether and how intervention is attempted.

There is considerable variation in the extent to which social workers may be involved with such struggles, either through social action roles in support of minority groups on home territory, or through participation in the international activities of pressure groups, and these points are returned to later.

The state and welfare

It was suggested earlier that one of the possible identifying features of statehood is the assumption by the state of some responsibility for the welfare of its citizens (over and above the maintenance of external security and internal order). The form and extent of such welfare arrangements varies considerably, and is determined in part by the economic wealth of a society. But, as a comparative examination of the diverse range and standards of (social) welfare provision in wealthy states demonstrates, economic status is only one aspect of the factors affecting this area of state activity, the others being related to the political philosophy of a given society interacting with the cultural norms and assumptions of the dominant group (Cochrane and Clarke 1993; Van Wormer 1997).

One of the first problems in progressing this discussion is the range of meanings attributed to the word *'welfare'* (sometimes preceded by 'social'). A precise but useful definition of social welfare is provided by *The Social Work Dictionary*: 'A nation's system of programmes, benefits and services that help people meet those social, economic, educational and health needs that are fundamental to the maintenance of society' and 'the state of collective well-being of a community or society' (Van Wormer 1997:4). At its widest then, (social) welfare can be taken to encompass a whole range of services and provisions, over which the state exercises regulatory power and/or makes resources available, such as education and health services, but also including income maintenance policies, 'social housing', policies and provisions for particular categories of 'disadvantaged' or dependent groups (for example, ethnic minorities, or pre-school children), and even labour market and unemployment policies.

Elsewhere, the term 'social welfare' has been used more narrowly to denote the fiscal arrangements (including tax, pension and income support) which states make for the financial security or survival of their populations (Esping-Anderson 1990; Wilson and Wilson 1991), although another text taking a comparative approach at that time included reference to health policies and those related to the family (Ginsburg 1992). These and other texts in the 1990s have contributed to debates about the nature of *the welfare state*, a feature of many Western countries in the post-war period (and also previously of the USSR and China, in a different form). Much of the debate has centred on the apparent 'threat' to the continued existence of welfare states since the 1980s (Munday 1989), with the shift in political spheres to a favouring of 'free market' principles and monetarist policies, and widespread attempts to reduce public expenditure. Glennerster (1995) dated this latter preoccupation from the oil crisis and resultant economic problems of the mid-1970s.

Traditional definitions of the welfare state had suggested that it incorporated a number of characteristics, including state ownership and control of economic activity as well as the guaranteeing of minimum standards and use of the state to bring about social change. In this conception Sweden, for example, was clearly seen to support a welfare state while the US did not. However, Esping-Anderson's text (1990) was important in offering a more sophisticated comparative analysis, and despite its Eurocentric basis, examples of the models proposed could be identified in modified form in other countries (for example, North America and Australasia): it was also widely used as the basis for later analyses of 'welfare states'. Esping-Anderson suggested three dominant models of political economy underpinning the state's approach to welfare, summarised as the Liberal (or Beveridgian); the Social Insurance (or Bismarkian); and the Social Democratic (or Nordic) models. The first of these models was in evidence in the UK and Canada, and derived from the 'poor relief' tradition. While affording some universal benefits (for example, education and traditionally, health care), it also used means-tested 'benefits' to guarantee minimal standards in some areas such as pensions.

The social insurance model, derived as the alternative name suggests, from the insurance principles established by a German chancellor, Bismark, at the end of the nineteenth century, was also identified in other corporatist states such as Austria, Italy and France. Its strong links to status-specific occupational insurance schemes gave unique sets of rights and privileges to sub-groups within society, including those classified as civil servants; the principle of subsidiarity (derived from Catholic social doctrine) was important. The third model was most in evidence in the North European (Nordic) states and marked by a substantial range of universalist provision to a high standard. It was based on a universal insurance system and high taxation in societies where most people worked and the state assumed greater responsibility for family functions, including child care, than would be true elsewhere (with the exception of states still or previously based on communist principles). Welfare in such countries has been seen as both underpinning opportunities to work and also necessitating high levels of economic activity of the population to support welfare costs.

A fourth variant was subsequently proposed, and referred to as the Latin rim (or Catholic) model. This acknowledged the important role of the Catholic Church in charitable and welfare activities and also the significance of the family and informal sector in providing social care. Portugal, Spain and Ireland are examples and similar traditions are evident in Greece through the Orthodox Church (Abrahamson 1993).

Apart from theoretical critiques (including from a feminist perspective), which have been usefully summarised by Hill (1996), this 'classification' has since been undermined by the significant changes which have taken place in the economies and welfare policies of all advanced industrial societies in the 1990s. Notwithstanding the changing fortunes of labour markets and employment prospects, countries, including the UK and US, have begun to develop policies which link welfare provision (in the form of child care) to work, in an attempt to break a dependency culture which was deemed to have been created in both a society with an established welfare state, and one with only a residual approach to welfare. Many countries have adopted market principles in welfare (for example, the Netherlands) and even countries with apparently well-established universalist policies such as Sweden have been affected by political shifts and harsher economic conditions and have moved towards targeted (selective) welfare provisions, with implications for the role of social professionals (Van der Laan 1998; Sunesson et al. 1998).

The notion of degree or level of state intervention in the welfare sphere therefore is significant, and it has been suggested that even strongly capitalist countries, such as Japan and the US, can be described as having 'weak' welfare states relative to examples of the stronger forms which have been evident in some European countries (Van Wormer 1997). The development of targeted welfare programmes is also important, both because, while apparently channelling scarce resources to those most in need, it fragments societies into 'competing groups', and also because it challenges those in the social professions to support the policies and provisions aimed at particular groups, while also making connections between different forms of disadvantage and discrimination.

The above discussion has relevance also to the bases and forms of welfare provision emerging in some of the newly industrialised countries of the world, and to the aspirations of some in the less advanced countries. It seems apparent that there is no absolute or best model of welfare state or provision, and the idea of a 'welfare mix' has gained significant ground, globally, towards the end of the twentieth century. The exact balance of state relative to independent sector provision and to informal care varies according to the economic means and the political goals and cultural assumptions of each society, including about the role of the family (discussed in Chapter 4).

However, there are some respects in which the 'beliefs' and therefore policies of some countries may have some influence on the views and behaviour of other states in close association to them, whether, for instance, through 'origins' and language, or through specific political arrangements. Two examples can be suggested. The first concerns the extreme moves to the political right and 'dismantling' of state welfare provisions which took place in New Zealand in the early 1990s (Kelsey 1995), and which were echoed in Australia; doing the unthinkable in some countries may open the way to others reviewing their assumptions and policies.

The second example concerns the apparent spread of the principle of *subsidiarity* in Europe. This propounds that the state should only intervene when the capacity of the family to meet its members' needs has been exhausted and that (welfare) needs should be met by the lowest level of competent authority (the state being the highest): 'responsibility should remain as near as possible to the people involved' (Cannan et al. 1992:32, citing Lippa 1983). This principle has gained wider importance in the context of the European Union's developing (social) policies, and in a climate favouring a shift to more pluralistic forms of welfare provision. Thus, whereas in countries such as Germany and France, welfare provision has traditionally been made through a large and well-established independent sector (in addition to some state provisions), countries such as the UK and Denmark have for the past half-century seen an increasing range of welfare provision made by (large) statutory agencies, with only more recent shifts or returns to some reliance on voluntary and private sector agencies.

This later development has been accompanied, for instance in the UK, by a renewed emphasis on the role of the informal sector (family, friends, neighbours) in meeting the needs of 'dependent' members of the family or community. A (commendable) policy of deinstitutionalisation was followed by the implementation of 'community care' policies. With some notable exceptions, such as the development of small scale group homes and encouragement of independent living schemes, this has often meant the resumption or continuation of care for dependent relatives by 'the family', a trend which some would see as being at variance with proclaimed goals of equal opportunities for women, including through paid work. Such debates and policy moves are not unique to the UK and resonate in other European countries (Lewis 1993; Hantrais 1995), and also in other parts of the world including the East (Stockman et al. 1995), and are further discussed in Chapter 4.

Returning to the more central theme of the role of the state, this can also be considered in terms of the relationship between the state and the independent sector (voluntary and private agencies) in particular. Wide variations can be observed and the role accorded to the voluntary sector is shaped by the previously mentioned economic, political and cultural factors. Even countries such as the UK and Ireland, with apparently similar origins of welfare in Poor Law traditions, have taken different routes in development. Thus the post-1921 establishment of welfare arrangements in Ireland was heavily influenced by the Catholic Church, and in the 1990s the idea of subsidiarity is reflected in the relative strength of the independent and informal sectors (relative both to the state sector and to the position in the UK).

An analysis of the role of the voluntary sector in the UK in the 1970s (when state power in the welfare sector, including deployment of the social professions, reached its height) suggested a number of possibilities ranging from complete autonomy, through a subservient position, to one based on innovation but carrying risk, to a mature interdependence and stimulating interaction (Darvil 1975). Echoes of this analysis may persist, but it does not describe the position which pertains in some other countries (including Germany and the US), where the voluntary sector constitutes the dominant organisational form for some aspects of welfare provision. Even in the UK in the 1990s, it is a large and diverse sector, with increasing requirements for accountability and efficiency. Additionally, some countries have long had, or have recently witnessed, the growth of private provision, adding another dimension to the notion of the independent or non-governmental sector. Therefore, taking a global perspective, three models of state/independent sector relationship can be suggested, namely, some dependence on the independent sector but limited regulation, recognition and regulation of it, and antagonism or conflict with it.

In the first model, the state has only a limited capacity (in economic terms) to meet the welfare needs of its citizens and therefore places considerable reliance on the efforts of the independent and informal sectors. Thus, in many less developed countries, such as Bangladesh and Papua New Guinea, there is an acceptance that those who can pay for private welfare services (including education and health care) do so, while the state provides only minimal levels of welfare, usually in the fields of health and education, for the majority of the population. Such governments are more or less amenable to the intervention of (overseas) NGOs and more locally based voluntary organisations in providing community development programmes or hospice care or child care schemes, for instance, though usually without any degree of funding or regulation from the state. To some extent, this model applied to the developing systems and services in the FSU and Central Europe in the early 1990s, particularly with regard to services and projects by external and indigenous voluntary agencies, although states such as Romania are increasingly claiming a regulative responsibility (Deacon 1993; McGrath 1998).

In the second model the state accepts (and the economy can support) an essential role in welfare provision, at least in the form of public education, some health provisions and minimal income support programmes, but also looks to the private and voluntary sectors to offer 'complementary' services (for instance, the private sector's role in health, some aspects of education, pension schemes and elder care in the US); and the voluntary sector is encouraged to meet a wide range of welfare needs for selected groups in the population. This model includes some use of subsidies and grants, and/or the direct purchase of services through contracts which regulate costs and standards.

So, for example in Germany, in the post-war period the role of the voluntary sector has been seen as important in providing an alternative power bloc to the state, and the 'big six' welfare organisations, including CARITAS and the Jewish Welfare organisation, offer a wide range of (social) services and projects across the spectrum of client groups (Cannan et al. 1992). Taking a very different example, in Hong Kong, apart from the establishment by government of the Social Welfare Department (in 1958), there was 'a burgeoning of voluntary agencies in the early sixties' (Chi and Cheung 1996:1). The independent sector (both private and voluntary) has since had an important role in developing welfare services, and in extending into new areas of work, for example, employee assistance programmes or some child care provisions, which are contracted directly by industry, rather than by the state.

With regard to the third model, it can be suggested that in some countries, while the state's own capacity or inclination to meet the welfare needs of the mass of the population may be limited, the goals and activities of voluntary agencies (and less formally defined 'movements') may be viewed as antagonistic to, or in conflict with, those of the state. This was the case in Chile during the period of military rule (1973–1990) (Jiminez and Aylwin 1992) and continues to be the case now in other countries, subject to despotic, arbitrary and/or corrupt rule.

It may be appropriate finally, to comment more particularly on the role of religions in contributing to welfare systems and initiatives. It was acknowledged earlier that religious establishments and motivations were often an important factor in the origins and development of any kind of welfare provision (including education and care of the sick), and this has continued to be the case in some societies, for instance the work of Muslim and Hindu groups in Bangladesh (Mumin 1998). But secularisation of states and welfare services has been a significant feature of the twentieth century, globally, and some states have discouraged political activities and associated welfare provisions by religious parties. According to press and radio reports (1997/8) Turkey has recently banned the Islamic Refah (Welfare) Party, although there were undoubtedly other considerations in this action than who should provide welfare services. Nevertheless, religiously inspired individuals and groups continue to play a part in the provision of welfare, whether through, for example, community development work in Brazil, or the provision of a hostel for battered wives in the US, or the care of the sick and dying in hospice work around the world.

The state and social work

A number of points in the preceding sections have relevance to the organisation and roles of the social professions, both nationally and at international level. The variation in welfare arrangements and different relationships between the state and independent sector give some clue as to the range of sectors and settings in which social professionals might be employed, and the roles which they might perform. Additionally, discussions about the nature of citizenship and the rights of minorities, as well as about the socio-economic divisions which exist within societies, raise questions about how social workers are trained and how far they see their role as addressing problems related to civil and human rights and social justice.

This section, therefore, considers some aspects of the employment and roles of social workers in global perspective, and also discusses some variations in the relationship between social workers and the state, including their regulation, and the scope for congruence or conflict related to values. Hokenstad et al. (1992) have provided some useful comparative examples of the numbers and location (fields) of social workers in a variety of countries, and these, together with other material and personal knowledge, have provided a basis for the following brief overview of employment patterns and areas of work.

The extent to which social workers are employed by the state, usually in the form of locally organised social service/welfare departments varies significantly. For example, a text produced in the early 1990s illustrates the high percentage of social workers employed in the public sector in Norway, reflecting the heavy investment in a welfare state based on universalist principles (Tutvedt and Young 1995), and this situation is replicated in other Nordic states.

Even in the UK, following a prolonged period when the goal of government was to reduce the role of the state in welfare, nearly 80 per cent of qualifying social workers took up posts in local authority social service departments in the 1990s, and others entered other forms of statutory work, with little movement between sectors (Lyons et al. 1995; Wallis Jones and Lyons 1997). Their role is mainly concerned with assessment of need or risk (in relation to children or vulnerable adults), and intervention aimed at alleviation or protection. While there is no direct link with income support services, there is a recognised connection between their work and the control or support of people experiencing poverty and social exclusion. However, in many cases, the commissioning and regulation of services has assumed a greater importance in the social work role than direct work with clients.

Conversely, although some social workers are employed by departments of human services in the US, larger numbers of social workers are located in the voluntary and private sectors, offering specialist services on a contracted basis. Grossman and Perry have described attempts in California to halt or reverse the flow of graduates away from the public services, in the face of trends towards direct intervention, which they suggest, have created a profession 'increasingly alienated from a mission of service to the poor' (1996:43) but Gilbert (1998) has suggested that current welfare reforms may exacerbate this trend.

Employment of social workers in departments more formally connected with income maintenance systems are less in evidence, but exist in the welfare departments of Germany, for instance. Also, Jiminez and Aylwin described the majority of social workers in Chile as working in public sector institutions in programmes specifically aimed at combating poverty (1992:37). But the problems of poverty are not only to be addressed through the statutory sector, and in Russia, for instance, an estimated 80 per cent of social workers are employed in voluntary organisations, many of which are aimed at the alleviation of the worst effects of poverty on selected populations.

Earlier mention was made of the origins, in some places, of social work in association with other institutions of welfare and these secondary settings (usually in the public sector but sometimes as voluntary or private institutions) persist as the site of social work in many countries. Thus, hospital social work is a well-established and widespread form of social work (including, for example, in Singapore and Australia), while, for instance in Greece and Chile, social work is related to primary (preventive) health care services, and in some countries field social workers are employed in health departments (or boards, as in Ireland). Social work, sometimes under the title of 'probation' services, exists in many countries in relation to justice/

correctional systems (for example, Australia and Jamaica); and schools or education systems also provide a base for social work activity in some countries (school social work is strong in some US states, for instance, and some German social workers are involved in projects with pupils after school).

Employment in relation to the housing field is more varied, but the need for social workers to pay more attention to (adult) homelessness or to the (protected or rehabilitative) housing needs of specific groups, for instance, women escaping domestic violence or people with disabilities discharged from long-stay hospitals, has been widely recognised in many advanced industrial countries. More general concerns about environmental health and living conditions are a feature of social work in some less developed countries, such as Brazil or India. (A serious related but different problem, that of street children, is mentioned in Chapter 4; and work in relation to the housing, health and other needs of refugees in Chapter 5.)

Another area of activity which shows considerable national variation is in relation to the personnel or labour welfare field, although this is well established in countries with widely contrasting social structures and welfare systems (such as Chile, Hong Kong, India, Netherlands and South Africa), and this comprises a substantial proportion of employment of social workers in the private sector. Not unrelated to this has been some growth of (privately contracted) social work services specifically aimed at offering counselling and support or rehabilitation to members of the helping professions, including social workers, who are increasingly recognised as being under stress and sometimes subject to violence and/or vulnerable to drug or alcohol abuse, in relation to their work.

This can be seen as a development of the considerable trend in some countries towards social workers as individual or (small) group therapists, often with a base in private practice, rather than in the statutory or voluntary sector. A survey of members of NASW in the US found that 22 per cent of its members derived their primary source of income from private practice (Ginsberg 1995). The 1990s have also seen the growth in the number of social workers who are mainly self-employed as consultants (sometimes operating outside their national borders), in relation to the organisation and management and/or training of the social work workforce, for example, in the UK.

To some extent, these trends are in line with wider trends in the labour market and employment patterns in the West, also reflected in unemployment of social workers, along with other sectors of the population, including graduates (for example, in Germany and Greece). The incentive to become part of the enterprise culture through securing funding to operate independently or in small-scale projects is therefore increased. However, such trends also sometimes reflect the opportunities available through the increase in the number of programmes (funded, for example, by the European Union) to promote the development of social work and welfare services in the FSU, and other central and eastern European countries.

Such developments raise questions about the accountability and regulation of social work. Traditional and more recent debates about accountability have suggested that the social worker's accountability is to the employing agency (which, as described, may be statutory and/or itself subject to monitoring and regulation) and that this should afford the necessary safeguards for clients. But professional judgements about client needs and appropriate forms of intervention do not necessarily accord with agency resources or guidelines. Accountability to the profession, through membership of a professional association and adherence to a code of ethics, may promote standards of practice and development of policies across a range of client groups and social problems, while also supporting social workers individually and collectively.

In some countries, issues of public accountability have been addressed through formal regulatory mechanisms, operated by the national or local states, including through quasi-autonomous councils. Thus, the term 'social work' sometimes has restricted use and connotes particular forms of state-approved activity, with the provision for disciplining in cases of unprofessional behaviour. This regulation was given impetus by the EEC Directive (1989) mentioned previously, and social work is now a regulated activity in most member states of the European Union, as well as in most US states. Elsewhere, usage of the term social work is much looser, though it may be associated with work of a particular kind and in a particular sector. For instance, in the UK social work has become associated in the public mind with child care work in the statutory sector and has received a bad press following the deaths of children in families under supervision of social workers, or abuse of children in public care, or dispute about the suitability of individuals wishing to foster or adopt children.

It can be suggested that, in a country such as the UK, the term has become overly identified with the statutory role of social workers in the child care field, to the detriment of support for pro-active and preventive strategies and the identification of more varied forms of social work. Adherence to a more inclusive or broader definition of social work would sit more comfortably with other models developed in Europe or emerging in less developed countries. However, this view has to be set against trends observable in a number of countries towards lower welfare expenditure, resulting in concerns about the devaluing of social work roles and deprofessionalisation (Van Wormer 1997).

Elsewhere, more diversity has been maintained and a more varied and positive image fostered through the greater emphasis on employment in the voluntary sector and the maintenance of work and projects aimed at prevention and alleviation as well as empowerment and change. But it is perhaps in the nature of social work – in the values it espouses and the client groups it seeks to help, if not necessarily in the methods it uses – that the relationship between social work and the wider society is not always an easy one and that, in some circumstances, social workers are in conflict with the state. Ideally, skills such as negotiation and conflict resolution can be brought to bear on various levels of familial, organisational and political systems, but there have been examples of social work being out of step with the values of a strong political leadership and/or apparently the wider society.

The development of anti-discriminatory or anti-oppressive training, following on from anti-racist concerns in the 1980s in the UK, can be cited as an example of this. The resulting emphasis on anti-oppressive practice in the early 1990s, together with the public lack of confidence, gave the government of the time the opportunity to discredit and undermine social work and to require reforms to its training (Jones 1996). It has also been questioned, partly in the context of ERASMUS and subsequent SOCRATES programmes, how far this approach might be relevant to other European countries. However, in the light of earlier comments about the rise of nationalism, and the presumed need for social workers to be concerned with social injustice related to race or ethnicity, it is suggested that this focus is of wider relevance than simply to countries like the UK and US with their demonstrably multicultural populations (Lyons 1997).

Additionally, anti-oppressive practice can help counteract the tendency of targeted welfare programmes to 'split' society into groups, since links are made between the differing but overlapping bases for discrimination or special treatment; and may encourage actions to reconcile groups in competition or conflict. Indeed the Council of Europe report on social work education (1995) agreed to a focus on human rights and the problems of minorities to guide its enquiries.

In other times and places the relationship between the state and social workers has been even more strained. The potential for the subversion of social work itself, under the control of extreme right-wing governments, has been commented on by Lorenz (1994) in the German context and Mazibuko et al. (1992) stated that state social work in pre-apartheid South Africa was associated with the oppressive white regime. Similarly, Jiminez and Aylwin (1992) suggested that Chile, during the period of military dictatorship, was not a safe place for social workers who openly disagreed with the government; clearly in some circumstances, social workers have been amongst those who take flight or fight. In other places, such as Brazil and the Philippines, there have been more recent examples of 'Church' and other workers, undertaking social action roles, coming into direct conflict and danger *vis-à-vis* the state (Davis 1989; O'Gorman 1992). Not all such workers consider themselves to be, or are seen as, social workers, but clearly there are similarities between them and some secular professionals in the goals and methods used to achieve welfare ends.

The possible need to defend the (human) rights of particular individuals or groups, and/or to assist communities in securing a fairer distribution of economic resources, clearly pose moral and ethical dilemmas of a very acute nature for social workers in some situations. They are likely to face decisions about whether resistance or attempts at change can be achieved by peaceful means or whether violent measures would be understandable or perhaps justified, and to make judgements about whether rebels against state power are terrorists or freedom fighters. The previously mentioned IFSW Commission on Human Rights has sometimes had to take such perspectives in considering whether to support the cases of social workers who have themselves been 'accused of offences prejudicial to the state' (IFSW 1994).

In reports to the IFSW executive in 1993 and 1994 (points from which were subsequently consolidated into a Position Paper), the Secretary of the Commission outlined the principles on which IFSW would intercede on behalf of such social workers. These were that such social workers were judged to be at risk of torture or death while in custody (regardless of the charge against them and their guilt or innocence) (that is the actual conditions of detention contravened the Geneva Convention); and/or, if on the basis of a situational judgement, violence might have been justified in the light of the violence of the regime. On these bases the IFSW has pursued individual cases referred to it and has raised issues of concern with particular governments. These principles can be viewed in relation to the earlier reference to criteria for international intervention in a state's affairs; and also as having relevance to the intervention of social workers more generally in support of human rights.

Conclusions

It has been suggested that social workers who wish to develop an international perspective to their practice or who engage in cross-national or international social work need to have some understanding of the debates about the nature of statehood and issues such as citizenship and minority rights which are current in the late twentieth century. This would be particularly true for social workers engaged in work promoting social development, human rights, and/or peace and reconciliation within or between nations in conflict.

A comparative perspective on the nature of 'welfare states' illustrates the wide range of considerations and assumptions which have a bearing on the welfare/well-being of individuals and groups. The diversity of welfare arrangements in turn gives rise to a varied and complex picture of converging and diverging trends in the employment, regulation and roles of social workers. Specifically, the extent to which social workers are employed by the state is variable, even between countries of similar economic capacity. Further, the degree to which such employment is compatible with the ethics and goals of social work also varies, and tensions can be observed between state-employed and other social workers in different times and places.

Additionally, comparative perspectives on social work organisation and on some forms of practice, illustrate some similarities in concerns and approaches, between countries and even continents, but also highlight the difficulties of arriving at a definition of social work internationally, other than one broadly based on particular values. Even the emphasis on the values identified may not be universally 'owned' or seen as relevant to particular circumstances. However, the values which support activities aimed at peace, justice and more equitable distribution of resources form a basis for the actual and potential growth of international social work as a specialism, whether in the form of experienced personnel assisting with the development of welfare programmes outside their own countries, or through participation in networks or organisations which promote these goals at international level.

4 International perspectives on 'the family'

Introduction

'The family' is a global institution, found in some form or other universally, but even within national contexts it has often ceased to be the homogeneous entity which the term might imply. This chapter explores some of the variations in family form and function associated with different political and cultural assumptions and socio-economic conditions.

The rapid pace of change towards the end of the twentieth century has also ensured that the family, no less than other social institutions, is itself subject to change, with varying consequences for roles and relationships of individual family members, as well as changing expectations of the collective unit. In particular, the role of women, attitudes to children and policies which are aimed specifically at families are explored in this context.

Finally, given the traditional and continuing concern of social work with vulnerable members of society, including children, there is some consideration of the role of social workers relative to families, from a comparative perspective. Families constitute the micro context or focus of much social work intervention at national level and are also sometimes, and perhaps increasingly, the focus of cross-national or international activity, as indicated in the concluding section.

Changing family forms and functions

The term 'family' has been used 'in various ways to include both a variety of social arrangements and ideological constructions' (Papadopoulos

67

1996:171). Conventionally, distinctions have been drawn between the *extended* family and the *nuclear* family. The former consists of three generations and/or a network of relatives (kin) living as one household (or in very close proximity), and was assumed to exist in pre-industrial times and to continue in countries where rural and/or traditional norms still prevail. Nuclear families, in contrast, are considered the norm in urbanised and economically advanced societies and consist of an adult couple, normally married, who have split off from their families of origin to establish their own family unit with their offspring.

But this is too simplistic a picture of family forms globally. There is evidence both that the extended family is 'breaking down' in countries where it might be assumed to be prevalent; and that it still exists, though in a more dispersed form and with emotional rather than practical functions, in many advanced societies. Similarly, the notion of the 'ideal' nuclear family has less currency in many post-modern and post-industrial societies. For instance Rapaport (1989) noted a decline in the conventional nuclear family across 14 European countries. Alongside this there has been the identification and acceptance of more varied family forms, and changes within the role-relationships, even within conventional nuclear families.

Gergen (1991:30) suggested that a range of changes have made the definition of the family more ambiguous and proposed the notion of the 'floating family'. This recognises the possibility of conflict and breakdown in adult couple relationships, resulting in the likelihood of lone parenthood and of 'serial partnerships', which in turn result in the existence of step or reconstituted families. The composition of individual families has thus changed in much shorter time-frames than those associated with conventional accounts of the family life-cycle and there is often less clarity about who is in and who is out of 'the family'. Such decisions are also no longer related exclusively to household form or spatial proximity of family members. Additionally, changing sexual mores have enabled the recognition in some societies of homosexual or lesbian partnerships in households which may include the children of one or both partners or adopted or fostered children.

Such variety in family form is probably associated more with Western, particularly Anglo-American, countries than other parts of the world, but it is clear that, for at least a generation, economic, scientific, political (legal) and demographic changes have been taking place which are not exclusive to advanced countries, and which have had a bearing on families globally. Pausing to consider family functions, these can be summarised as the regulation of sexual behaviour; the reproduction, care and socialisation of children and care of other dependent members; the meeting of physical and emotional needs of family members, and the transmission of religious and cultural norms. The family previously also met the educational and training needs of children, in preparation for adult work roles, and also provided health care for its members. While in many societies these latter functions have been largely replaced by the provisions of the state, elsewhere these aspects may remain with the family to a greater or lesser extent. The relative *strength*, that is, stability and ability to carry out expected functions, of the family has been a focus for debate and analysis. For instance, Papadopoulos (1996:182) identified the Greek family as demonstrating a 'web of relationships [forming] a special mix of solidarity and dependency' and, in a comparative analysis of Eurostat figures, demonstrated various criteria (including low divorce rates, lone-parent households and births outside marriage) on which the family could be said to be a strong institution in Greece. Papadopoulos suggested that the low level of Greek welfare state provisions (relative to other EU countries, Australia, Norway and the US) resulted in stronger familial expectations and obligations. Thus, the family was seen as a social and economic unit, a vehicle for mutual support and social mobility. Whenever possible, families invested in education for their children, seeing this as a route to betterment and security for the whole family. This analysis might hold true in many other countries (for instance, Thailand and Papua New Guinea), and arguably the strength of families is associated with the stage of transition from rural to urban societies and the values of a given society, rather than with the strength of welfare states specifically.

Cultural (including religious) values therefore have a significant role in determining the accepted forms and expectations of families in given societies. A range of observable differences (for example, the basis on which sexual partnerships are agreed or arranged, the likely age at which adults form families, the likelihood of care for elders or family members with a disability, the expected roles of women inside and outside the home, divorce levels, family size related to the possibility of birth control or abortion) depend as much on cultural factors as on economic factors. It is this cultural dimension which underlies a distinction that has been drawn between the more individually oriented ambitions and roles apparent in the West relative to an orientation to the needs and interests of family groups identified in the East (Tam and Yeung 1994).

A consideration of changes in family form and functions requires also some appreciation of *demographic* changes, since these both reflect and shape other societal changes impacting on families. Globally, there have been a number of significant trends but two in particular have been singled out for brief discussion. The first is a reduction in family size accompanying a shift to nuclear family households, noted, for instance, over a decade ago by Seager and Olsen (1986:107); the second is a universal rise in the number of people over 65 years, marked, for instance, by a special edition of the *Asia*

Pacific Journal of Social Work (1993) and discussed in Van Wormer (1997). These two factors are related in so far as the increase in elders is both an absolute rise, related to greater longevity, and a proportional rise, relative to the number of children and adults of working age.

The distribution of children relative to elders in any population (the age dependency ratio) is extremely varied and changing. UN predictions for the position by 2025 were cited by Graycar (1993) as follows: 118 people over 65 years in Japan to every 100 children under 15 years (or 111 elders in Singapore), to only 12 or 15 people over 65, relative to every 100 children in Afghanistan or Bangladesh, respectively. Such balance or imbalance in sectors of the population who might be dependent has direct implications for the policy decisions about forms of welfare expenditure and provision as well for individual families, and concerns centre on the numbers of increasingly frail elderly people to be supported (financially and practically) by a decreasing pool of adults of working age.

Universal trends towards smaller family size reflect the decrease in the number of children being born as a result of scientific advance (efficient contraception), changes in the position and choices of women, and also, in some cases, significant state interventions in family life and individual choice, through population policies. Thus, while cultural and religious values have sometimes worked against the encouragement of family planning (for example, it is forbidden in Saudi Arabia and Chad, and not favoured by some in Ireland, Greece and Bolivia), elsewhere policies and practices to limit family size have been actively encouraged, if not enforced. Family planning strategies have been linked with child survival interventions through primary health care as the most important factors in improving the quality of life for children and families, as well as the socio-economic development prospects of countries, and Thailand and Indonesia have been described as the leaders in population control in a number of countries surveyed in South East Asia (Davis 1994:11).

It was recently estimated that Thailand's active birth control measures (pursued since 1970 in association with programmes to improve maternal and child health) have prevented 20 million births over the past decade (*Today*, BBC Radio 4, 2 November 96). In Indonesia (with the fourth largest population in the world), Davis described how the family planning programme, initiated in 1967, was not just about demographics or a clinical matter of contraception but an endeavour to bring about changes in the value system and norms of the society. A Presidential speech in 1989 had paid tribute to the role of 'the guardians of socio-cultural norms ... such as religious leaders and other prominent members of the community' in effecting a shift in societal attitudes to children and families. The activities of village groups were identified as important in encouraging and monitoring family planning efforts of all members of the community with the (largely successful) aim of creating small families as the norm (Davis 1994:15). The critical nature of China's population growth has also required stringent control methods, and birth rates have been reduced to a 'one child per family' norm through mandatory abortions and sterilisations, achieved through threat of fines and withdrawal of benefits in relation to any subsequent births (Davis 1994:23). However, the imposition of this policy and the favouring of boys over girls has had unanticipated consequences in female infanticide or abandonment, also observed in India, where some public authorities have placed cots in hospitals where 'people could deposit unwanted children' (Goldenburg 1995). This has resulted in an imbalance in the national gender ratio in these and other countries, including Bangladesh and Pakistan.

It can be noted in this context that scientific advances in infertility treatment and genetics are offering increased opportunities for couples in advanced industrial countries to have (healthy) children, with associated ethical and political dilemmas about the choices and costs related to such possibilities.

Women, children and policies for families

The composition and responsibilities of families in different societies, as indicated above, vary according to a number of factors. Two variables which have continuing importance are the position of women and attitudes towards children, both globally and nationally. These in turn affect the cluster of policies which most directly address the needs and opportunities of families, within any wider welfare provisions which states make, whether directly or through the agencies of the voluntary and private sectors.

Considering first the position of women, the women's suffrage movement was beginning to take root in some parts of the world around the turn of the twentieth century; by 1917 women in Australia, most Nordic countries and the FSU states had gained the vote, with New Zealand having led the way in 1893. Further developments occurred in the 20-year period from 1918, extending rights to women in Brazil, Burma and Thailand as well as many European countries and North America. A further period of political emancipation occurred in the years 1941–60 affecting the rest of Europe, about half the African states and most countries of Asia, and South America, while, in most remaining countries, women have achieved the vote since 1961 (Seager and Olsen 1986). In South Africa, universal suffrage was only achieved with the ending of apartheid and the first democratic elections in 1994.

But the granting of political rights does not necessarily ensure equal representation or the development of social and economic opportunities, as the inferior position of women in many parts of the world still testifies and, as the existence of female infanticide suggests, many societies continue to view girl children as a burden. This is related both to cultural practices, such as dowries which entail heavy costs to the families of girls, and to their potential economic value in employment terms, but also reflects the lower social status accorded to women in some Asian and African societies (Goldenburg 1995).

However, since the 1960s, with developments in contraception and improved access to educational and health opportunities in most advanced industrial countries, there is some evidence of governmental attempts to protect and promote the rights of women. This has been in part the result of campaigning by feminists, from a wide range of ideological perspectives (Williams 1989), with the active sponsorship of the UN through the Decade for women (1975–85) and the more recent world conferences on and for Women (for example Beijing in 1995).

Many countries have seen a rapid rise in women's participation in education, including at higher levels, and also in labour participation rates, such that in much of Europe and North America, it is the norm for women to undertake paid work outside the home for much of their adult lives. However, even in these countries, and with equal opportunities legislation in place in relation to employment, the differentials in pay levels, promotion opportunities and the uneven distribution of women in different occupational groups has been well documented (Green 1991; Lewis 1993; Stockman et al. 1995).

Such differentials go back in part to assumptions about the role of the state and the position of men. So Lewis (1993) could suggest a categorisation of European Union states according to whether they illustrated strong, modified, or weak male-breadwinner countries, ranging from Greece at one end of the spectrum to Denmark at the other. It can be suggested that such a classification could be correlated with tendencies towards acceptance of patriarchal authority or family democratic patterns, and might also be related to the influence of religious values, since religions around the world tend to support a particular home-based and family-orientated role for women.

Even in countries where waged work and Western-style 'careers' are less available, women may play a significant role in community development, or in political activity at national level, as evidenced, for instance, in some Latin American countries (Green 1991, Julia 1994). In other societies women and young females are seen as making an important contribution to family incomes, though this may mean them leaving their families to find work, either moving to urban areas, as for instance in Ghana (Agarwal et al. 1997) or to other countries, as in the case of Filipino women (Bagley et al. 1997).

But women are still widely viewed as having the major responsibility for the care of children and for the maintenance of family systems and households. Even when women themselves are economically active in the informal sector or the formal labour market, there has been little evidence in any society of more equal distribution of domestic roles (Lewis 1993; Stockman et al. 1995). This may impact particularly heavily on women in less developed countries where traditional expectations about women's roles sometimes include tending a plot to grow some of the foodstuffs needed by the family and adhering to time-consuming cooking methods, without the conveniences of water on tap or Western-style cooking facilities, for instance, in Papua New Guinea (Schneider 1993).

Elsewhere, the encroachment of the outside world, including the demands of businessmen and sexual tourism, may provide a source of income to rural families in poverty whose daughters can earn money through prostitution in the cities, as in Thailand (Mensendiek 1997), although countries in the West and Central Europe have also seen an increase in prostitution (mainly by young, single women), in the face of lack of employment opportunities or very low wage jobs. Additionally, even where other forms of employment might be found, relatively few employers operate 'family-friendly' policies, and increasing numbers of lone parents have sometimes felt under pressure to 'get off benefits' but to find work for which training is not needed and which can be fitted round child care responsibilities (as in the UK).

When problems occur in relation to children – concerns about educational attainment or about physical or mental illness or delinquent behaviour or even child abuse by a male relative – it is still often the case that women are seen as 'responsible'. Indeed, the breakdown in traditional family forms is sometimes laid at the door of 'feminists', including women who have apparently put 'self-fulfilment' or earning money to assist the family economy above the needs of the family. The changing position of women has challenged patriarchal assumptions inside families as well as in the wider society, and, while some would argue that many families have become more democratic institutions in the process, others would see this as part of a wider breakdown of respect for authority in societies (Gergen 1991).

Against a degree of societal 'blaming', for instance in relation to working mothers, must be set the conflicting policies, referred to previously, which assume that women's earnings will be needed to support the family (as in the Nordic countries), or that women (as well as men) are to be discouraged from receiving state support to raise their children (as in the US and UK).

Additionally, the shift to community care policies in relation to elders and adults with disabilities, evident in so many advanced industrial countries, once more assumes a caring role by women, although there are less women in families to share this responsibility, and many in the likely age group are themselves in paid work outside the home. For instance, according to Graycar (1993), 61 per cent of married women in the age group 45–54 years are active in the labour force in Australia. Additionally, increased divorce rates and changing family structures may alter the sense of obligation felt to offer care for instance to 'in-laws' or step-parents, as suggested by studies in Australia and the US (McGlone 1997)

Turning now to the position of children, their care, as stated, has generally been regarded as a natural responsibility of families, especially women in families, but to be supplemented or supplanted by alternative arrangements should such care fall short or fail in some way. An international concern with the rights and protection of children originated with the founding of Save the Children Fund in 1919 and its extension to the international scene by 1923, in response to the plight of refugee children. This organisation drafted a Declaration on the Rights of the Child, adopted (as the Geneva Declaration) by the League of Nations in 1924, and in 1948, the United Nations agreed a revised version. In 1959, the UN further developed the Declaration, including civil rights (for example to name and nationality) and introduced the phrase 'the best interests of the child'; in 1989, after a lengthy redrafting process, it was given the status of a Convention (Hill and Tisdall 1997:27).

The preamble states that children have equal value to adults, but need special safeguards and care; that they should grow up in a family environment, with due regard for cultural values, and that international cooperation should aim to improve the living conditions of all children. The Convention contains '54 articles concerning civil, economic, social and cultural rights' and defines children as below the age of 18 years. By 1996 all but six countries had signed the Convention (Hill and Tisdall 1997:28). The UN Convention has been important in setting standards to be attained but it has also been criticised on a number of points, including being both gender-blind and ethnocentric; and lacking relevance to the lives of the majority of children in the Southern hemisphere: it cannot of itself cure the plight of children in extreme poverty or affected by war, nor prevent negligent or harmful parenting. However, it has been a spur to the development of children's advocacy schemes, for example, Children's Rights Councils in Brazil; to national consultation and participation exercises, for instance in Slovakia, India and Denmark, and to a general raising of children on policy agendas in many countries (Hill and Tisdall 1997).

Hill and Tisdall (1997) also examined the concept of children's needs, predominantly from an Anglo-American perspective of psychological needs, while Kennedy et al. (1996) carried out comparative research on the economic circumstances of children across ten (advanced industrial) countries. They identified the continuing existence of child poverty, even in affluent societies such as Australia and the US, with children of lone-parent families being substantially the worst off. Ruxton (1996) has also surveyed the literature and statistics about a wide range of policies and provisions relating to children in the European Union.

However, Davis (1994) provided a different perspective on the needs and circumstances of children, in this case in South-east Asia, where 50 per cent of the population will be aged under 15 years in 2010. This and other material is important in reinforcing the fact that, just as attitudes to the family and women differ, so do attitudes to children, as well as the resources to meet their needs. In many countries, provision of clean water, sufficient food and very basic education and health care would be priorities for some families and agencies, and Western sensibilities about children's psychological development, would indeed seem irrelevant or inappropriate, or would at least need to be addressed in relation to the physical and cultural environment. (This perspective, for instance in relation to child labour is discussed further in Chapter 5.)

Turning now to 'family policies', Papadopoulos (1996) observed that 'family policies affect the extent to which certain notions of "the family" are reenforced and reproduced as ideological constructs', and identified a number of definitions supplied by earlier writers, concluding that 'the term "policies for families" is probably more adequate as it refers to different forms of the family' (1996:171–2). This is certainly more useful in the context of discussion about family forms and policies internationally, since it is clear that some of the key features identifiable in 'family policy' in advanced industrial societies, and even in some newly industrialised countries (such as income support schemes and (formal) child care provisions), may not be features of less developed countries.

As already suggested, in less developed countries, policies for families might be concerned with reduction of family size, the development of programmes for child and maternal health, informal education programmes aimed at child nutrition and development and/or alternative means of providing for families other than through children's earnings. Thus, programmes which fall broadly under the remit of 'health' and 'education' policies would have greatest priority and might be seen as for the good of communities and society, rather than for individuals and families, as such.

In advanced industrial countries messages about favoured family forms and about the responsibilities expected of families have been conveyed by

recent policy trends. Thus, in the Anglo-American world and the majority
of European countries, legislative and fiscal measures have aimed to discourage lone parenthood and to extend the period during which parental
responsibility to maintain children applies. So, for example, policies have
promoted the entry to the labour market by lone parents (usually mothers)
(the US); absent parents (usually fathers) have been required to continue to
provide financial support to children (Germany, UK); parents of children
who truant or commit crimes can be held responsible (France, UK), and
parents have been expected to maintain or assist their older children, whether
they be unemployed teenagers (UK) or young people (over the age of
majority) in higher education (Australia). Additionally, in some countries,
(social) housing legislation has tended to assist families rather than other
vulnerable groups within society.

As Cannan et al. (1992) identified, even within the European (Union)
context, a comparative perspective on 'family policies' reveals different
attitudes to the importance attached to the 'privacy' of the family (as in the
UK) relative to a view of children as future national capital, for whom the
wider society also has responsibility; and in the encouragement to be given
to family formation and maintenance (for example France has well established pro-natalist policies). The difference in approach to families, particularly between the UK and other European countries, was further illustrated
in a study carried out for UNICEF (Hewlett 1993) of advanced industrial
countries. This identified two models of state attitudes to children and
families (as reflected in their policy outcomes), described as the European/
Japanese model and the Anglo-American model. The first was seen as
supportive to families and maintaining 'family values', while the second
was described by David Barsamian as being 'basically at war with children
and families and [having] destroyed them', through the pressure on parents
to work resulting in 'latchkey children, television supervision, abuse of
children by children, violence against children' (Chomsky 1996:32–33).

The implication here seems to be that societies in which both parents
work risk the health of families. While this view certainly has some currency, states can be supportive to both parents having choices about work
and child-care arrangements, as demonstrated in the high levels of good-
quality and varied day-care provisions for children in the Nordic countries
and their well-established schemes for parental leave (both for care of babies and young children and for older children who are sick or have special
needs) (Kahn and Kamerman 1994; Ruxton 1996).

Additionally, superficially pro-family attitudes can be damaging if carried to extremes, as illustrated previously in the case of Romania. Encouragement of large families during the Communist regime (not least through
a ban on birth control and abortions), with minimal practical or fiscal sup-

port for them, resulted in dire poverty for some families, in damaged health for women who resorted to illegal abortions, and in a high number of 'orphans' or abandoned children in state care (McGrath 1998).

Social work with children and families

As may be apparent from the preceding discussion, the range of interventions under the broad heading of social and development work in relation to families, deemed necessary and/or appropriate globally, is considerable, although they might be seen as having a unifying framework in the concepts of *protection* and *empowerment*. Additionally, it is likely that effective interventions, which support and protect children and families, wherever undertaken, require collaborative work with other systems concerned with child and family welfare, such as health and education, and sometimes also with the labour market, housing authorities and/or the income maintenance or criminal justice systems.

A number of areas of concern could be identified as providing a focus for interventions aimed particularly at children and families, including the following: children and families in poverty and/or marginalised on grounds of race or ethnicity, children and families affected by disabilities or specific health problems, families where domestic violence (to either women or children or both) is an issue, and the provision of alternative care for children. The first of these is mainly addressed in the context of a wider discussion about poverty in the next chapter, and interventions in relation to minority families follow on from a discussion about migration and the particular circumstances of refugees in Chapter 6. This section therefore provides a comparative perspective on the remaining areas, and also mentions new developments arising from technical developments and the increased likelihood of cross-national or international activities in relation to children and families.

Turning first to families where *disability* or *ill health* present problems, Ruxton (1996) identified a dearth of statistical information on an international or regional level about the scale of the problem of children with disabilities or particular health care needs. However, it is an area where there is a close association with the health and education sectors, and a variety of responses by the social professions are observable in many countries. These demonstrate the different roles of social workers, including those based in hospitals and other health care settings, as well as in the residential sector.

In a number of societies, the needs of children with disabilities, including in less developed countries, have traditionally been identified and responded to by the voluntary sector (including religious groups) and provision has mainly been in the form of residential care. This form of 'care' (by the state) was also the norm in the countries of the FSU and Central Europe. While in some cases such children are still cared for in institutions, a brief article in 1995 had described the early establishment (since 1989) of a community-based respite care scheme in Poland and a later study by the same authors illustrated some development of community-based social services and social work in this field (Gammon and Dziegielewska 1995, 1997). More recent developments elsewhere, for instance in Romania, have also favoured the closing of institutions in favour of return to and support of families of origin or substitute care (McGrath 1998) in line with trends in Europe more generally (Ruxton 1996)

Ruxton (1996) also identified concern by parents of children with disabilities about levels of discrimination and the need for more financial and practical support. In some EU countries, principles of normalisation have become well established and interventions by the social professions are aimed at integration, although small-scale, high-standard, specialist residential and day-care provisions as well as fostering schemes are also available (in Denmark, for instance). In the UK the concern with abuse within the family, has detracted from a wider definition of children in need, resulting in this group being relatively neglected or served better by the voluntary sector and self-help organisations than by the helping professions.

Relative neglect by the public welfare sector also seems to be the case in the US, since an otherwise wide-ranging text about social welfare makes little reference to the situation of children with disabilities, beyond noting that there is inadequate financial help for families with needs of this kind, and that children may have to be fostered or adopted to meet the costs of specialist medical care (Van Wormer 1997:299). However, in other respects, principles of normalisation and integration have been widely accepted, and in some states, for example, school social workers in Illinois have clearly defined roles in the assessment and support of children who have special needs related to physical or psychological/emotional impairment. There are also a number of well-established agencies in the voluntary sector offering social work and other services to children with special needs and their families (FRCD 1994).

A more recently recognised issue in some European countries, in relation to ill health or disability in the family, is the extent to which children and young people themselves may undertake significant care roles of adult family members or siblings, at the expense of their own health and development – and with little practical or social support, although Ruxton (1996) noted some recent initiatives in the UK, mainly through the voluntary sector. An exploratory comparative study in Britain, France, Sweden and Germany found little official recognition of the issue and suggested the need for increased awareness as a precursor to development of services (Becker 1995).

The other area of recent growth in provision and intervention concerns families where parents and/or children have contracted HIV/AIDS. This is a significant problem (in terms of numbers) in some African and Asian countries, for instance, one in forty adults in sub-Saharan Africa is estimated to have contracted the HIV virus (Van Wormer 1997; see also Brooks 1996). In Thailand, government programmes to prevent and treat AIDS, including in children, are well established, if stretched relative to needs. A Thai press report (*The Nation*, 5 January 98) described how social workers employed by the AIDS Network Development Foundation (Aid Net) assist children caring for parents with AIDS or orphaned. Much of the work is based on community development projects but 345 children orphaned by AIDS have received educational scholarships under a more individually focused Foster Parent Project. However, many more children live in poverty and face lack of education, or discrimination in the school system related to their (or their parents') condition. Similarly, an earlier report in the British press (*The Guardian*, 9 November 96) had signalled concerns about a 'huge surge in AIDS orphans' (estimated at over 500,000 children by the year 2000) in Indonesia, following a study which demonstrated much higher rates of AIDS-related adult deaths than indicated by government statistics.

In the EU, there were estimated to be nearly 5000 children infected by AIDS in 1994 (Ruxton 1996:234), with highest levels identified in Spain, France and Italy and the UK and very low reports of cases in other EU countries. A European Forum has been established, together with a new Commission programme (1996–2000) to promote programmes concerned with prevention, treatment and education. Outside the European Union, the high number and serious plight of babies and children with AIDS in Romania has received international attention and resulted in the establishment of some treatment provisions, including hospice care, by NGOs (McGrath 1998).

Turning now to violence within the family, the situation initially identified as 'baby battering' in the US in the early 1960s (Kemp et al. 1962) was more generally developed into a conception of child abuse, with a related need for child protection. Slightly later, in the 1970s, the abuse of women by their partners became recognised as domestic violence, and by the 1990s this had increasingly been recognised as also having an impact on children. Both forms of abuse, whether physical (including sexual) or emotional can be seen as a form of abuse of power within the domestic environment. Specialist services have been developed (usually separately) to address these problems in advanced industrial countries and there is also increasing attention to both issues in some less developed countries.

In relation to domestic violence, Dobash and Dobash (1992) examined the range of legal and practical responses to this problem in the UK and US. This response was largely through the voluntary sector and operated partly on a self and mutual help basis, with little initial response to the problem by the statutory social services or trained social workers. This perhaps reflects the earlier mentioned societal view of the family as a private institution, in which state services and functionaries should play no part. It also reflects a situation which can be observed elsewhere, where the initiative to support other women has to come from 'the community', that is, other women, rather than from state-approved and funded services, as evidenced in a study of violence to women in Israel (a state apparently supportive of the family and placing value on women's role in it). The authors also noted tensions between the perceptions and responses of the helping professions relative to activists informed by feminist perspectives (Edelson et al. 1992). Elsewhere, getting the issue of domestic violence onto the public agenda at all may be difficult, as Van Wormer (1997) and others have suggested is the case in India, for example.

Even before the 1989 Convention on the Rights of the Child, the recognition of child abuse and development of responses has been far more widespread, and has taken a dominant position in the development of some (Western) social work services. As mentioned previously, this is evident in the UK where child protection work – assessment and intervention in reported cases – over a decade or more had taken priority in both the allocation of resources and perceptions of social work in the public mind. Negative public attitudes to social workers have been based on 'scandals' reported in the press of children under social work supervision being killed by their carers, and by revelations about child sexual abuse, sometimes thought to be exaggerated by social workers.

While child sexual abuse came onto the public agenda in the late 1980s in the UK, Van Wormer (1997:326) suggested that an autobiography by Maya Angelou (1969) 'broke through the wall of silence'; child sexual abuse (including incest) is now widely accepted by some as having been a well-kept secret for generations in societies around the world. It can also be linked to more recent concerns about a growth in child pornography, for instance on the Internet, and paedophile activities which sometimes cross national boundaries and require international and interprofessional responses.

An interesting example of the possible mismatch between perceptions of need between professionals and the wider community, in relation to child protection in a very different society, was illustrated in a study visit to Papua New Guinea in the mid-1990s. A small group of academic and professional workers were trying to raise the profile of child abuse (in various forms) and gain official agreement to intervention. However, it was clear that the capacity of the state or voluntary agencies to address this problem in individual cases, in the context of a dearth of resources for welfare provision and the persistence in much of society of traditional attitudes to the (inferior) place of women and children, and suspicions of people who might be seen as interfering, created a very difficult situation in which to develop responses; it became clear that broad-based policies aimed at public education and attitudinal change and community-based sanctions were required (Ferea 1995).

Returning to the European scene, the work of Heatherington et al. (1997) in a comparative study of child protection strategies in eight European Union countries, has illustrated the varied nature of official (including social work) responses, according to perceptions of children and the relationship between the family and society, in which some countries have clearly seen the provision of 'support services' as having a preventive role. There have been recent signs of a shift in British thinking to promote such policies which need to be mirrored in social work practice, whether in the state or independent sectors. In this context, various writers have suggested that the West/North also has much to learn from approaches developed in the East/South: a brief note by White (1998) about a child-oriented focus and community development practice in India illustrated this point.

However, there are clearly cases where, in the interests of child protection or for other reasons (including sometimes severe disability), and, notwithstanding social work ethics which usually favour the maintenance of the family unit whenever possible, *alternative care* on a permanent or respite basis has to be provided. Most societies, even ones which might previously have provided substitute care through the extended family or village, now have such provision, sometimes run under the auspices of religious groups or international aid agencies (that is, not formally part of a response by the state and professional social workers to social needs). In the EU, where residential and day care provisions are provided by local authorities (or agencies under contract to them) there is variation in the extent to which they employ professionally trained staff, and the range of qualifications considered appropriate (Ruxton 1996).

Residential provision or alternative care through fostering or adoption has traditionally related to two groups of children and young people, those in need of care and protection and those seen as needing punishment, containment and/or treatment because of offending behaviour, though in some countries this distinction has been blurred if not abandoned in practice (except for young people needing secure accommodation because of the nature of their offence/severity of disturbance).

In a study of alternative care policy and practice in the EU, Colton and Hellinckx (1994) identified a number of common trends. These were summarised as the decrease in residential care relative to an increased use of fostering; but an increase in the severity of the problems presented by the children and young people in residential provisions. In addition, there has tended to be a move away from large-scale residential establishments towards smaller units in 'home' communities, and increased differentiation in the residential and fostering provisions; increased professionalisation of residential and foster carers, and greater use of an ecological perspective in the work. Finally, some alternatives have been developed, such as day care and independent living schemes. They noted that the pace of change across Europe is uneven, and more marked in the northern countries, Denmark, Germany, the Netherlands and the UK.

A similar study by Madge (1994) illustrated particular features of residential care in a wider range of European countries, and suggested that Sweden had the highest proportion of children fostered (80 per cent, including children with a wide range of special needs), although comparisons were rendered difficult by the different bases on which statistics are kept, and the very limited information available in some countries (for example, Italy). There are also different legislative bases for children being cared for, although many countries have provision for voluntary as well as statutory admissions. Additionally, there has been varied development of systems which aim to ensure the representation of both children and young people, and their parents or carers, although the balance between the two groups varies. Van Wormer suggested that in Norway the child's interests take precedence while Germany and the USA veer towards the rights of parents (1997:337).

On a global scale, four issues in relation to alternative care can be identified as needing more attention. The first concerns the educational needs of children in care, though Weale (in the IASSW Newsletter No. 4 1997) noted 'pockets of pioneering work', for instance in Australia, Canada, and the Netherlands. Conversely, some countries have stronger traditions of linking education and training programmes to care provisions (for example, Germany, India). The second concerns the needs of young people leaving care, and this group has been identified in Europe as more vulnerable than others in the population, in terms of employment, finance and accommodation – that is the transition to independent, adulthood, although the Nordic countries have better established systems of after-care than other states (Ruxton 1996).

Thirdly, the rights of foster or adoptive parents, relative to the possibility of maintaining contact with children's natural families has become a focus of concern in some countries, though attitudes and practice vary, for instance between the US and Israel (Mosek 1993). Also, the extent to which fostering is seen as a professional activity is increasingly under debate and the differences in thinking underpinning alternative care through foster placements has recently been examined internationally across 22 countries (Colton and Williams 1997).

Finally, another contested issue concerns the placement, including for adoption, of children from ethnic minorities. In the UK, for instance, they have been noted as being over-represented in the care system and more vulnerable in terms of the three issues already mentioned. There has also been considerable debate about the relative merits of trans-racial relative to same-race placements, with the latter generally being preferred. In fact, UK legislation since the 1989 Children Act requires social workers to pay due regard to factors such as the child's ethnicity and religion, as well as other characteristics, in assessing need and appropriate intervention.

Child care practice in other countries has also been criticised for lack of regard to cultural and ethnic origins, or for actual racism and break-up of communities (in line with colonisation), as illustrated in the removal of Aboriginal children from their families in Australia, a practice which only ceased with the passing of the Aboriginal Child Placement Act in 1986. However, O'Connor (1994) has suggested that this practice has effectively been continued through the operation of the juvenile justice system, through which disproportionate numbers of Aboriginal youths are being institutionalised in the penal system (a situation evident also in the UK and US).

Concerning the situation of young offenders more generally, Lane (1998) reported on a recent European seminar which suggested that common trends in patterns of offending were evident across eight European countries, related to similar likely causes. Not least of these were underachievement in the education setting and lack of preparation for a very competitive job market (for instance, he cited 25 per cent of young people in Germany as unemployed), with resultant problems in relation to finance and accommodation, and establishing a role in the adult world. Drug use was also widely linked to problematic behaviour, and a variety of strategies in relation to prevention, intervention and correction were in evidence. These reflected differences in the age at which children and young people are judged to be liable for criminal behaviour and differential attitudes to custody (as opposed to community based punishment and treatment) and to regimes within correctional institutions (Ruxton 1996). Lane (1998) concluded that more research and development of innovative solutions were required, in the face of generally rising levels of anti-social, criminal and violent behaviour.

Some concluding thoughts: new developments and implications for international social work

Globally, 'the family', in various forms and notwithstanding concerns about its relative strength, remains the cornerstone of care for children and vulnerable members of society. The UN, at a recent conference about social development, declared that supporting families was not just a matter of welfare policy but a long-term social investment (IFSW Update 1/97). But how individual states treat families and their expectations of them, depend on a complex mix of religious and cultural traditions and values, in the context of economic capabilities and political ideologies, not least in relation to women. In most societies, support for children and families is evident to varying degrees through development programmes and legislative and fiscal measures.

Similar problems and trends are observable across many advanced industrialised countries (although organisational responses may vary); related concerns are sometimes evident in less developed countries, where responses may need to be significantly different and/or rooted in community and voluntary initiatives rather than addressed through the state. Where state services and social work are more established, intervention by the social professions can sometimes be viewed as aimed at family support and amelioration of social problems while, in other cases, it is clearly a measure of the extent to which particular children, young people or families are viewed as deviant in some way and in need of treatment or control.

Relatively new areas of concern and intervention are apparent in a number of countries related to scientific and technical advances. While the spread of HIV/AIDS challenges the medical profession and social support systems throughout the world, developments in reproductive technology have prompted the establishment of infertility and/or genetic counselling services. The growth in telephone help-lines has had direct impact on child care and family work. For instance, a telephone service for children in the UK answered more than a million calls in 1997, 14 per cent more than in 1996 (Child Line Annual Report, 1/98); Lazar and Erera (1997) reported on use of a national telephone helpline (ERAN) in Israel. Similarly, the Internet is now being used to offer some self-help services (Wilson 1996), and is used by some child care workers, for example in Denmark and other European countries, to secure foster placement and exchange information about missing children (Shahid 1998).

In some countries and regions, international influences (for example, tourism) and underdeveloped or uncompetitive local economies have had a particular effect on family life and the roles of individual members, as can be noted in increased pressures on women and children to contribute to the family economy, sometimes in ways which are contrary to their own interests and/or which involve intra or intercountry migration.

Higher levels of population mobility in general and increased rates of 'mixed marriages' have produced new opportunities and new stresses for individuals and families. The result has sometimes been conflict over the care of children, particularly if such marriages break down and one partner returns to a country of origin, possibly 'kidnapping' the children (Hegar and Greif 1991). In the UK child abductions increased from 11 cases in 1986 to 145 in 1993, and a newly formed organisation, Reunite, prompted the establishment of a parliamentary working party on the subject in the early 1990s. Some of the necessary responses and changes are legal or diplomatic but social professionals may also be involved.

Another area with international dimensions, related to ethnicity, concerns the question of cross-national adoptions. This is not in itself a new phenomenon, though periodically particular events or cases have brought it to public attention. Some would argue that it is legitimate to 'rescue' children from otherwise certain poverty or institutional care (for instance, in recent examples from Peru or Romania), while others consider that removal of children from their country of origin deprives them of their cultural heritage, with profound implications for identity formation. Finding solutions to the needs of children within their own societies would certainly seem to be the preferred solution (not least because of the small numbers who can be 'helped' by cross-national adoptions relative to the scale of need), but failing this, attention needs to be paid to the conditions under which children can be adopted and are likely to be raised, including opportunities to learn about their own culture (Bagley 1993; Greenfield 1994).

This chapter has taken a predominantly comparative approach to a discussion about the nature of families and associated social problems and responses. However, there are also global dimensions to the root causes of problems affecting some families. These can be identified as *poverty* and the unequal distribution of wealth within and between societies, and also the unequal power relationships between people of different nationality, race and ethnicity in the context of increased *migration*. Additionally, families in particular societies are more or less susceptible to natural or manmade (*sic*) *disasters*, and the increased amount of population mobility has increased the international dimension, for example, of transport disasters, with effects on families and communities across a number of countries. These three themes are the subject of examination in Chapters 5, 6 and 7.

5 Poverty – a global problem

Introduction

Poverty is a universal problem rooted in structural divisions and personal differences in every society. But the concept of poverty has changed over time and means different things to different people, not least related to their national context. In the industrialised countries there have been concerns about causes, solutions and how to measure poverty since the nineteenth century, when forerunners of the social professions were engaged in efforts to address poverty, whether at individual or policy levels. The twentieth century has seen the growth of awareness of poverty outside Europe and North America and attempts to respond through international initiatives, particularly in the second half of this century. 1996 was declared the International Year for the Eradication of Poverty, following a World Summit on Social Development in 1994, and there has been some change in approach to development theories and work in the 1990s.

This chapter considers some aspects of the nature and scale of the problem, seeing it as having international, regional, and national dimensions, and considers the relationship between notions of poverty and social exclusion. It then considers how the international community has sought to address the problem and some of the research and policy developments which have impacted on specific countries. Finally, it considers the implications for the social professions and illustrates their concern and responses to particular problems resulting from poverty.

The nature of the problem

The major divisions in the world between rich and poor, the 'haves' and 'have-nots', can be demarcated along various lines – West/East or North/ South, urban/rural, white/black – more generally between the advanced industrial nations and the less developed (agrarian) countries. However, such divisions hide a range of disparities, including those within countries based on class, gender and ethnicity, as well as those based on cross-national or regional comparisons. Such divisions immediately raise questions about what constitutes poverty, since clearly the situation of traditional communities, where the local economy is based on subsistence farming and barter, is vastly different from the position of the urban poor in the cash economies of Europe and North America. Indeed, the former communities may not consider themselves poor in some circumstances.

An initial distinction needs to be made therefore between the concept of *absolute* poverty, where people are without any form of income or means of support such that their very survival is threatened, and that of *relative* poverty, as suggested in the UK by Townsend (1978) and generally deemed more useful in the context of advanced industrialised countries. Townsend linked relative poverty to a range of deprivations and defined it as 'the absence or inadequacy of those diets, amenities, standards, services and activities which are common or customary in society'. There has thus been a growing acceptance that poverty has a social dimension in addition to an economic form, and is relative to a given time and place. This thinking has subsequently been extended into a more general framing, in Europe, of the concept of *social exclusion*, acknowledging that economic hardship is only one aspect of the experience of discrimination, powerlessness and lack of access to and participation in civic society of particular groups.

Poverty is related to decisions by those who hold power (whether economic or political) about how resources are shared and the range of international and national policies which determine opportunities for income generation and (re)distribution. It therefore has a moral dimension, and its amelioration or eradication can be related to public and political will as well as to economic resources. A UN Draft Declaration (1994), following the World Summit for Social Development (WSSD, Copenhagen, 1994), stated

> The struggle against poverty constitutes a moral obligation to ensure that all human beings enjoy at least the basic food, shelter, social services and human relationships that are necessary for health, dignity and social participation ... All poverty results from social, economic, legal and political structures and not just from the limited capabilities and misfortunes of individuals. Efforts to reduce and eliminate poverty must be based on a continuing examination of the

structures and processes that determine the distribution and redistribution of income in a society. (United Nations 1994:20–21)

Statements about the nature of poverty have also been related to questions about its extent. The world has been described as having a one-third/two-thirds split:

> The poor of the less developed and third world countries and increased numbers from the industrialised first world nations make up the deprived poor of the 2/3 world. The privileged majority of the industrialised countries, together with those at the top of the social pyramids of the poor countries comprise the 'haves' of the 1/3 world. (O'Gorman 1992:xiii)

The measurement of poverty has received periodic attention since early, local attempts to assess its scale at the end of the nineteenth century. It has sometimes resulted in the formulation of a 'poverty line', relating income available to costs of meeting needs, and suggesting a level beneath which people might be considered poor. In Europe, currently, this is taken as being less than 50 per cent of the average earnings in a given society, and this formulation allows for some movement over time and place. Additionally, an indicator of costs and standards of living has been established, Purchasing Power Parities (PPPs), which enables comparisons between the states of the EU (Donnellan 1998). But globally, the use of a range of other indicators has frequently been used to illustrate the differences between countries and regions, in the scale of problems which either reflect or determine the socio-economic status of sectors of the population. Such indicators include statistics about education, health, water supplies, land holding, employment and trade, as well as income levels, illustrating the wide range of factors which are seen to interact with poverty.

Additionally, debates about *population policies* also have a place in any discussion of poverty, reflecting questions about the ability of natural resources to sustain the world's population. In 1974 the UN organised a first World Conference on Population, amid concerns about growth rates. By the time of the third World Conference on Population, in Cairo, 1994, the population had risen from 4 billion to 5.7 billion and, despite significant stabilisation or even downward trends in some countries' projections, was still rising (Harrison 1994). Seven out of ten of the world's most populated countries are in Asia, including the two 'giants', China (1100 million) and India (850 million), and reference has been made earlier to their stringent population control measures. Traditionally, high birth rates could be seen as a 'rational' response to poverty, given high infant mortality rates, subsistence farming or limited formal work opportunities, and very little (if any) support from the state, in relation to disease, disability or old age. But countries like Bangladesh (population over 100 million, and one of the poorest nations in the world) are beginning to see population control as in the interests of national survival and development, and its government has been promoting birth control alongside efforts to improve educational and health provisions (Ghazi 1994).

Also, Harrison (1994) noted that high rates of population growth have not been restricted to the less developed countries, and the US was cited as having a faster rate of growth than nine developing or newly industrialised countries, including Uruguay and South Korea. In general, low birth rates are associated with wealthier countries and high ones with poorer societies but this is not an automatic correlation, as high birth rates in the Middle East and low birth rates in Sri Lanka illustrate. Thus, the link between birth rates and poverty or economic development is complex. Although some countries have demonstrated an apparent relationship between a fall in birth rate and improved economic performance (for example, Thailand), other factors, such as educational levels, health care and women's rights, also have a bearing on the equation (Harrison 1994).

In relation to other indicators, *literacy* and *under-five mortality rates* have been seen as significantly associated with poverty levels and show a close association with each other. UNICEF statistics in the mid-1990s showed a literacy rate for advanced industrial countries approaching 100 per cent and under-five mortality rate of 10 in 1000, compared to 40 per cent and 125 in 1000 in South Asia, or 50 per cent and 170 per 1000 in sub-Saharan Africa, with East Asia and Latin America between these extremes. The links between poverty and health have been long established and periodically reiterated, including in advanced industrial countries. For instance, the right of people to basic health care (including provision of family planning, safe drinking water and sanitation) was enshrined in a UN Declaration on Primary Health Care dating back to 1978, and in a recent interview, Townsend suggested that the 1980 Black Report, virtually ignored in the UK, influenced policy directions promoted by the WHO (Richards 1996). The UN's belief in the importance of education as a basic public service (related to the health and welfare of whole societies) was reflected in a World Declaration on Education for All (in 1990), and has been an important element of many aid programmes since (see next section). Lack of education has been correlated with high poverty levels in both urban and rural societies.

In the latter case, rural poverty has also been seen as related to land ownership and use. For example, a news item on the UK radio (*Today*, BBC Radio 4, 22 November 96) stated that in Brazil 1 per cent of the population owns 50 per cent of the land, the most unfair distribution in the world. Apparently, efforts by the Brazilian Land Commission to redistribute land were being resisted by wealthy land owners (engaged in forestry or ranching): more than 1000 people had been killed, and an area the size of Belgium had already been deforested. (Issues of land use and misuse will be returned to in Chapter 7.)

Problems of rural poverty have, in some cases, resulted in continuing migration to urban areas in search of work and greater security, and the shanty towns and slums on the outskirts of major cities in Africa, Asia and Latin America have grown apace, usually without any infrastructure of sanitation or other amenities, and only physically and economically remote chances of work. For instance, 20 per cent of Bangladesh's population is now urban and the population of Dhakar has doubled in 20 years to eight million, three in ten of whom live in cardboard shanty towns, where private landlords resist efforts by NGOs to improve living conditions (Ghazi 1994). Even in the affluent West, rates of homelessness among adults have been rising (for instance, estimated at 7 per 1000 by the European Observatory on Homelessness); and problems of street children and homeless youth are now common to all continents, despite differences in scale (Davis 1994; Ruxton 1996; Van Wormer 1997). Concerns about housing and homelessness are reflected in the UN's Global Strategy for Shelter, aimed at improvements by the year 2000 (UN 1994).

But migration to the city has not ensured work in the less developed countries, and unemployment is another indicator of poverty which has also been rising in the West. UNDP material (1995) cited an International Labour Organisation (ILO) estimate that 30 per cent of the labour force globally is not productively employed and that the average rate of unemployment in the OECD countries grew from 3 per cent in the mid-1970s to 10 per cent in 1992. In sub-Saharan Africa this figure was nearer 15–20 per cent. Additionally, jobless statistics do not tell the whole story and there are significant problems of under-employment, particularly in countries lacking a safety net of state benefits. In the Philippines the official figure for unemployment is 15 per cent, but it is probably nearer 30 per cent if those employed on a casual basis in the informal sector are taken into account. In many societies, people, including children, in poverty have to find some means of making money, whether it be through scavenging, street hawking, begging or prostitution, and it has been estimated that more than 60 per cent of the African labour force in cities is in this informal sector (UNDP 1995).

Furthermore, those in work may have falling incomes. For instance, in Latin America in the decade to 1991, the value of the minimum wage fell by 35 per cent (UNDP 1995); employment generally has become far more precarious, with big employers (including global companies) pursuing 'core and periphery' labour policies and subcontracting work to smaller firms where employment conditions are often less secure. The UN has predicted that the labour force in developing countries is growing by over 2 per cent a year in the 1990s and that there would need to be over one billion new jobs by the beginning of the twenty-first century to absorb this growth. This is at a point when labour market trends are running in the opposite direction, as discussed in a special edition of the ILO Review on the nature and future of work (ILO 1996).

Apart from attempts to estimate and compare levels of poverty around the globe according to different indicators, there has also been some attention to the dynamics of poverty, that is, the extent to which individuals, families or societies remain in poverty or are able to improve their lot. For instance, it was suggested in the UK under Thatcher that poverty was for many a temporary condition, but more recent research has confirmed that, for the vast majority of those in poverty, even if some individuals and families rise above the poverty line sometimes, most either stay (or return) below it (Browne 1998). Similarly, the amount and degree of poverty in some societies has increased in the 1990s and there are persistent patterns of inequality between countries, which show little sign of changing for the better or have even deteriorated. Townsend and others have cited research which demonstrated that the gap between the richest 20 per cent of the world's population and the poorest 20 per cent had doubled between 1960 and 1994, increasing in dollar equivalents from 30:1 to 60:1 (Richards 1996).

Inequalities and poverty in the West have also apparently been increasing, as illustrated by an editorial in the American professional journal *Social Work* which suggested that 'A generation of children have grown up in a culture of unprecedented and publicly condoned greed ... but the economic position of some children has regressed [and] almost a quarter are now growing up in poverty' (Ewalt 1994:149). Across the Atlantic, Eurostat figures released in 1997 showed a significant increase in poverty between 1988 and 1993, with only France, Germany and Italy showing some decrease. The biggest proportional increase in the number of individuals living in poverty was in the Netherlands, although the highest number overall was found in Portugal, and the average increase throughout the EU was 10 per cent. More children in Britain were likely to live in poverty than in other EU countries, 32 per cent compared with a minimum of 5 per cent in Denmark (Donnellan 1998). Reports from the FSU and Central European countries have also suggested a significant worsening of living conditions for many since 1989.

Everywhere, some sectors of the population are more at risk of poverty than others and old age, poor health or disability, and ethnic difference are all pre-disposing factors which increase the risk of poverty. Additionally, the feminisation of poverty has been remarked on by a number of writers

(Lewis 1993; Pearson 1992; Van Wormer 1997). This is partly related to the fact that women usually live longer than men and are more likely than men to be raising children alone, but also reflects the increased feminisation of the work force in many countries, as the bases for employment have changed. For example, women constitute 90 per cent of the workforce in garment factories in Bangladesh, and are also more likely to be employed in the service sector and some forms of manufacturing in advanced industrial countries, but, in general, pay and conditions for women are inferior to those of men (Pearson 1992).

There is, therefore, no room for complacency in relation to the nature and scale of poverty and it may be useful to consider how international activities exacerbate or attempt to address the problem.

International influences and interventions

Townsend recently stated, 'the key question of our time is how to deal with the structural problem of social polarisation' (cited in Richards 1996:13). This view would apparently be endorsed by the UN, through its restructuring and refocusing of the Development Programme in the mid-1990s, stating that 'social progress is the supreme objective of the international community' (UNDP 1995). In a British press report on poverty in 1996, avenues for change were identified as through international NGOs, legal frameworks, campaigns, education and trading links. While acknowledging the possibility of exploitative trade, the report also advanced the slogan 'Trade not aid' as more likely to lead to development based on economic independence of the poorest countries, than aid, with its overtones of charity and 'strings attached' (Hunt 1996). This view tends to be supported by the UN literature and shifts in policy of some of the major NGOs. However, the debate is complex and some of the arguments in relation to both trade and aid, are briefly examined here.

In the early 1990s, an economist advanced the view that states could choose to be 'public spirited' in their actions and traced the pattern of aid and trade over four decades. Halloran Lumsdaine (1993) noted that aid to less developed countries dated mainly from a speech by the American President, Harry Truman, in 1949, advocating technical aid to the 'third world', so that, from the 1950s in particular, American aid was switched from assisting the European economies. While the US government had some political motivation during the Cold War period, Halloran Lumsdaine suggested that some other countries had established aid on humanitarian grounds. This view can be compared with a recent comment by the then

British Minister responsible for overseas aid, Lynda Chalker, who stated that aid had been administered under UK law since 1991 'to promote good government' (BBC Radio interview, 1996).

OECD figures for the period 1986–94 showed variations in the extent to which regions are heavily dependent on either aid or trade. Thus, sub-Saharan Africa was dependent on aid ($25 billion relative to less than $5 billion in trade), whereas both Central/South America and Asia showed a significant increase in trade, relative to aid (over $40 billion : $10 billion and over $50 billion : $20 billion, respectively). Additionally, it has been suggested that the furore in 1994 over the Pergau Dam deal between the British government and Malaysia (in which aid was apparently linked to arms trade deals) tipped the balance from the British government favouring large-scale aid for infrastructure projects to smaller-scale NGO-sponsored schemes (Durham 1994b).

Also in 1994, the then British Minister for Overseas Development stated that an increasing amount of aid was being directed through NGOs, which could give better value for money. She claimed that the amount of money thus directed had doubled in the early 1990s, but it still only stood at 10 per cent of the Overseas Development Aid (ODA) budget in 1993, the remainder being distributed through bilateral schemes between governments, or in partnership with other governments, or through the European Union (Chalker 1994). In fact, the money contributed in aid to less developed countries from British and American governments has declined significantly since the early 1980s, attributed by Halloran Lumsdaine (1993) to the view of neo-liberal economic policies which equated aid with dependency. The UNICEF Annual Report (1997) noted that official development aid (from governments) was at its lowest since statistics were first collected in 1950, with Denmark showing up as the most generous nation as measured by percentage of GNP and aid per person.

In general, large-scale schemes have sometimes been criticised on economic, financial and environmental grounds: the role of the global financial institutions in helping governments invest in infrastructure and industrial projects has been recognised as important in many cases but the IMF in particular has come under criticism from various quarters. As has been suggested previously, the IMF wields considerable power in less developed countries, but can be seen as an instrument of the governments and capitalists of the West and Japan. All 182 participating members (including 75 less developed countries) have voting rights, but these are weighted in favour of the largest financial contributors, and the IMF and World Bank orthodoxies of full liberalisation and privatisation have been regarded by some as misguided and harmful.

Sachs (1998) described the IMF as 'a lifeline' to capital markets, foreign aid (including emergency loans) and respectability for less developed countries. However, he questioned the assumed infallibility of the IMF and suggested that in recent cases of loss of confidence in particular economies, the IMF, instead of assisting in restoring confidence and stability, had contributed to the financial panic by blaming national governments for improvidence and calling for bank closures. In a useful analysis of the recent problems in some Asian economies, he cited Mexico (1995), Bulgaria (1996), and Thailand, Indonesia and Korea (1997) as examples of financial crises which had been exacerbated by the IMF's intervention rather than ameliorated. While collapse of financial markets may seem to impact most on those with enough money to invest, the human costs and spin off to poorer sections of society have been considerable in all the countries mentioned.

Sachs concluded that this secretive international bureaucracy should be more open and held accountable; and that aid programmes should be designed by national governments with the advice of the IMF, rather than at its behest. (Concerns about the powerful role but undemocratic nature of the IMF at international level are mirrored at regional level in criticisms of the Central Bank in the European Union.)

Another source of criticism of international financial arrangements is the huge cost to less developed countries of *debt repayments*. In 1996 the G7 states agreed to write off 80 per cent of the debt burden of some countries under a new initiative, the Heavily Indebted Poor Countries (HIPCs) scheme. At that time Uganda, for instance, was paying one-third of all government revenue to its debtors – ten times the amount of money being spent on primary health care – in a country with one of the highest rates of HIV/ AIDS infection in the world, and where defence expenditure had risen from 13 to 20 per cent of the budget between 1991 and 1996. A spokesperson for OXFAM hoped that the money 'saved' could be channelled into health and education programmes but also that there could be some rebalancing of the budget to reduce military expenditure (Thomas 1996).

This example raises the issue that, whether the source of income is aid or trade, national governments bear responsibility for how economies are managed, and resources allocated. Concerns in relation to the arms trade provides an illustration. Not only are resources diverted from use for development, but it is also possible that military strength will be used against local populations, as happened in Rwanda in the mid-1990s. In the less obviously harmful field of petroleum extraction, 'respectable' global companies have been involved in deals with governments which have put local (poor) populations at a disadvantage and even risk of serious violations of human rights, as in the case of Shell in Nigeria, or BP in Colombia, also in the mid-1990s. These examples illustrate the extent to which the economic goals of the West, as represented by global companies, are in direct conflict with humanitarian and social development goals, promoted by the UN and apparently supported by advanced industrial countries.

Logging is another example of trade which may benefit governments of less developed countries (or individuals within them) but where any gain fails to 'trickle down' to the people impoverished by displacement from their land. For instance, Snow and Collee (1996) noted that logging in the Solomon Islands was bringing in about half the government revenue but saw this as a very short-term and misguided 'gain', given minimal regulation and cheating over extraction rates by the Asian logging companies, and deforestation rates which are unsustainable as well as socially disruptive. This issue partly crosses into concerns about the environment (and disasters, further discussed in Chapter 7) but there are practical consequences for local populations, as evidenced in the shift which has occurred from a subsistence and barter economy to exploited labour, in some parts of Papua New Guinea, or in the threat to the continued existence of the indigenous population, for instance, the Yanomami Indians in Amazonia. Although international agencies and Western governments have been beginning to express concern about environmental damage (after long campaigning by NGOs), there has been no attempt at intervention in the logging trade on humanitarian or social grounds (Vogler 1997).

Tobacco sales illustrate how tax revenues and profits benefit governments and global corporations rather than promoting developments for people who work on the land; world markets generally tend to promote an over-reliance on cash crops by less industrialised countries rather than developing internal markets and associated industries. This makes such countries vulnerable to changes in world commodity prices, reductions in which may plunge poor countries even deeper into poverty. Less developed countries are also likely to suffer from trade barriers and tariffs imposed by the West to protect domestic production or more favoured trading partners. It was suggested in the mid-1990s that the work programme of the World Trade Organisation should reduce trade barriers to increase export opportunities of developing countries (UN 1994), but there has been little evidence of substantial change in trading policy or practice since that time.

However, some global companies have begun to suggest that trade does not have to be exploitative, and a recent joint initiative between Anita Roddick of the Body Shop and a British university has established a course promoting *ethical business* which relates responsible business practice to concern about people (social equity) and the planet (environmental quality) as well as profit. In acknowledging the power of global corporations – of the ten largest economic enterprises in the world, half are companies – the course recognises the need for cultural change within companies, and a shift in business values. This small initiative may have implications for relationships between companies and governments and between the 'developed' and 'developing' worlds, but such changes are complex and need to be supported by other developments. For instance, as Roddick observed, 'refusing to buy from companies that employ children can mean throwing whole families into poverty' (Slavin 1998:8), a point returned to later.

Turning back to aid, it was suggested earlier that the emphasis of the UN and of some governments has shifted from large-scale interventions to a preference for small-scale, 'bottom up' projects; in some cases, these are best promoted by NGOs acting in concert with national governments and local communities. But the financial basis of much NGO activity is insecure and both charitable donations and government funding can be criticised as being erratic and mean.

For instance, a report by a consumer group noted that the British public gave £4 billion to charity in 1996 but that this was a 20 per cent decrease since 1993 (Consumers' Association 1997). The charity sector had expanded considerably in the UK since the early 1980s, including the establishment since the late 1980s of initiatives such as Comic Relief and Band Aid, which provided funding to NGOs engaged in international activities (Comic Relief 3 in 1991 raised £22.5 million, of which three-quarters went to aid projects in Africa ('World on her Shoulders', *Observer* Supplement Report, 16 October 94)). But in the early 1990s the combination of a recession, 'donor fatigue' and the establishment of a national lottery were taking their toll.

There has also been some disillusionment with aid, as corruption in this field has come to light. For instance, in 1996 the Charity Commission in the UK appointed receivers to take over the Humana 'charity'. This Danish-owned organisation had been operating in the field of private education and recycling donated clothing to the Third World in the UK since 1986 and for longer in other parts of Europe. However, there had been concerns about its probity over two decades (the European Union had withdrawn funding in 1985) and it had been investigated by Interpol for suspected money laundering and gun running. But it had continued to operate, defrauding donors of about £50 million per year and failing to promote the projects in the less developed countries which it claimed to be helping (Durham 1994a).

This, and other concerns, for instance, about how the money of legitimate charities is used in the receiving countries, has led some people to believe that aid should only be channelled through governments or through very well-established and experienced NGOs such as the Red Cross, Save the Children and Oxfam. There has been support for greater regulation of charities and for the monitoring and evaluation of aid projects. The decrease in aid has also led the UNDP to call for a 'global 20/20 compact' under which advanced industrial countries would raise current levels of aid and require that 20 per cent of it be spent on social projects while developing countries would undertake to allocate 20 per cent of their gross domestic budget to human priorities. It was suggested that this did not necessarily mean an increase in resources, rather a reallocation of how resources are used, including a shift from military purposes to developments rooted in solidarity and mutual co-operation.

Other reports and literature have documented the benefits of relatively small investments in health care and education (particularly of girls and women) as a means of raising living standards overall. The UNDP (1995) suggested that a new legitimacy should be accorded to the idea of public works and active labour market policies, such that more people can become economically active and self-supporting. The report advocated the development of pluralist systems of providing public services, the creation of space for a civil society and support for the development of self-help initiatives (UNDP 1995:55). The UN's support for social programmes allied to economic developments has been echoed elsewhere: it has been suggested that developing countries need to re-establish social control over capital and subordinate markets to social purposes.

There are some indications that greater credence is also being given to the view that 'outside aid' may not be necessary and that the West/North may have things to learn from less developed countries, that is, that the donor–recipient relationship implicit in most aid transactions is not a one-way relationship.

The Grameen Bank can be cited as a particular example of this. This was formally established by a Bangladeshi economist, Muhammed Yunus, in 1984, after nearly a decade during which he developed the idea in the face of lack of support from conventional banks and officialdom. He initially lent the equivalent of about US$30 each to 42 people in 1976. His view was that sometimes the people who were least likely to get credit from a bank, that is, the poor, only needed small loans for specific purchases, such as a sewing machine or a cow, to improve their position, and that resorting to money-lenders was an extortionate way to raise money. He was further prompted by a recognition that about 75 per cent of aid to Bangladesh was being returned to the West in the form of payments for consultants, services and equipment, and that 'self-help' was a better option.

In a radical departure from local tradition, Yunus decided that women should be allowed to have credit, and that they were likely to be more reliable than men in 'investing' such loans in improving the lot of their families and in repaying them, a belief borne out in practice. He also recognised the need for mutual help and worked with small groups of women (about five) who could provide peer support and regulation of the scheme: this became an important feature in subsequent developments. By 1994 the Grameen Bank had helped about 2 million families (with average loans of about US$100) and had over US$1 billion turnover and was regarded as one of the main agents of social change in Bangladesh (notwithstanding criticisms that the repayment periods are short, rates of interest relatively high and some families can be left worse off if their investment fails) (Ghazi 1994).

Following meetings with Hilary Clinton and other significant women at the UN Women's Conference in Beijing, Yunus attended a Micro-Summit Conference in Washington in 1996 to launch a global movement to lend money for small businesses to 100 million families by the year 2005. Even before this, microcredit had been recognised as a powerful tool to tackle poverty and economic dependence, and partly through promotion by international NGOs, the concept has been transplanted to 52 other countries (starting in Malaysia in 1985). Replication projects are sometimes supported by the Grameen Trust, an NGO established to provide training, capital and advice to new programmes.

Other developments have followed in Bangladesh, in the form of Grameen Telecom and Grameen Shakti (energy from solar power), enabling villages to be connected to the Internet. The scheme now has 1057 branches in 36,000 villages, with 2.1 million borrowers, the majority of whom are women. It has been estimated that average incomes of participating families have been increased by 53 per cent over three years, and repayment rates run at about 98 per cent. One of the spin-offs of this development has been increased levels of voting by women and increased levels of literacy, as women were required to learn to sign their names when taking out loans, and, as borrowers, they have wanted to keep records (Johnston 1997).

Perhaps in some ways the idea is not so different from that of credit unions, well established in rural Ireland since the 1960s, and now being actively promoted in urban areas in the UK, and about 500 schemes similar to the Grameen Bank now also exist in the US. But the leap of faith required of one person in Bangladesh in the 1970s, when women in poverty had no education or involvement in financial matters, cannot be underestimated, nor can the achievements of the spread of the idea, and the change in women's position and improved circumstances of families and communities which it has promoted. However, a down side recently reported has been a backlash by men against the changed status and increased powers of women in the domestic economy, in situations where men often are without paid employment (personal communication). This illustrates again how change efforts can have unanticipated as well as intended consequences, and require work with both parties or all sectors of communities likely to be affected by change.

Poverty and the social professions

The position of people in poverty in both the 'developed' and 'developing' worlds outlined above presents challenges and opportunities to those in the social professions, which call upon use of skills and organisational abilities at local levels, as well as negotiation and intervention in systems which are national or international in their remit. In such work a traditional casework principle, of deciding 'who is the client', is supplanted by more important considerations about who has the power/resources and how can these be shared or redirected. Additionally, the power and resources of poor people themselves have increasingly been seen as vital in any development processes, with people's own assessments of their needs and desired directions of change as a starting point for interventions.

It is also apparent that the range of people engaged in such change efforts is not restricted to people formally trained on courses labelled 'social work' or 'community development' or something similar and who, in any case may be thin on the ground in less developed countries or rural areas), but extends more widely to people in government posts or employed or volunteering in NGOs. This reinforces the need to establish allies, and to avoid duplication or antagonism; and also informs the following discussion of examples of interventions, including by NGOs.

A classification of types of social intervention by client group or method or setting is difficult in relation to the broad field of poverty given the overlapping and interrelated nature of the problems faced by people in these circumstances, but some discrete areas have been identified for the purposes of this discussion. These are interventions in relation to street children, sexual exploitation and child labour, and community development. In each of these areas the guiding principles of protection and promotion of human rights and social justice inform the policies of agencies and the practice of individual workers or volunteers.

Concerning street children, Van Wormer (1997) cited an estimate that 40 million children are living on the streets world-wide, 25 million of them in Latin America. This is also an established and significant problem in Southeast Asia (Davis 1994), and the UN Centre for Human Settlement recently identified an increasing number of African children living on the streets (IFSW Update 2/97). A research programme in 31 countries in Europe by the Council of Europe in 1992/93 also identified a significant increase in numbers (Cemlyn and Vdovenko 1995) and, while the term 'street children' is not generally used in North America or Australia, the numbers of children and young people who are homeless has also increased (Van Wormer 1997; Standing Committee on Community Affairs 1995).

The UN defined street children as those 'for whom the street (in the widest sense of the word ...) has become [the] habitual abode and/or source of livelihood; and who are inadequately protected, supervised or directed by responsible adults' (Lusk 1992: 294). It is thus a broader concept than simply homelessness, and such children and young people are not necessarily orphans – in fact some studies in Latin America suggest that about 95 per cent have at least one living parent (Raffaelli 1997). However, they lack food, shelter (and warmth) as well as access to health and education. In addition to lacking basic rights, they are likely to face isolation and stigmatisation, although they can also be seen as resourceful and pursuing survival strategies. They are susceptible to exploitation and abuse, including involvement in crime and drugs (whether as victims or perpetrators), and may be at risk of death through starvation, cold or violence, including that which is officially perpetrated (Lusk 1992; Cemlyn and Vdovenko 1995).

The Council of Europe Report (cited in Cemlyn and Vdovenko 1995) identified that many European governments were reluctant to acknowledge the scale of the problem and that NGOs were better informed and more likely to address the issue in ways concerned with protection and human rights rather than repression – this is also the case in the less developing countries. Such children and young people represent the casualties of family problems (including violence) and/or a breakdown in traditional social controls and of extreme poverty in the face of urbanisation or changed political conditions. Their increase in more advanced industrial societies has also been attributed to a lack of preventive measures to maintain families and communities.

Cemlyn and Vdovenko (1995) summarised the Council of Europe's declaration of principles on which intervention to assist street children should be based. These include approaches which are outreaching, non-intrusive, validating, supportive of family ties, and provide practical and psychological help aimed at reintegration to society. Additionally, the need for co-ordination across services and sectors was stressed. The authors gave specific examples of official and NGO responses to the problem in St Petersburg which illustrated differences between the priorities accorded to protection or rights; this account and those discussing the situation in Latin America demonstrated the likely connection between street children and the criminal justice systems (Lusk 1992; Raffaelli 1997). Raffaelli also suggested that the particular circumstances of children and young people surviving on the streets was diverse and that more differentiated responses are required to address the problem.

Studies have also highlighted an overlap between the issue of street children, and that of child labour, since many of the children 'work' on the streets ('as shoe-shine boys, ... beggars or car watchmen', Lusk 1992:299) to contribute to family incomes. More recently Swift (1998) has illustrated some of the practical and progressive practices, including a legal defence system and children's news agency, which have been developed with street children in Brazil, in the context of efforts to promote a more democratic and less divided society in which even the poorest children can participate.

Other texts have also highlighted the link with sexual exploitation of children (for example Davis (1994) in the South-east Asian context), although establishment of a regular pattern of prostitution may well provide an alternative means of livelihood and chance of shelter for some children and young people. At a local level, Ghazi (1994) described the growth of prostitution in Bangladesh, despite its illegality and contravention of cultural norms. Of an estimated 150,000 illegal prostitutes, most are teenage girls, without other means of support, who run the risk of harassment, rape, violence and sexually transmitted diseases. Here, as elsewhere, it tended to be NGOs, such as Concern, Worldvision and Marie Stopes, which have set up programmes, usually aimed at 'rescue and rehabilitation'.

The problem of sexual exploitation and violence is not restricted to the less developed countries, but associated with poverty everywhere. Barbaret et al. (1995) cited the case of youth prostitution in Spain, including involvement of immigrants from North Africa and Latin America, and noted that the link between prostitution and the justice system was not helpful, but that relatively few examples existed of more constructive approaches, such as out-reach work, drop-ins, advice-lines or action research projects aimed at helping the young women involved identify the nature of the problem and possible responses. The need for structural change and the difficulty of addressing the issue at a policy level was also mentioned, as was the place for a lead agency to co-ordinate social interventions in this area.

There has been some increase in international activity to address this problem following the Agenda for Action set by the World Congress Against Commercial Exploitation of Children held in Stockholm in 1996 and the establishment of ECPAT (End Child Prostitution, Pornography and Trafficking in Children). IFSW is co-operating with other bodies to develop data banks, joint studies and operations, and is preparing a manual, 'Lives at the Crossroads', on strategies and psycho-social methods aimed at prevention and recovery of children abused through sexual exploitation (IFSW Newsletter 3/97–1/98:10).

Issues of structural change and the role of NGOs are also linked to concerns about child labour. The International Labour Organisation (ILO) estimated that 250 million children between 5 and 16 years were working in developing countries in 1996 (including 120 million working full-time) (Hill and Tisdall 1997) and the problem is also of concern, though on a much smaller scale, in advanced industrial countries. The NGO Group for the UN Convention on the Rights of the Child (a coalition of about 40 international NGOs) has established a subgroup on child labour which has produced guidelines on 'Working with companies to prevent the exploitation of Child Labour' (1997). This explored some of the definitional issues of the age at which children might work and the conditions under which such work might be acceptable. It took child labour to signify conditions which are exploitative, and potentially damaging to a child's development, and defined employment which is injurious to health or prevents education of children under 18 years as exploitative.

However, the guidelines acknowledged the difficulty around the age at which children might be regarded as young people able to work, and quoted the UN's own acceptance that this age may be as low as 14 years in countries where the economy and educational facilities are less developed. It also noted that companies should adopt codes of practice which are not counterproductive to the children's interest, apparently supporting the point made by Anita Roddick, noted earlier. Even children of five or six years might make useful contributions to the income of very poor families (who in any case may not be able to send such children to school), and employment of children and young people may promote responsibility and contribute to the inter-generational transfer of skills (Hill and Tisdall 1997). Thus, the issue becomes more complex than simply trying to prevent the employment of children in sweatshops or their engagement in aspects of the informal economy.

One example of an understanding of the socio-economic importance of child labour was provided by a study by Agarwal et al. (1997). This found that girls as young as eight years old might be employed as 'kayayoos' (head-load carriers) in Accra, and sending remittances to their families in Northern Ghana (despite legislation which forbids employment under 15 years of age); but it raised the question of how the lives of these children could be improved, rather than assuming suppression of the practice.

Taking another example, the number of child labourers in Bangladesh, aged between 5 and 14 years (and not receiving an education) was estimated at about 6.3 million in 1996 by the Bangladesh Bureau of Statistics, of whom over 80 per cent were in rural areas and 96 per cent were in the informal sector, including young girls employed as maids by wealthy families. While the government and NGOs are working together to address this problem (including through targeting global companies which employ children) reports in the press suggested that parents regard their families as dependent on such incomes and were fearful for the families' positions if the children no longer work (Mumin 1998). Therefore, some NGOs have devised programmes which provide incentives (in the form of food) to families who let children attend school, or which provide informal education to older children, in particular girls aged 10–13 years, which fit round their working hours, rather than expecting them to cease work (Ghazi 1994).

Nevertheless, trends in the West are to bring pressure to bear on global companies which employ child labour abroad or which buy supplies from such companies. One such example recently noted, was the Ethical Trading Initiative, launched in 1997 by the UK government, with the backing of several major companies to promote a voluntary code of conduct for such companies (Woolf 1997). While the overall goal of improving the lot of children by ending child labour may be laudable, a less direct strategy (noted on the NISW international social work network, 17/2/98), prompting social workers to engage in lobbying of global companies to 'invest' more of their profits in welfare and development programmes, might achieve this goal and have wider benefits.

But child labour is not only a problem of the less developed countries, and there have been signs of increased concerns about the issue in advanced industrial countries (although its nature and scale differs). In 1994 the EU issued The Young Workers Directive which sought to regulate the conditions under which young people are employed, although some national studies have suggested that of young people working, many are outside regulatory frameworks.

For instance, in a British study up to three-quarters were 'under age', in prohibited jobs and/or working illegal hours: despite this the British government chose to 'opt out' of implementing some of the Directive's provisions until the year 2000 (Ruxton 1996). Raheim, writing in the American context, suggested that 'Micro-enterprise development forms an important element in new thinking about social welfare' (1996:69), and advocated that social workers should acquaint themselves with existing projects and opportunities on behalf of their clients (including young people). However, such an approach, while possibly helpful to some individuals, may not be appropriate for all people in poverty, and fails to address the more fundamental causes of poverty rooted in the unequal distribution of resources.

At an international level, the 1989 Convention on the Rights of the Child is seen as offering some protection for children and young people if it informs national policies and practices. Additionally, other developments aimed at raising the status and 'earning capacity' of women (as discussed above) may have direct implications for child labour and school attendance rates in the less developed countries. Thus, community and social development approaches which address the root cause of the problem, poverty, and raise standards of health care and literacy, are seen as having an important part to play (UNDP Human Development Report 1995). Finally, international talks have recently been held about the issue, including representatives from the IFSW and an ILO body, IPEC (International Programme on the Elimination of Child Labour) (IFSW Newsletter 3/97–1/98, p.10).

Turning now to social and community development these approaches have been advocated not only in the less developed countries but also in relation to some of the most deprived communities of North America and Europe. Midgley, writing about practice in relation to economic development, noted that social work 'needs to transcend its narrow concern with remedial practice and promote activities that make a positive contribution to social well-being' (1996:14). The adoption or extension of a (group/community) developmental perspective, already held by some Latin American workers and social professionals trained in other traditions in Europe, would be consistent with a renewed commitment to social development apparent in some UN literature and proclamations, and the EU policies aimed at social integration.

Midgley has suggested that intervention aimed at social development should be focused on promoting people's material welfare, and should have a threefold focus: programmes fostering human capital development (for instance through mobilising communities to establish centres giving access to information and supplies in the fields of basic health and literacy); programmes aimed at development of social capital (such as clean water supply for a village and other forms of infrastructure of immediate and lasting benefit to communities), and finally through assisting vulnerable individuals or groups to engage in vocational education programmes or other strategies aimed at enabling them to be self-supporting (Midgley 1996).

Elsewhere, in the context of experience in Brazil, and with simple examples, O'Gorman (1992) has elaborated a fivefold approach to social change which ranges from the remedial (the sticking plaster), providing resources to meet needs; through facilitating self-help (the ladder); through neighbourhood and community development programmes (the patchwork); through community networking and linked programmes for citizen empowerment (the beehive); to a transformational spiral (the beacon) which incorporates the other four approaches and brings structural problems to attention in ways which inform the world's agenda. The book has a certain 'missionary zeal' to its style but the 'transformation' of people from dependent recipients of welfare or groups who are marginalised and ignored, to people who have self-respect and are active participants in their own communities, with some appreciation of wider concerns, is a goal espoused by most social workers, and as relevant to some of the cities of Europe or North America as to the rural and urban areas of less developed countries.

Drawing conclusions

More than one in five people live in conditions of extreme poverty on only about one American dollar a day. Poverty travels across borders in the form of drugs, diseases, pollution, migration, terrorism and political instability. It is a complex and multidimensional phenomenon resulting from deeply imbedded structural imbalances in all realms of human existence – the state, economy, society, culture and the environment (UN 1994).

Poverty has been a central concern to many of those in the social professions over a significant period of time, and in many different (geographical) situations. Increasingly, the lack of improvement in the material circumstances of vast numbers of people around the world, and indeed deteriorating conditions for some, can only be understood in an analysis which includes reference to the political motivations of governments and the economic goals of commercial enterprises, in a global context. It has been suggested that the continued existence of poverty, alongside many indications of modernisation and economic growth, can be characterised as 'distorted development' (Midgley 1996:6), and that it is time for social workers to turn their attentions (back) to interventions aimed at ameliorating and challenging the effects of such distortion.

Elsewhere, approaches which stress human and civil rights, and empowerment of individuals and groups, are consistent with strategies to combat poverty and social exclusion. However, one of the most significant challenges facing policy makers in the welfare field and, *inter alia*, the social professions, is the change taking place in the field of 'work', at a time when more emphasis is being put on self-reliance and work as the key to individual survival and well-being. This was prefigured in UNDP papers in the mid-1990s which suggested a need to rethink the traditional assumptions (at least in the Western world) about life being divided into three stages concerned with education, work and retirement. Such divisions have never been so clear-cut or available to the majority of the population in traditional societies, which nevertheless in many cases, are striving to emulate the standards of education and employment rights of the West.

The renewed interest in social development, not least by the UN, and increasing attention to new problems, such as environmental concerns, suggest that the social professions, along with others, need to consider whether there are other ways in which roles and activities which are traditionally undervalued or taken for granted, together with new responsibilities, can be valued and rewarded, such that people can participate in, contribute to and, when necessary, be supported by society. Additionally, the impact on particular societies of global markets and economic decisions need to be better understood and some of the global mechanisms of distribution made more accountable.

The eradication of poverty and establishment of equality in societies and between nations may be a pipe-dream, but, quite apart from any moral arguments, the effects of poverty are ultimately damaging to wider groups than just those experiencing it. Notwithstanding Halloran Lumsdaine's views (1993) on the humanitarian motives of some governments in giving aid, altruism is not a fashionable concept, but policy makers in the past have periodically appreciated that attending to the needs of the poor is ultimately in their own interest. It would be timely for the social professions to engage (or re-engage) with the poor in ways which enable them to make their voice heard.

6 Migration and refugees

Introduction

Movement of peoples has been a feature of every age since the first hunter-gatherers. But modern concerns about migration and the status of people attempting to resettle date from the establishment of national boundaries and legislative and fiscal devices to encourage or discourage population movements. This chapter examines aspects of recent and current migration patterns and identifies different forms of migration, with particular concerns around people seeking asylum outside their country of origin. The extent to which migration is now a global phenomenon, with every continent involved in both sending and receiving migrants is noted.

Apart from actions by individual governments, aimed at controlling the inflow of immigrants and asylum seekers, or which, in some cases, promote emigration, the international community has played an increasing role in the regulation of population movement. Some examples of international legislation and other means by which migration is regulated are considered, and the growth of regional policies is also mentioned.

Finally, there is some discussion of the expectations of the social professions in this field. Examples illustrate a wide range of possible roles in the statutory and voluntary sectors in response to both the crises of individual asylum seekers and the longer-term concerns of established immigrant communities. Reference is also made to international principles and perspectives which might guide work in relation to refugees and migrants.

Population movement: socio-economic and political aspects

The causes, forms and extent of migration have varied considerably over time and place, and have been influenced by, and contributed to, changing socio-economic and political conditions within and between states. Migration across national borders has recently gained more prominence on the international agenda because of its increasing scale and consequent impact on world politics. Bali (1997:202) has attributed greater, especially cross-national, mobility to an increase in the number of states (creating political boundaries to be crossed); the growth of the global population, and the communication and transport revolutions (which have increased knowledge of conditions and opportunities elsewhere and relative ease of access). To these must be added the different rates at which national economies have been industrialised and modernised, and the individual and collective aspirations of people to seek a better life, through increased economic opportunities, security and/or freedom.

While such factors can partly 'explain' the historic and more recent motivation for what is sometimes termed 'economic' or voluntary migration, Kane (1995) put a different emphasis on a Worldwatch analysis of population mobility. He cited the increase in local conflicts and civil wars in the latter half of the twentieth century, as the cause of a more significant – and involuntary – form of population mobility, namely refugees. The rise in refugees from under 3 million in 1960 to about 23 million by the mid-1990s, particularly pronounced since the late 1980s, can be associated with an increase in the number of wars or conflicts resulting in more than 1000 deaths from about 11 in the 1950s, through 15 in the 1960s and to over 30 since the late 1970s (UNHCR figures, cited in Kane 1995:19).

The basic distinction often made between migration which is individually motivated and voluntary, and the involuntary movements of individuals or ethnic groups is sometimes further identified as related to economic or political considerations, respectively. But this is to oversimplify the causes of population mobility, whether at individual or collective levels, and in the past century or so, migration has been associated with a complex interplay of economic need (or greed) and political motivation or necessity. The varied and changing motivations and push–pull factors at work in different times and places have made a categorisation of forms of population mobility and analysis of directions complicated, but some broad trends have been identified in major population movements (Castles and Miller 1993; Bali 1997) and some approaches to classification suggested (Bali 1997; Kane 1995).

Historically, both political and economic motivations were evident in colonialism, which prompted large-scale movement of Europeans to Africa, Asia, North and South America, Australia and New Zealand (Bali 1997:203). The consequences for indigenous populations, and for their subsequent socio-economic development and relations with the incomers, are still reverberating in these societies, as evidenced by land rights claims and continuing efforts to secure equal opportunities by First Americans and Aborigines, for instance. Allied to colonialism, the effects of the slave trade (until its abolition in 1834), and then of the use of indentured labour, also resulted in significant forced migration from Africa, India and China, to over 40 countries world-wide, also with long-term socio-economic and political effects still prevalent (Bali 1997:204). By definition, migration of people, in whatever form, has resulted in the establishment of ethnic minority populations in 'host countries', although the balance of power between incomers and indigenous populations has varied.

In the twentieth century, emigration has continued from Europe, notably in the exodus of Jewish people, particularly to North America, from Germany and other Central European countries in the inter-war period and, from 1948, to the newly established state of Israel; and in the migration of large numbers of people from various European states to countries such as Australia and Canada in the late 1940s. But more complex patterns have also developed of migration into Europe and within the region; and from Asia to North America and Australia, subsequent to the easing of restrictions which favoured white (European) migrants, in the late 1960s (the US), and after 1971, in the case of Australia (Bali 1997).

The extent to which economic, social or political factors have influenced these large-scale migration patterns has varied. For instance, the Irish leaving for the US in the mid-nineteenth century were undoubtedly seeking economic betterment, but were also anticipating a life free from British rule. For Jews leaving Germany in the 1930s, fear of political persecution played a larger part than economic need (though this was also a factor for some); and people leaving Greece or the UK for Australia in the late 1940s, encouraged by assisted passages, were looking for new social and economic opportunities. Similarly, Europeans and Asians leaving communist-dominated countries, including the USSR and China, were seeking both economic improvement and a different political regime in North America or Australia, while those moving from South America to the US or Europe have at different times been fleeing right-wing regimes or poverty.

Clearly, economic factors have played a significant part in the movement of individuals and groups, but it is a moot point whether people 'choose' to leave a society where their economic prospects are limited, even when they are apparently 'invited' to a wealthier nation, and, in the twentieth century, many migrants have seen their sojourn elsewhere as temporary. Such circumstances prevailed in relation to people of African-Caribbean descent who emigrated to Britain in the 1950s and '60s; or in the case of North Africans to France, or Turks to Germany in the 1960s and '70s, and parallels and differences can be noted in the outcomes, including the extent to which such groups have become established citizens of their adopted countries.

In other situations, more acute forms of (economic) need have resulted from natural disaster or political upheaval. Bangladesh can be cited as a country prone to natural disasters which has seen considerable emigration of people from largely rural backgrounds to urban centres in Britain and elsewhere in Europe, over the last few decades. There has also been some migration of Asians to newly industrialised countries within the region, since the 1970s, when immigration rules were generally being tightened by the majority of advanced industrial countries.

More recently, the economic crises resulting from the demise of communism in Central Europe and the FSU states has resulted in involuntary migration for some women, for instance to Israel, amounting to a modern-day form of slavery. A recent media report suggested that 'thousands of women' from Lithuania, Hungary and Russia were being brought into Israel by criminal elements (the Russian Mafia) and then kept as prisoners and forced into prostitution. Periodically, swoops by the Israeli vice squad 'rescue' such women who can then stay in 'shelters for battered women' (*sic*) pending repatriation (*Correspondent*, BBC2, 4 April 98).

Turning to a classification of forms of migration, Bali (1997:201) suggested three categories of voluntary migration: permanent settlers, temporary settlers (including 'overseas students' and expatriates working in global companies or the Gulf States), and illegal migrants, that is, unauthorised by the receiving state, sometimes called 'undocumented'. Bali also suggested that one form of migration might lead to another, for instance, Sikhs who came to the UK and established communities on a voluntary basis were later joined by Sikhs who were facing persecution.

Appleyard (1992) suggested a more extended classification, relating to a wider range of migrants and based on their legal status. This included people who were permanent settlers (and whose family members were also granted right of entry), temporary contract workers (unskilled), temporary professional workers, illegal migrant workers, asylum seekers and refugees (that is, granted refugee status according to the 1951 UN Convention). The UN Convention Relating to the Status of Refugees defined a refugee as a person

who, owing to a well-founded fear of being persecuted for reasons of race, religion, nationality, membership of a particular social group or political opinion, is outside the country of his nationality and is unable or, owing to such fear, is unwilling to avail himself of the protection of that country. (UNHCR 1997)

This is the basis on which government decisions are made about asylum applications, and has become an increasingly important test as the number of asylum seekers has risen and immigration opportunities to many countries have diminished.

The involuntary aspect of migration featured even more strongly in Kane's suggested classification, which he based on the immediate reasons for departure as well as the possible consequences. He thus cited persecution (which qualifies a person to seek asylum) and warfare (which may cause internal or external migration but does not guarantee refugee status) at the top of a list which included also lack of work (leading to either legal or undocumented movement to another country as well as internal migration), environmental degradation, redrawing of political boundaries, forced resettlement, famine, poverty and political disempowerment (Kane 1995:12–13).

While Kane suggested that some of these factors are more likely to cause internal rather than external migration (and thus might seem to have less relevance in the international context), nevertheless some would give rise to situations of concern to the international community, or might be the prelude to external migration. It is also possible that some people who have been displaced, following one of the above events would be the subject of international humanitarian aid, as 'refugees', even if they are not formally applying for asylum in another country.

In the mid-1990s, Worldwatch attempted to calculate the numbers of people caught up in different forms of migration and identified or estimated the following figures: 23 million official refugees (registered by the UN as having fled and/or under the protection of the UN), 27 million internal refugees (uprooted under similar conditions but had not crossed any national borders), 100 million legal immigrants, 10 million illegal immigrants (clearly, there are no official figures for this) and 10 million oustees (people displaced by public works projects for instance, but remaining in their own countries). It was also suggested that as many as 20 million to 30 million people may move for economic reasons within their own countries but not feature in international calculations of migration. Worldwatch therefore suggested that in 1995, about 35 million people 'migrated' within their own countries, while about 125 million people moved outside their country of origin (Kane 1995).

In relation to refugees, the figures can be elaborated on with statistics from the UN High Commission for Refugees. A recent Public Information Sheet (UNHCR 1997) stated, 'the UNHCR protects and assists more than 22 million people who have fled war or persecution' and this figure was increased to 50 million if the number of people displaced within their own countries was included. The UNHCR also provided a breakdown between continents showing that Africa and Asia each accounted for over 4 million refugees, while there were 3 million in Europe, but less than 1 million in North America, and less than 100,000 in both Latin America and Oceania. Further, the figures for Africa, Asia and Europe were virtually doubled by the addition of internally displaced people, returnees and others 'of concern' to the UNHCR.

The rapid rise in the number of refugees as a proportion of migrants dates from the mid-1970s, coinciding with the oil crisis and the downturn of some economies of advanced industrial countries. While conflict in the Middle East affected that region and Europe, there were also victims of conflicts in Vietnam, Cambodia and Laos who fled (mainly) to other Asian countries such as Hong Kong, Indonesia and Thailand. The 1980s and '90s have seen the growth of wars and local conflicts with resultant migration from Afghanistan, Sudan, the Horn of Africa and Rwanda, as well as Argentina, Chile and Sri Lanka. While some people, from the last three countries in particular, sought political asylum in Europe, the vast majority of refugees from the other conflicts crossed neighbouring borders, placing a disproportionate burden on less developed countries. Some of the Mediterranean countries have also become important centres for involuntary migration from former Balkan States, eastern Europe and the Middle East; Greece, for instance, has significant refugee numbers, relative to its overall population size.

UNHCR figures demonstrated that, of the 'top ten' countries of asylum in 1997, five were in Africa (including the Sudan and Ethiopia); and the largest 'receivers' overall were Iran and Pakistan (with over 2 million and 1 million refugees respectively, particularly from Afghanistan, from which over 6 million refugees were recorded by the UNHCR in the peak year, 1992). Germany and the US also featured in this list, as did the countries of the former Yugoslavia. In the case of the last, this was partly accounted for by the internal redistribution of an ethnically mixed population to new political entities apparently more sympathetic to specific groups. Even so, there are still examples of people living as refugees, such as the thousands of Muslims living in hostels on the Dalmatian Coast of Croatia, since being displaced from their own farms and villages by Serbs in 1991 (Seacombe 1996). This example illustrates the extent to which refugee problems may be both local and protracted, and short-term solutions to immediate crises can turn into longer-term concerns.

The top ten countries of origin also illustrate the scale of the problems arising from conflicts, as does the list of countries containing internally displaced persons of concern to the UNHCR, with some countries featuring in both lists (Afghanistan, Bosnia-Herzegovina, Liberia, Sierra Leone). The Rwandan conflict in the mid-1990s led to a mass exodus to neighbouring countries (over 2 million people in 1994) and produced some of the worst examples of poverty and violence in refugee camps which the international community and voluntary organisations (and the world through the media) have witnessed, but, while there was still concern in the late 1990s, a substantial majority of people had been repatriated (UNHCR 1997).

Other characteristics and consequences of population mobility include the growth in the number of women and children involved in migration. This is partly a result of increased economic activity outside their home countries by women and also a consequence of the greater extent to which civilian populations have been caught up in conflicts, necessitating flight. In either case, women may find themselves vulnerable to violence and/or sexual exploitation. Examples have been cited in the press of Filipino women in the UK and the Middle East engaged as domestic helpers but then deprived of their passports and abused. Women in refugee camps may have their needs ignored and be excluded from any decision making, and sometimes also be subject to abuse.

There has been increased concern about the number of refugees who are minors, including children seeking asylum in their own right. Problems were recognised by the UNHCR which issued Guidelines on Refugee Children (in 1988, updated in 1994) grounded in a philosophy of the rights of the child. Ruxton (1996) found statistical data about unaccompanied minors in Europe in short supply, but one European survey suggested that the numbers of unaccompanied minors varied from 27 children in Greece relative to over 2000 in Germany, over a three-year period up to 1992 (Ruxton 1996); and, according to the Commission for Racial Equality, 486 children applied for asylum at UK points of entry in 1995 (CRE 1997).

At the other end of the spectrum, changes in the labour market and other aspects of globalisation have given some men – and women – the opportunity to engage in temporary or seasonal forms of migration which enable them to earn high salaries or engage in leisure-related work. Examples range from people such as Irish nurses or Norwegian oil men in the Gulf States (where, according to Bali (1997), 70–85 per cent of the labour force is foreign); to Australians who work as representatives for ski companies, spending the winter season in the European Alps and the Southern winter in the ski resorts of Australia or New Zealand. There have also been examples of the return of guest workers from North European countries to establish their own businesses (sometimes in leisure and tourism).

Migration therefore is not a unitary concept, nor necessarily a wholly 'negative' phenomenon. In the international context, political and trading relations between countries can be strengthened by the existence of an established ethnic minority group which maintains close links with the home country and, apart from the value of remittances to some less developed countries (increased overall from US$40 billion to US$61 billion between 1982 and 1989), access to the knowledge and economic power systems of the West may be attained through the efforts of immigrants in advanced industrial countries (Bali 1997:207–8). But inevitably, the focus of national and international regulation and of intervention by the social professions is on aspects of migration perceived as problematic.

International, national and regional frameworks for regulation

Responses to the historic waves of migration have largely been a matter for national governments, but the plight of refugees came onto the international agenda through the League of Nations in the inter-war years. Responses were devised with sympathetic governments to the needs of people (outside their country of origin and without the protection of their own governments) fleeing communism and Nazism (Bali 1997:218). Since the Second World War, the United Nations has assumed an increasing role in relation to the regulation and relief of refugees, through the particular efforts of the High Commission for Refugees. This body now has 246 offices in 122 countries and employs nearly 1000 staff at headquarters, and over 4500 in the field (UNHCR 1997).

Three major protocols have been developed since the war which relate to the rights and treatment of refugees, including, initially, the Universal Declaration of Human Rights (1948). This grants anyone the right to exit from their own country and the right to seek asylum from persecution. Despite this, some countries, including Iraq, Burma and Sudan, as well as the remaining communist regimes, still restrict exit (Bali 1997). The Convention Relating to the Status of Refugees (1951) was designed to deal with the large numbers of displaced persons in Europe after the Second World War and, apart from defining refugee status, it specified that people should not be returned to a country where they might face threats to life and liberty. But the onus is on people seeking asylum to prove that such fear is well founded, and national governments have some discretion in their responses and in any special measures (for example, quotas) to assist refugees. A further protocol has been in force since 1967 and 126 states have signed both documents, while eight others have signed one or the other (UNHCR 1997).

Apart from its negotiating and procedural roles, the UNHCR has specific functions in relation to relief work. From a total budget of US$1.216 billion in 1997, the UNHCR assisted with a range of special programmes and emergencies, for example contributing nearly half the costs of Rwandan refugee programmes (US$50.4 million of US$114 million) and over half the repatriation costs of refugees to Myanmar (US$7 million of US$11.2 million). By far the largest single item of expenditure went towards the costs of programmes in relation to the former Yugoslavia (US$134.9 million of US$233.8 million). The major contributors to the UNHCR budget were the US, the EC and Japan (with contributions ranging from US$262 million to US$130 million), while individual European governments donated sums up to US$72,000 (Sweden) (UNHCR 1997).

Another role of the UNHCR is to arrange the safe repatriation of refugees to their country of origin, and this area of work has assumed increasing importance during the 1990s. For instance, over half the refugees from Afghanistan (peaking at more than 6 million in 1992) were repatriated in the period 1989–97. The repatriation of Rwandan refugees was almost 100 per cent in the period 1994–97, and a high proportion of Iraqi refugees were repatriated in the period 1991–97. The UNHCR statistics also illustrate some much longer-term refugee situations, with relatively lower rates of repatriation: 110,000 refugees have returned from Hong Kong and Indonesia to Vietnam in the period since 1979, and 27,000 Laotians have returned since 1975, but figures suggest that in the latter case up to about 100,000 have remained in Thailand (UNHCR 1997).

However, as the foregoing and previous discussions have suggested, the policies of individual countries are significant in determining the responses to individuals and groups, whether they be voluntary or involuntary migrants, and there have long been variations in the extent to which immigrants, and more recently refugees, have been granted permanent stay and citizenship rights. In general terms, the US, Canada and Australia were seen as the most 'liberal' (but note earlier caveats about favoured groups); countries such as Britain and France tended to grant full rights only to immigrants from their former colonies; other countries such as Germany, Belgium and Switzerland operated 'guest-worker' systems giving only restricted rights to immigrants, and the Gulf States have been described as having harsh policies and no permanent resident rights in relation to foreign workers (Bali 1997:211).

Bali (1997:209) has also pointed out that even countries needing labour may choose to protect the homogeneity of society rather than encourage immigration – Japan is a case in point. General economic and migration policies favour firms moving to countries where labour costs are lower, rather than promoting immigration; and, while it makes a significant contribution in monetary terms to the UNHCR, formal programmes for asylum seekers are relatively recent and limited (Hirayama et al. 1995). There are, however, small ethnic minorities within Japan (including Koreans and Vietnamese) and individual skilled workers can secure temporary contracts, but Japan has not been a large player in the migration scene, either as a sending or receiving country. The wish to preserve homogeneity and ensure the dominance of 'national culture' can be observed in most other societies and is periodically the basis for particularly nationalistic or fascistic tendencies in policies towards existing or potential immigrants, including in Europe and the US (Lorenz 1994; Van Wormer 1997).

With regard to one of the largest traditional 'receiving' countries, 30 million people migrated to the US between 1861 and 1920 and a further 24 million in the period up to 1987 (Castles and Miller 1993:51). But entry was not unregulated and the Chinese Exclusion Act (1882) was passed to prevent an increase in the number of Asians then entering the US, and affected immigration patterns for nearly ninety years (Wong 1997). Recent legislation has suggested a marked change in approach and been seen as discouraging further immigration of both Asians and Latinos (from Mexico in particular) and as discriminating against existing migrants. The main elements of the Illegal Immigration Reform and Immigrant Responsibility Act (1996) include tighter border control, higher penalties for illegal entry, tougher measures aimed at exclusion and streamlined deportation procedures. The Act has been described as 'particularly unwelcoming to those seeking asylum' by Seidl (1997) who also noted that the US rejects 80 per cent of asylum applications, relative to an 80 per cent acceptance rate by Canada.

The recent passage of the English Language Empowerment Act (1996) (declaring English the official language of the US) has also indicated a hardening of attitudes, in a country which previously prided itself on its multiculturalism. This has been related to the fear engendered by the rapid increase in Spanish-speaking Latinos who, according to US Census Bureau projections, are set to become the largest minority by 2010, relative to their current position as constituting 9 per cent of the population (Van Wormer 1997). Further, the Personal Responsibility and Work Opportunity Reconciliation Act of 1996 threatened to cut off legal immigrants from eligibility for food stamps and Supplemental Security Income (SSI), unless they applied for US citizenship. In this process, the English-proficiency portion of the naturalisation test also seemed prejudicial to the position of some established Latino migrants (Prigoff 1997), as well as Asians and East Europeans. Wong (1997) noted that lobbying and alliances between different ethnic groups had resulted in the partial restoration of the SSI benefit.

Countries also have very variable records in relation to refugees and a number have recently set quotas to maintain levels which are nationally acceptable (although regional policies are also becoming more influential, as discussed later). Up to the mid-1990s, Sweden had been identified as the country in the OECD with the highest proportion of asylum seekers, relative to both total immigrant numbers and the overall population size (Ginsberg 1994), although in 1997, the US and Germany both had higher overall numbers (UNHCR 1997). Concerns about the number of immigrants, including asylum seekers, and a general tightening of restrictions were evident in legislative changes in a number of European countries, following a rapid rise in numbers in the late 1980s.

One example was the UK's Asylum and Immigration Appeals Act (1993), a particular feature of which was the requirement that new arrivals seeking asylum, formally request this at the time and point of entry. This Act has apparently resulted in the cutting of successful applications for asylum from 53 per cent to 22 per cent between 1992 and 1994. Despite an intention to reduce the time taken to process applications, the average time has remained quite high at about ten months, and the number of appeals against decisions has increased. In 1995 only about 1 per cent of these were allowed (CRE 1997). The UK Carriers Liability Act gave the government powers to impose a fine on airlines transporting migrants without proper entry documents, a practice likely to be extended to prevent undocumented arrivals via the Channel Tunnel.

The impact of particular ethnic or national groups, as *established* minorities who have achieved some economic and/or political power within a society, can be noted as affecting other aspects of policy, including foreign policy. In the US, for instance, Irish nationalist sympathisers have lent financial and political support to the aspirations of those aiming for a united Ireland; pro-Israeli sympathisers have influenced US foreign policy in the Middle East. Elsewhere, the relationship between immigration and the security or foreign policy of receiving countries has also been apparent in other ways, for example, when political instability in Algeria spilled over into Algerian communities in France (Bali 1997:213).

Specific countries can also be seen as pursuing particular policies – or failing to enforce restrictions – which impact on their neighbours. For instance, Turkey (as well as generating its own refugees in the form of Kurds) has been identified as a route into Europe for illegal immigrants (via boats which then land in Italy) and it has been alleged that smuggling rings have been operating for about ten years to send Africans and Asians to Europe. A new tough policy has recently been announced by the Turks under pressure from the EU (Hanson 1998). However, in a counter-claim, Turkey had suggested that the Italian policy of granting political asylum to Kurds was itself encouraging illegal immigrants. Italy was reported as having accepted over a thousand immigrants from Turkey in the first week in 1998, and regarded them as fleeing repression in Turkey. (The Turkish government outlawed the Kurdistan Workers Party and the speaking of the Kurdish language in the mid-1980s.) Half a million Kurds (including from Iraq and Iran) are already living in Germany, which is keen to prevent any further migration. Germany was urging Italy to prevent illegal entry to the country from Turkey, not least given Italy's position as a member of the Schengen group (Chipaka 1998), illustrating the way pressure may be brought to bear on one country by another in relation to a third.

Mention of the Schengen groups leads on to a brief consideration of the development of *regional* policies in relation to migration (including asylum seekers), for instance, in Europe. Even before the development of policies aimed at political and social, rather than economic, goals in the then European Economic Community, the more broadly based Council of Europe had established a European Convention on Human Rights (1950) which included some provisions relevant to migrants, some of whom have had recourse to the European Court of Human Rights, including in the 1990s (Ruxton 1996). At a more general level, Seacombe (1996) questioned Croatia's admission to the Council of Europe (as its fortieth member), since admission conferred an undeserved 'cloak of respectability'. Seacombe suggested that the country's government was not democratic and that the plight and rights of minority Muslim 'refugees' were being ignored. Additionally, an international warrant for the arrest of an indicted war criminal had been ignored, and respect for human rights generally seemed at variance with the Council's goals. Council of Europe membership has also sometimes been seen as a prelude to later application for admission to the EU.

The European Union 'has increasingly seen the harmonisation of immigration and refugee policies of Member States as necessary in order to create an impregnable outer border round the EU and prevent an uneven distribution of asylum seekers within [it]' (Ruxton 1996:426). The origins of this policy were signified in the formation of the Trevi Group in 1976, when a group of Ministers and police chiefs was established to counteract 'terrorism, radicalism, extremism and violence'. Its remit has since been expanded to include all 'security and policing aspects of freedom of movement' (Ruxton 1996:432), implying an association between migrants and criminals which is inappropriate and even prejudicial in the majority of cases.

A decade later, a move towards harmonising of immigration laws was initiated by a Ministerial Group on Immigration, in preparation for the establishment of the Single Market, with its intended free movement of goods, money and people. The resulting Schengen Agreement on intergovernmental processes in relation to population movement within the EU was established in 1990. It has since been ratified by nine Member States (Germany, France, the Benelux and southern European countries), and came into effect in 1995. Apart from the abolition of border controls between the signatories, it introduced common visa and carrier liability policies, detailed checks on entries by non-EU nationals, a list of 'undesirable aliens' and a stipulation that asylum seekers must apply in their first country of entry and, if refused, are not eligible to seek asylum elsewhere in the EU. (This last provision was established by the Dublin Convention of 1990.) The 1991 Maastricht Treaty on European Union, in force since 1993, also referred to asylum and immigration policy, although asylum policy is outside the jurisdiction of the European Court of Justice (Ruxton 1996).

These policies have laid the EU open to charges of creating a 'fortress Europe', pulling up the drawbridge against people seeking improved economic conditions and/or political protection and rights. They have also been seen to have racist implications in the context of growing evidence of public racism, despite the issuing in 1986 of a Joint Declaration against Racism and Xenophobia by the EC institutions. Over a decade later, concerns about the effects of increased racism have been reiterated in the previously mentioned policies in relation to social exclusion. Also, in launching the European Year against Racism (1997), the Commissioner for Employment and Social Affairs acknowledged the multicultural and multinational character of the EU and the insidious effects of racism, and hoped that the year would promote new initiatives and good practice in anti-racist strategies (EC Newsletter 30 January 97). One aspect of the year was a European Conference, 'Celebrating Diversity', which examined the diversity of ethnic minority populations in a number of European cities; it compared national legislations, highlighted the contributions made by ethnic minority groups in the labour market and illustrated the importance of joint working relationships (Page 1997).

However, apparent attempts to recognise the needs and contributions of established migrants have not lessened the concern to deter further immigration. This was illustrated by press reports of a shift in expenditure of the European Aid Budget from Third World projects to ones in North Africa and the Middle East with the suggestion that such funding was directly aimed at creating a prosperous region around the Mediterranean and reinforcing democracy, 'in the hope of damming the flood of illegal immigration' (Kemp 1996). Under a five-year programme (1995–99) the Meda budget (nearly £4 billion) would be spent on projects in 12 South Mediterranean and North African countries (although funding to projects in Turkey was blocked because of concern about the country's human rights record). The shift was seen as being at the expense of the poorest countries in the world (sub-Saharan Africa), and as promoting EU foreign policy rather than alleviating poverty and suffering. Additionally, some of the projects in the

Mediterranean region were described as 'questionable' and the Court of Auditors were called in to examine the accounts.

The above case might be seen as an example of a strategy which has been advocated by Worldwatch, that is, that rather than concentrating on ways to prevent entry of immigrants to specific states, or alleviation of mass refugee situations, the advanced industrial countries and the international community should put more resources into preventing the conditions which create migrants, whether voluntary or involuntary (Newland 1994; Kane 1995). (Although the EU example marked a shift in resources from the very poor to the poor in a way which could be judged as serving its own interests more directly.) This relates back to some of the earlier discussion about aid and trade in relation to poverty, though clearly there are also important political and human rights dimensions in the case of civil wars and other conflicts, and totalitarian regimes. But even assuming some shift in strategies and resources towards more fundamental prevention, migration has given rise to social problems associated with or attributed to established ethnic minority communities and newly arrived asylum seekers which have become the focus for intervention by some workers in the social professions, as discussed next.

The role of social professionals

It has been suggested that social work in the US had a 'historic stake in the plight of immigrants' at the turn of the twentieth century (Richan 1997); as was noted earlier, on the other side of the Atlantic, the impetus for the establishment of a major international children's welfare organisation, the Save the Children Fund in 1919, was rooted in concerns about the needs of refugee children fleeing the Balkan crisis (Ruxton 1996). To this day, workers in the social professions have undertaken a number of roles in statutory and voluntary sectors, in residential settings and in the community to alleviate the problems or advocate for the rights of particular minorities. Richan suggested that some of the issues relating to work in this field are little different from a century ago, but that new questions have also arisen in the modern environment and in the light of a more sophisticated understanding of cultural and class diversity.

Most countries have developed welfare systems (whether formal or informal) suited to the needs of the indigenous population, or in the case of the countries subject to European colonisation, to the dominant white majority. The establishment of ethnic minority populations resulting from economic migration or people seeking asylum has challenged states and the social professions to consider the needs of more diverse populations and to make appropriate provisions and responses. The range of motivations for migration, origins of migrants and varied experiences of the migratory process and settlement in a new country require sensitive and differentiated programmes and interventions geared to the needs of particular groups, as well as more general provisions which do not discriminate against minorities.

Recent policy changes and historical occurrences in many countries have demonstrated how economic downturn in individual societies can negatively affect perceptions of established minority groups and newcomers who have often been 'blamed' for socio-economic problems. This has been apparent in the deteriorating treatment of Gypsies in Central European countries in the 1990s, and was also illustrated, for example, by press reports of attacks on Chinese shopkeepers in disturbances related to the economic crisis in Indonesia in 1997/8. But migrants are often the most likely people to experience the worst effects of limited, low-paid and insecure employment, poor housing conditions, strained health and education services, and restrictive financial aid (should any be available). In fact their access to any of these resources may be restricted because of their status (for instance, in the UK people seeking asylum were not allowed to work, although in 1997 a High Court decision ruled this unlawful), or because of their own fears about eligibility and stigma, or ignorance about availability. Additionally, pressures may impact differently on different family members, resulting in strains within family systems and minority communities.

While some of the social work literature relating to work with minority groups has focused specifically on work in relation to particular established communities or with refugees and asylum seekers (including unaccompanied minors), Sherraden and Martin (1994) made a useful case for the adoption of international perspectives in a range of interventions related to migrants, including the need to have some understanding of the national and cultural roots of the particular individuals and groups, and the realities of welfare provision which might have prevailed in the countries of origin. These would have a bearing on the likely expectations of the newcomers, and might suggest adaptations to provisions and approaches to make services more accessible and acceptable to particular communities.

Additionally, Sherraden and Martin identified the importance of developing an appreciation of the effects of the process of migration (including the specific circumstances surrounding the departure of individuals and families and their arrival in their new destination). Other studies of particular migrant groups have also illustrated the importance of this understanding, for instance, Schindler (1993) regarding the migration of black Jews from Ethiopia to Israel, and have illustrated the usefulness of evaluating the expectations as well as the initial experiences of new migrants, when planning services (see, for instance, Chow and Ho (1996) in relation to the arrival of new migrants to Hong Kong).

At a psychosocial level, the theme of *loss* is a significant dimension in the experience of migrants, and may be a focus for counselling or other forms of therapeutic intervention. But the extent to which this is a constant or damaging factor varies according to the particular circumstances of departure, the new situation and the extent to which positive links can be maintained between relatives and former home countries. For some, notions of loss are kept at bay by the reality or assumption that this is only a temporary separation, but for others the loss can be of substantial and irreversible magnitude. The extreme loss of a young Bosnian man interviewed in a refugee centre by a social work student of a similar age, struck home when the asylum seeker spoke of the loss, not only of family members, but of his country (personal communication).

Mental health may also be affected by the need to achieve, and the fear of failure which may be particularly strong in some migrants, especially if relatives 'back home' are dependent on remittances. One study suggested that the poor adjustment and mental health problems of a minority of Filipino domestic workers in Hong Kong could sometimes be attributed to the extent to which debt and family problems in the Philippines weighed on them at a distance. Other stress factors included abuse by employers and limitations placed on their association with a peer network. While supportive group relations are generally readily available to Filipino women in Hong Kong (including through informal, outdoor Sunday gatherings), such opportunities are likely to be more limited or non-existent in some of the other 140 countries where Filipino women are now employed as domestic workers (Bagley et al. 1997).

In many situations, the practical needs of newly arrived migrants take precedence over their psychological needs, and Hirayama et al. (1995) described the differences in response to South-east Asian refugee resettlement in Japan and the US. Perhaps the Japanese approach – institutionally based programmes in Refugee Resettlement Centres, rather than the individualised programmes common in the US – reflects stronger tendencies towards group care in other forms of Japanese social services, rather than inherent differences in the needs of the migrants themselves. Common features of both approaches (and of refugee resettlement programmes in many other countries) were programmes concerned with language needs, cultural orientation, vocational guidance, cash assistance with housing and advice about education and health facilities.

The article also stressed the common goals of resettlement work in both countries as 'assimilation and self-sufficiency' (Hirayama et al. 1995:164), and these terms raise interesting questions. While the expectation that migrants should be (or be assisted to become) self-sufficient, the notion of assimilation may imply adaptation to, and absorption by, the host cultures in ways which are not healthy or appropriate for the migrant groups. Policies and practices which promote integration, multiculturalism, marginalisation, segregation or diversity have been apparent to varying degrees in all receiving countries, and 'fashions' informing how migrants should be regarded and treated have changed over time. In general, there seems to have been a more widespread official recognition of the pluralist nature of many societies in the 1990s, and of the strengths as well as possible tensions surrounding bi-culturalism for instance, but often the defence and promotion of minority cultures and rights is, in part, a responsibility of the social professions.

Brody (1990) identified the adaptations which the migratory process frequently requires of people: from traditional settings and cultures to modern secular societies; from societies where traditional skills have been passed on and are useful, to those where technical skills have to be learned; from extended families in homogeneous societies to isolation and segregation in heterogeneous societies, and from societies stressing family obligations to those stressing independence. Such 'enforced modernisation' can impact on gender roles and marital relationships and also on the expectations and identity development of children and young people. Such strains may be alleviated by informed professionals working in mainstream services but may require differentiated services from workers who are more familiar with the cultural values of specific ethnic groups.

Although the 'valuing of diversity' has been espoused by global companies and many governments, the empowerment of individuals and minority groups who are economically disadvantaged or who have experienced fear and violence (or both) remains a major task for workers in the social professions. This may require a shift in the professional 'mind-set' from seeing migrants as people with problems or in need, to seeing them as people who are essentially resourceful and resilient, (but) who have experienced the double disadvantages of difficult (and perhaps dangerous) circumstances in one country, and discrimination in another. It is also evident that, notwithstanding some of the commonalties of the migratory process, there are significant differences between migrants themselves, including in terms of previous educational attainment and work experience. However, while some migrants are equipped for responsible and skilled jobs, most are assumed to lack skills, if only because of lack of fluency in a new language, and may have difficulty gaining employment or find themselves underemployed.

This, in turn, raises the question of the extent to which migrants, and particularly asylum seekers, can 'manage themselves' and, when necessary, help and advise other newcomers. Much of this already occurs informally, but it can also be formally built into the working and employment/volunteer practices of resettlement programmes, whether run by the state or NGOs. Additionally, social service agencies working with migrants in the community can decide how much of their resources should be allocated to the particular problems and needs of individuals, and how to promote collective and pro-active approaches to common concerns such as poor housing, discriminatory health or educational policies, or proposed legislation, as illustrated earlier in the case of the US (Prigoff 1997; Wong 1997).

Different characteristics of, and opportunities available to, long-established minority groups have also been demonstrated, for example in a recent summary of data arising from the British 1991 population census. This showed differential rates of school success between Asian and African-Caribbean children resulting in different opportunities in the workplace. It also illustrated the higher likelihood of African-Caribbean children being in care, and of black youths entering the juvenile justice system, phenomena long familiar to many social workers, even if solutions are more elusive. Perhaps inevitably, the data also showed that migrants who arrived from the poorest and most rural societies, such as Bangladesh, are more likely to be struggling, in socio-economic terms, and still living in larger families in poorer areas than those who arrived with higher educational qualifications. However, unemployment – or underemployment – is generally higher among migrants than the white population, although there are also differences in the extent to which different groups are self-employed (Peach 1996).

With regard to special services and social work intervention in relation to refugees, a rather minimalist approach in the UK, where the official response is off-putting and voluntary responses are under-resourced and poorly co-ordinated, can be contrasted with the situations in most Nordic countries, which illustrate a high degree of centralised planning and pro-active intervention including by social professionals. In Denmark, for instance, the Danish Red Cross (under contract to the government) assumes a central role in service provision and co-ordination of services by other voluntary organisations, and social workers are present when asylum seekers are interviewed by immigration officials. But there are concerns about the extent to which such a streamlined and centralised approach may foster a dependency culture in migrants.

Apart from the possible involvement of people in the social professions in the work of the UN and some of the major NGOs concerned with refugees, such as the Red Cross/Red Crescent, Oxfam and Save the Children Fund, the IFSW has drawn up a Policy Statement on Refugees (11/97). This provided a background and definition of the problem and also identified the key areas of knowledge for social workers involved in this area of work as relating to the trauma of uprootment, separation and loss, hardship and persecution; a knowledge of the world conditions which have led to displacement, and knowledge relating to cultural factors and the effects of xenophobia in the host community. It identified the goal of resettlement programmes as being to enable refugees to become self-sufficient, and recognised a tension for social workers between meeting basic needs and avoiding encouraging dependency.

In particular, the statement recognised the plight of people caught up in mass and long-term 'holding' operations and advocated a multidimensional approach to policy and programmes, including for refugees 'in limbo', where particular attention to creating a sense of community and improving/maintaining morale in the face of long-term uncertainty would be particularly important. It stressed the need for the active participation of refugees themselves in the running of camps and in discussions and decisions about their future choices.

It also discussed the needs of refugees and the likely focus of programmes at the (re)settlement stage in a new country, noting the need for recreational facilities, child care facilities, special services for vulnerable groups, and re-adaptation programmes for refugees who opt for voluntary repatriation. A third phase of work identified was the provision of ethnically sensitive services to assist the longer-term adjustment of refugees to their new environment, including help with housing and health care, facilitating self-help groups, career counselling, development of interpreter and paraprofessional helping services drawn from the minority, mental health programmes and public education.

The IFSW Statement supports the principle of coexistence, or integration into pluralist societies (rather than assimilation) and the development of specialist services where necessary and possible. It also advocates collaborative work with organisations such as Amnesty International and the Red Cross to lobby for change, and develop strategies aimed at prevention as well as intervention. It identified work with refugees as a current or potential area of work for many in the social professions and therefore something that should be part of mainstream education and training for social work.

Conclusions

An examination of the different facets of migration illustrates the importance of economic issues as well as political conflict in the contemporary world, and the complex inter-relationships between diverse nations. The growth of non-indigenous ethnic populations in many countries around the world has helped to blur the distinctions between domestic and international boundaries (Bali 1997:220). Immigrants reflect the gulf between living conditions in the advanced industrial countries and the less developed countries, and refugees highlight the denial of democratic freedoms and human rights which others might take for granted. Migration has brought the concerns of countries stricken by poverty or war to the television screens, and sometimes to the doorsteps of more settled and prosperous societies.

Migration is an important facet of modern life, and two figures put the phenomenon into perspective: it is rare for as much as 10 per cent of a national population to emigrate (Bali 1997), none the less, globally, one in every 120 people is a migrant (UNHCR 1997). It seems likely that, as with the pace of change in other areas, the extent of migration and cultural diversity within societies far outstrips anything imagined in previous times of significant population mobility, and the prospects of increased circular movement and intermarriage are considerable, with implications for individuals, families and societies. Governments and international bodies have been challenged to devise policies and programmes which meet the particular needs of people displaced by conflict or natural disaster, or motivated to seek change and opportunity elsewhere.

The causes and forms of migration are complex, and, apart from the particular situation of asylum seekers, a simple 'push–pull' calculus, related solely to job opportunities and wage differentials, overlooks a wide range of other personal and structural factors (including labour recruitment and immigration policies) which inform the departure decisions of individuals and groups, and impact on their capacity to adapt and settle in new conditions. While many migrants are personally capable and resourceful, some succumb to the dual disadvantages of previous problems and new discriminations.

Social professionals are found in a variety of roles and settings concerned with migrants, ranging from assistance in refugee camps, resettlement programmes for new arrivals and statutory responsibilities for unaccompanied minors, to programmes associated with the special needs of migrants, for example, related to youth unemployment, disabilities or mental health problems, HIV/AIDS, or the consequences of torture abroad or domestic violence at home. There are also increasing concerns about the needs of migrant elders in some societies, and about the widespread discrimination of a permanent migrant group, Gypsies/travellers. Apart from direct work, some workers and agencies see their task as more concerned with addressing the structural factors which cause migration or which disadvantage migrants in particular countries, and undertake research, public education and lobbying at national, regional or international levels. Whatever the particular roles of social professionals, work in the field of migration requires international perspectives and particular knowledge about cultural difference.

7 Disasters in international perspective

Introduction

While human agents are thought to direct the path of technological change, and of economic, political and social developments, there are nevertheless occasions when accidents or events occur, which are outside human control. When the consequences affect numerous individuals or whole groups, communities or societies, the term 'disaster' is used. Such events result in loss: death and bereavement; injury and disability; loss of homes, livelihoods and sometimes local power, transport and civic infrastructure, and varying degrees of emotional trauma for survivors, relatives and the helping personnel.

This chapter considers the varied forms which disasters take and how they might be classified, including a basic distinction as to whether they are 'natural', or resulting from human action or inaction – or a combination of both. The *Oxford English Dictionary* defines a disaster as 'anything ruinous or distressing that befalls; a sudden or great misfortune or mishap; a calamity'; and one of the immediate consequences is chaos, 'a state of confusion and disorder'.

To an increasing extent, disasters, wherever they occur, have become a matter of international interest through the press and media, and in some cases there are also international responses. Sometimes the form of disaster, such as an air crash, can be seen both as an aspect of increasing globalisation and also as having international dimensions and implications, as discussed later.

In some countries, disasters are outside the general experience of most social professionals. However, a minority of social workers are involved in

131

preparations for potential disasters and/or in responses to actual occurrences. This may be as part of central or local government teams or in positions within (international) relief organisations, and in some circumstances their roles involve cross-national communications, as illustrated below.

Classifying disasters

Disasters, or major emergencies, are 'overwhelming events' (Raphael 1986) and come in many forms, of varying scale. While the immediate effects of a major emergency may be relatively local and involve only tens of people, other disasters cover a wider geographical area and may affect thousands. Additionally, people not immediately affected become involved in their roles as relatives, neighbours or official or informal helpers, creating a ripple effect to the wider society (Gibson 1991), or sometimes globally. Some disasters have a progressive onset or more immediate warnings, while others are hard to predict and plan for. All result in disruption of normal routines and services, uncertainty and lack of information, and sometimes a breakdown in communication and transport networks which challenge helping responses.

Disasters can be classified according to whether they are *natural*, of which earthquakes and volcanoes are examples; or *manmade* (*sic*) (the result of human action or inaction), of which war, civil conflict, terrorism and technical failure are the most obvious. However, it has also been increasingly recognised that a range of disasters, including drought and famine, while apparently 'natural', are partly related to human behaviour and political and economic decisions which have impacted on the physical environment, including the climate. In the case of floods, these may be the result of natural causes, as in the case of tidal waves resulting from earthquakes, or may be an example of a combined effect, as illustrated later.

Apart from the above distinctions, disasters can also be classified according to *scale*, both in terms of the number of people involved and whether the event is seen as having predominantly local, national or international implications. Berren et al. (1989) suggested that a 'small disaster' might only involve twenty deaths, while medium and large-scale ones would involve up to or in excess of a hundred respectively, but it is probably more helpful, if using this criterion, to think in terms of tens, hundreds and thousands of deaths. Also, the extent to which a disaster is small or medium scale in numbers may not correlate with its national or international significance. For instance, in the crash of a scheduled flight in 1989 from

Europe to the US, near Lockerbie in Scotland, the fact that the crash was caused by a terrorist bomb had international repercussions which have still not been resolved (White et al. 1997).

Other ways of classifying disasters can be related to the possibility of *prediction*, the length of likely warning, the duration of the disaster, and the likelihood of re-occurrence. Thus some 'manmade' disasters, such as the Lockerbie bomb, are instantaneous in time-scale and might be unpredictable and unlikely to be repeated (at least in the exact form and place), while many natural disasters (and some which partly result from human actions) can be predicted to varying degrees, and are also liable to recur in the same area. Earthquakes and volcanic eruptions are difficult to predict but the possibility or likelihood of them occurring in certain regions or sites is known. More advanced technology in the fields of seismology and vulcanology, and sometimes other signs, might give some indications of earth movements or impending eruption, although in recent events these have not been understood in time to enable evacuation.

In the case of the Kobe-Osaka earthquake, in Japan in 1995, the unusual behaviour of birds, animals and fish in the Tsunami (Pacific coastal) area had been noted ('Savage Earth', ITV documentary, 9 December 97); other warning signs which might indicate an earthquake include radon gas leaking from the ground, sudden changes in the water table, electromagnetic signals from rocks or slight ground tremors prior to the quake. Nevertheless, the Kobe-Osaka earthquake was apparently unanticipated, measured 7.2 on the Richter scale and killed over 5000 people. This was the most recent of nearly thirty major earthquakes in just over two decades, affecting countries/states on the west side of North and South America, and in and around the Pacific and Asian subcontinent, as well as some countries in the Middle East and Balkan areas and bordering the Mediterranean. The consequences of these massive earth movements depend partly on the population density of the areas affected as well as the design and building materials used in dwellings and other constructions, relative to the severity of the tremors. For instance a quake in Maharashtra in India (1993) was estimated to have killed 10,000 people, while only about sixty people died in the Los Angeles earthquake a year later ('Earthquakes', *Guardian Education*, 24 January 95).

Volcanic activity is, if anything, even less predictable, despite considerable study around the world. Depending on the size of the country or region, relative to the prevalence of volcanic activity, questions arise about the viability of particular areas for settlement. For example, in 1997, a volcanic eruption in Montserrat caused significant destruction and disruption of the local economy and highlighted the extent to which small nations with limited resources might expect assistance after the event from the international community, or from particular countries (in this case, the UK). This might include the need for resettlement of people displaced and for whom returning or staying in the region seems not to be an option. However, volcanic soil is fertile (as are alluvial plains which are liable to flooding), and the temptation or necessity of settlement and cultivation of such areas has been a significant factor in the scale of some disasters.

One of the best-known examples of volcanic activity in the European region is Mount Vesuvius in Italy, with records of eruptions dating back to AD 79 (and earlier according to other evidence). It has now been dormant since 1944, but it is predicted that further volcanic activity is imminent, with up to three million people over a five-mile radius being at risk from the superheated ash, poisonous gas and flow of molten lava. In 1995 the Italian government established an emergency plan for evacuating the area over a seven-day period but experienced vulcanologists consider this an unrealistic time-scale given the difficulty of forecasting the eruption and the speed at which events unfold when it occurs. Significant monitoring arrangements are now in place (electrical currents are used to probe the area) but final warning signals may only be possible a few days or hours in advance and some people have therefore advocated a wholesale evacuation of the area sooner rather than later (Matthews 1998).

Still considering natural disasters, those related to *climatic extremes* can be forecast with varying degrees of accuracy (for example, the likely path and strength of cyclones and hurricanes), and events such as droughts (resulting in famine) are protracted rather than sudden and short-lived in their form. In both cases, particular localities and regions are known to be 'at risk'. In some places adaptations have been made to settlement patterns and land use, to avoid or mitigate the possible effects, but other areas are well-settled with consequent risks to established populations. An apparent increase in the number and severity of floods and drought, in particular, have raised questions about the extent to which human use of the earth's resources has affected both global climatic conditions and local ecosystems.

Climatologists and other scientists have recognised that global warming is discernible (0.6 degrees overall in this century but up to 2 degrees in Canada, for instance). This has been attributed to interference with the natural habitat, not least deforestation which has had measurable effects on local rainfall patterns, river flows, droughts and floods. As well as the effects on agricultural production and the threat to human survival in the face of drought (inducing famine, as in the sub-Saharan area of Africa), severe drought has also been blamed for an increase in forest fires, including in Indonesia and in Australia, where huge fires have recently threatened the outskirts of Sydney.

Returning to the connection between afforestation and climate, large forested areas have traditionally acted like sponges, soaking up and recirculating water and, in mountainous areas, preventing soil erosion and rapid run-off of excess water: in this respect forests may be more important as a climatic regulator than as a resource. In 1988 logging was banned in Thailand because of landslides and erosion following torrential rain. Tree felling in the foothills of the Himalayas has increased flooding in Bangladesh during the monsoon season and led to the silting up of the Bay of Bengal. It has even been suggested that the destruction of large areas of forest in Ethiopia since the nineteenth century might have resulted in the extreme drought and resultant famines in the region since the 1980s; it has been speculated that, if enough trees were planted, it might be possible to reverse current climatic changes. So, for instance, efforts are being made to 'reforest' parts of Ethiopia (with the aid of irrigation schemes), and some have advocated an increase in the forest cover of the world's surface from the 1990 figure of about 25 per cent, although climatic change itself may make reforestation, or maintenance of forests in particular regions, difficult (Brown 1996).

Climatic conditions and change also have a bearing on the virulence and spread of some types of disease and infection and the increased possibility of epidemics, if not pandemics. For instance, it has been suggested that higher average temperatures in the UK might account for an increase in enterovirus infections which can result in outbreaks of serious or life-threatening diseases such as polio or meningitis (Hanstock 1991). Though such occurrences might not be on a scale to qualify as disasters in themselves, there is an association between some types of disaster, including floods and wars, and the likelihood of death through rapid spread of diseases such as cholera, because of breakdown in water supplies and sanitation. Additionally, environmental pollution, affecting both air and water supplies, threaten the health of whole populations. Environmental damage has resulted from technological development and failure, and from the policies of global companies and governments, concerned to 'off-load' inferior products or toxic waste.

An example of technological failure occurred in the explosion of a nuclear power station in Chernobyl in Byelorussia, in 1986, when, despite evacuation of the immediate area, deaths and injuries occurred. The after-effects of environmental pollution (the spreading of radioactivity) have been more widespread and long term. Over 100,000 people have been relocated and a 'Zone of Estrangement' established (Van Wormer 1997:454). Nevertheless, there has been an increase in cancer rates and other diseases over a wide area and affecting a new generation of children (Artobolevskiy 1991; Edwards 1994; Bamford 1998).

In relation to multinational corporate policy, the accidental release of pesticide from the Union Carbide plant in Bhopal, India in 1985 resulted in 2500 deaths and 200,000 people harmed. Rogge and Darkwa (1996) have pointed out that pesticides are often banned by advanced industrial nations but commercially produced and marketed in less developed countries. In such cases, the conditions for their manufacture and use are even less safe due to lack of health and safety regulations, and limited advice about risks and usage, perhaps negated by low levels of literacy or economic necessity. Additionally, the industrialised countries produce about 97 per cent of the world's toxic waste, but the less developed countries have become the targets for dumping because of Western governmental controls or opposition from lobbying groups.

Less developed countries, or poorer populations within them, are also more likely to be affected by the 'manmade' disasters of war and military conflict, or the economic sanctions applied against countries such as Iraq in the 1990s. Kane quoted UN figures which showed that 90 per cent of armed conflicts and refugees are to be found in the Third World (1995:20) and also illustrated the connection between wars, famines and migration. Modern conflicts may also be environmentally damaging through the use of nuclear or chemical weapons. There is also a much greater likelihood of civilian populations being involved. According to UN figures, civilian deaths rose from 5 per cent of the casualties in the First World War to 90 per cent in armed conflicts in the 1990s (Kane 1995:19–20).

This partly reflects the extent to which civil wars now predominate over inter-country wars – 79 out of 82 armed conflicts between 1989 and 1992 were internal (Kane 1995:21) – and a recognition, or assumption, that whole communities may be in opposition to a particular government or competing military forces. Julia (1994) has noted, for instance, how one in ten El Salvadorians were displaced and 75,000 people (including armed insurgents) killed over a decade when the Sandinista regime was in power, up to the early 1990s; events in the former Yugoslavia in the early 1990s also demonstrated a massive involvement of local populations as targets of 'ethnic cleansing' and rape tactics. Van Wormer has summarised literature about the vulnerable position of women in war and the use of rape as a weapon of war (1997:632).

The increased risks to children have also been particularly noticeable: UNICEF estimated that about two million children had died, up to five million had been disabled, five million were in refugee camps, and twelve million had been made homeless in over thirty conflicts around the world during the decade from the mid-1980s to the mid-1990s (*The Guardian*, 16 December 1994). A subsequent UN report (1996) suggested that children were at increased risk of being used as human shields, subject to rape or prostitution or enforced military service or espionage roles, or tortured or killed to demoralise communities or as part of ethnic cleansing. Perhaps at the chronic rather than the acute end of disasters, Ruxton (1996) has noted that children in Northern Ireland have lived through the longest period of conflict in modern times (since 1968, but with the possibility of a peace settlement at the time of writing, 1998).

Conflicts may also spread over into states or territories not formally involved, as in 'Operation Desert Shield', a six-week military operation by US and NATO forces against Iraq in 1991. In this case 40 Scud missile attacks reached Israel, resulting in the evacuation of over a thousand people and hundreds of injuries (but few deaths), as well as causing fear related to the threat of chemical attacks, and substantial damage to properties in the affected area (Lowenberg 1992). There are 'knock-on' effects to neighbouring countries in other ways, as illustrated by the thousands of refugees who fled from El Salvador to Honduras, or who crossed the national border at the height of civil war in Rwanda.

The last example of disasters which can be classified as of a particular type (though causes and scales vary), and which tend to involve both more affluent and poor populations, are *transport* disasters. These range from coach or train to plane crashes and the sinking of ferries (for instance the *Herald of Free Enterprise*, crossing between Belgium and England in 1988, but also many examples in less developed parts of the world). Particular features of such disasters are that the people involved are away from their homes and possibly come from different countries. For example, thirty nationalities were among the dead in the Lockerbie air crash (Gibson 1991).

Sometimes an air or sea disaster involves people from a particular area, as in the case of the 'Axminster' Air Disaster, in 1963, in which 108 people were killed when a charter flight carrying tourists crashed into a Swiss mountain. Most of the dead were women from a particular British village, with special implications for that community, but the fact that the crash happened away from home raised many of the common problems associated with transport disasters, which make these cross-national, if not international in scope.

Overall therefore, an apparent rise in the number of disasters can be attributed not just to the speed of communications (for example, the 1989 earthquake in San Francisco was reported within minutes of its occurrence on early morning news bulletins in the UK) and the amount of media and press reporting, but also to the possibility that larger numbers of people are gathered together in confined spaces (as in mass travel or sporting events); or that failures occur in advanced technology, as in the Chernobyl disaster. In some cases some warning may be possible and people are likely to take common preventive or protective measures such as gathering of the family unit (perhaps in a special place), rapid bonding of individuals in collective efforts to try to avert or escape disaster, and/or 'prayer and provision', including stockpiling of food supplies (Gibson 1991).

But in other cases no such activities are possible or useful, and disasters regarded as natural, but with a human component in their causation, are particularly likely to impact disproportionately on populations in less developed countries who lack resources to take preventive measures, even if these might be effective. However, there is increasing recognition that events and catastrophes in far-off places are often related to, or cause, environmental damage which has global implications. As with poverty and migration, advanced industrial societies cannot afford to ignore the symptoms of climate change or the consequences of distant conflicts, and international bodies have an important role in providing humanitarian aid and expertise in relation to disasters.

Common problems and international responses to disasters

A number of writers have identified the likely results of disasters in terms of the common problems and needs which arise in the immediate/short, medium and long term, and also suggested a range of helping roles and tasks (Gibson 1991; Newburn 1996). This section examines the particular problems and needs associated with different phases of intervention, and identifies some of the activities of a range of helpers and organisations.

In most types of disaster, in the immediate and short term, the problems and needs are practical and technical. In some disasters, such as earthquakes or air crashes, there is a clear need for the work of 'rescue' services, but conditions may dictate a breakdown of professional roles in which a range of individuals may become 'helpers by circumstance' before the arrival of 'assigned helpers' (Gibson 1991), in the form of fire and police services, health workers and perhaps the military, and voluntary organisations. Essential requirements at this stage are speed and co-ordination of responses. In many cases these will be local or national but in some large-scale or high-risk disasters international experts or organisations might be involved.

In the case of earthquakes, for instance, the first three days are regarded as crucial in the possibility of finding survivors alive, and technical equipment (for example, thermal imaging cameras) and expert personnel might need to be sought. Some criticism was levelled against the Japanese government in the case of the Kobe-Osaka earthquake, for slow response, bureaucracy and failure to make best use of all possible resources. International aid was not requested until the fifth day and then specialist teams found themselves faced with language problems and lack of co-ordination ('3D', Carlton Television Report, 2 March 95).

Specialist teams and experts come in many forms. Sometimes assistance is sought based on expert knowledge about the phenomenon or type of disaster (for instance, an American oil man, Red Adair, was flown in to assist with the Piper Alpha oil rig disaster in the North Sea). Some organisations have specific training and experience in rescue work: for example, the British-based International Rescue Corps consists of volunteers (from relevant fields such as the Fire Service, Mountain Rescue, Marines and Royal Engineers), which is recognised by the UN and might be requested to give assistance anywhere in the world. Other organisations are more clearly concerned with the medical needs of survivors, and organisations such as Médicins sans Frontières send teams when requested; and NGOs, such as the Red Cross and Red Crescent, often play a central role in the immediate care and support of non-hospitalised survivors and of the rescue services personnel.

Initial activities, apart from locating any possible survivors, are concerned with providing field hospital and/or mortuary facilities; shelter, food and clothing for any survivors, and establishing (or re-establishing) transport and communication links. A particular need which arises in the short term, and which may involve people in the social professions, is for information and communications, for instance with the relatives of people directly affected by the disaster, but in other respects social workers may not be found in the front line of immediate responses to disasters and their particular role is further discussed in the next section.

As previously discussed in relation to population mobility, the United Nations might be involved in situations creating substantial displacement of population, in setting up refugee camps, as well as in transporting supplies and people. The UN may have a role in implementing field policies to assist particular groups. For instance in the UN report about children affected by war (1996), it was suggested that programmes should be aimed at providing temporary security and substitute care, including health and educational provision, although these tasks might be the responsibility of NGOs.

With regard to transport disasters, Gibson (1991) identified the particular features of these. One feature is location: access may be difficult; rescuers may come from different places and nationalities, with implications for co-ordination, and there are likely to be greater difficulties and costs for relatives seeking information and dealing with the dead or injured in a different legal or health system. Another feature of transport disasters is a lack of group identity: the effects are likely to be spread over different communities and countries. Finally, there are problems of dispersal: survivors may be taken to different hospitals, and, in any case, are likely to return to different areas or countries in the longer term, making location and provision of any follow-up services more fragmented or less likely. This last point also results in a lack of continuity in helpers and the probable loss of the 'first significant helper'. This may have implications both for the people involved in the rescue operation, who are unlikely to know the outcome of their actions, and also for the rehabilitation of survivors.

A final point noted by Gibson concerns the problem of people who are 'missing, presumed dead', arising from disasters at sea or when bodies have no means of identification, to which can be added the problem of mistaken identity, when the wrong bodies are despatched to relatives for burial (as happened in the case of a coach crash in Europe in 1997). However, accounting for all the dead and missing is clearly also a problem in other types of disaster, and indeed in the case of massive flooding, for instance in Bangladesh, it may not even be possible to establish the exact numbers of people drowned.

Turning to medium and longer-term needs and responses, UN Social Development Newsletters in the early 1990s included items about 'Social Action in conditions of National Catastrophe' which suggested that the UN has an important role to play in the medium and longer-term responses to disasters, particularly where these are related to war or environmental disasters. Thus, UN personnel have become involved in rehabilitative work associated with peace-keeping, as well as in promoting international discussion about longer-term strategies aimed at prevention of particular types of national emergencies and large-scale disasters. The United Nations Protection Force (UNPROFOR) has a particular role in trying to re-establish normal living conditions for millions of people in war-torn areas.

For example, in Croatia a 'short-term programme of social reconstruction' was begun after UNPROFOR assumed control in the area of Western Slavonia. This had been, historically, an ethnically mixed area with a 40 per cent rate of intermarriage between Serbs and Croats. The aim was to provide support for efforts geared to peace and re-establishment of local living conditions, and to rebuild confidence and ethnic harmony among the local population. To this end UN personnel assisted with the re-establishment of the mail system, visits by displaced persons to their former homes, provision of temporary accommodation for returnees, and family reunions. An Action Plan was drawn up for community-focused reconstruction, with specific projects to meet the needs of children, youth, the elderly and people with disabilities. Efforts were also made to create employment opportunities to encourage men to give up military activity (UN 1993b).

In the example of returnees after civil war in El Salvador mentioned earlier, it was the Red Cross which assisted with the provision of very basic infrastructure to enable the repopulation and reconstruction of deserted villages. Julia (1994) also noted the provision of shared child care and communal cooking facilities to enable women's participation in the re-establishment of the agricultural economy and village life. However, a later article (Julia 1995) also noted a reversion to traditional roles and problems in the repopulated villages, suggesting that it may be difficult to sustain the personal coping mechanisms and social changes activated by some disasters.

Mention of the work of the Red Cross also prompts a more general consideration of the role of NGOs, volunteers and financial aid in medium and longer-term relief work with survivors of war and famine, particularly when provided to people in refugee camps. De Waal (1996) stated that the use of funding raised through Band Aid and other activities since the mid-1980s had resulted in over-optimistic claims about what could be achieved to address the consequences of specific disasters, and that in some instances its use had been counterproductive or unethical. That is, it had been more likely to fund military conflict and oppressive regimes – in Ethiopia, Rwanda, Sudan, Bosnia – than to relieve the suffering of famine victims or refugees, apparently confirming (from someone in the field) the links between famine, migration and military activity noted earlier.

De Waal also criticised the short-term use of untrained volunteers in refugee camps by 'one of the largest relief organisations in the world' and suggested that 'fighting famine, genocide and human suffering in war are too important to be left to aid agencies'. However, he recognised the professionalism and efforts of organisations such as the Red Cross, Médicins sans Frontières and Oxfam, but thought that regulation of NGOs was essential, for instance through the appointment of a Disaster Relief Commissioner, possibly from the UN, to investigate all aspects of humanitarian aid.

The UN already has an important role in addressing some of the medium-term problems raised by disasters through the UNHCR and other branches of the organisation concerned with peace-keeping, human rights and social development. It has also provided a focal point for discussions about (longer term) strategies aimed at preventing or ameliorating the conditions which give rise to some disasters, such as those related to environmental damage or military conflict. For instance, the UN report about children and war (1996) recommended the development of 'education for peace' programmes; the Swedish Save the Children has provided detailed training on children's rights for Swedish personnel operating as UN troops in peace-keeping operations.

On a different note, the follow-up of human rights abuses (including against children) through the International Criminal Courts has also been recommended by the UN. While the latter strategy apparently has widespread approval from member nations, there are practical problems associated with bringing alleged perpetrators of war crimes to trial. Apart from the roles of military leaders, some countries (for example, Belgium) prosecute their own soldiers if they are believed to have committed atrocities while on active service abroad.

Concerted international responses, involving national companies and global corporations are also needed to address the longer-term problems of global warming, to stabilise, if not to reverse, climatic changes (Hanstock 1991). The introduction of combined strategies which, for instance, regulate forestry policies and reduce levels of carbon dioxide emissions, have socio-economic implications, which impact differentially on 'rich' and 'poor' nations. As has been shown in relation to the Conventions on Human Rights or the Rights of the Child, even if the UN can obtain agreement in principle, compliance is not guaranteed, and sanctions may not be effective or have debatable consequences. The UN and campaigning groups, such as Greenpeace, are therefore important in publicising 'offences' and promoting public education.

The role of the social professions

While some of the preceding material may seem remote from the daily experience of many social workers, the concerns are consistent with those of the social professions. Indeed, the social professions have particular expertise to offer, not in some of the technical and dramatic responses to disasters, but in understanding and addressing the medium and longer-term effects of loss on individuals and communities affected by disaster, and also in responding to the stress sometimes experienced by the immediate/front-line helpers. In relation to less developed countries faced with larger-scale disasters, social professionals may only be present in small numbers, perhaps employed as part of international relief programmes, although they may also have roles in social planning, or lobbying, including at national and international levels, aimed at addressing the roots of disasters.

Apart from the role for social professionals in longer-term interventions, researchers have suggested that there is also a role for social workers in the early stages of disaster work and that a rapid and effective response at this stage may well facilitate effective use of services later (Harrison 1987; Newburn 1996). Caplan's work in the US in the 1960s identified the opportunity for *effective intervention at the point of crisis*. While 'crisis intervention' theories and techniques were developed in relation to the mental health field, they clearly also have relevance to situations arising from disasters. Disasters can impact on the physical and emotional well-being of survivors and victims' relatives (and sometimes helpers) and can affect their behaviour, relationships and capacity to work. The old principle holds true that a little help, rationally directed and purposefully focused at this strategic time, is likely to have greater value than more extensive help given at 'a period of less emotional accessibility' (Caplan 1968).

Other knowledge about the effects of stress or 'trauma' associated with disasters also derives from the US. The elaboration of post-traumatic stress reaction, with its possible development into a psychiatric condition (post-traumatic stress disorder or PTSD) was based on work with the American ex-military survivors of the Vietnam War in the 1970s. However, some critics have since suggested that the theoretical basis (a neo-Freudian approach based on psychiatric thinking of the 1920s) and the cultural/policy context in which it was developed (provision of help to veterans was dependent on a diagnosis and label), made this a construct of its time and place, and that it has become an over-used concept (Young 1997).

Whatever the debates about PTSD as a psychiatric condition, more commonly acknowledged stages in grief reaction have been attributed to the survivors of disasters. Thus, people are likely, initially, to be 'in shock', that is, numb and detached, with an increase in anxiety or anger or possible denial as realisation dawns. A phase of acknowledgement may result in pain, anxiety or depression related to mourning, and the adaptation to victim or survivor status may nevertheless be accompanied by flash-backs or nightmares (Gibson 1991). Such feelings are as likely to be experienced by the survivors of a transport disaster as those seeking asylum from the horrors of war, and are also likely to be shared, to varying degrees, by the relatives of victims, those involved in rescue and relief work, and a wider public.

In some types of disaster – war or hostage situations, for instance – people may survive but carry a huge burden of guilt in relation to their inability to protect others, or aspects of their behaviour which they regard as cowardly or unworthy. The effects on males of their inability to protect wives, mothers and sisters from rape in war, for example, has been seen as a way of demoralising a population (Van Wormer 1997) and a cause of subsequent despair in some individuals. Such after-effects as guilt and worthlessness, can constitute a 'survival syndrome' in some who escaped death, alongside friends or family members who did not (Gibson 1991). Trust within families and communities can also be irretrievably broken in situations of civil war, when people are divided about whether the acts of specific groups constitute terrorism or justifiable resistance/part of the struggle for freedom (Davis 1989; Gibson 1991).

Relatives are also far from immune. In an age when most disasters are widely reported on national radio and television stations, people who know or fear that family members might be involved might be unable to watch the television reports, or become obsessional about doing so; they may feel anger at politicians or military leaders or company directors who 'let this thing happen', and they are likely to be desperate for hard news about individuals and a conclusion to the event. If relatives do not return, for example from a journey or war, those left at home may feel overwhelmed by feelings of guilt or regret about things said or done – or not – and confused about which grief reactions are 'normal' or a sign of mental break-down. They may become fearful of their ability to cope and adapt to their new circumstances. Such feelings can afflict children as much as adults, and the former may also have the burden of words said on departure, of the 'look after your mother/little brother' variety (Gibson 1991).

It is, perhaps, the scale of the shock (including possible mass hysteria) and grief which follows disasters, which makes this an unfamiliar and daunting area of work for many in the social professions. However, in areas where natural disasters are a constant risk, it is a recognised part of some social workers' roles and it has also been developed in other countries in response to particular situations. For instance, in Chile 'social workers pro-vide material assistance and emergency services to individuals or groups whose survival is imperilled'. Apart from the effects of chronic poverty among some populations, 'earthquakes and floods ... occur regularly in the country' and social workers are involved in the responses to these and other emergencies, as part of their wider practice which stresses commu-nity participation and social organisation (Jiminez and Aylwin 1992:35).

In the second case, the 1991 war in the Middle East, mentioned earlier, resulted in the 'call up' of social workers in Israel for emergency duties. These were mainly concerned with assistance to people evacuated from the area affected by missile attacks and included the screening and establish-ment of records on the evacuees. In a subsequent note on this occurrence, Lowenberg (1992) questioned the possible use to which such records (in-cluding reference to the mental state of the evacuees) might be put, and suggested that it would have been useful if social workers had engaged in *planning* and development of guidelines for such eventualities before being called upon to offer services and make decisions which might have longer term implications.

Ryotaru Katsura, in an invited address to the IASSW/IFSW Congress in 1996, also suggested that one lesson from the Kobe-Osaka earthquake was that social workers needed to be ready for such events, and prepared to engage in the early stages in enquiries about missing people and the distri-bution of relief aid, as well as assisting in the development of new communities and offering specialist services for particular affected groups, such as orphaned children or people left with disabilities, in the longer term. Katsura confirmed that the disaster had challenged the welfare sector and other bodies to make changes to their crisis planning and management systems, and that co-operative work between informal helpers and the emergency and welfare services was also indicated in the immediate and longer-term responses.

In the UK too, models of practice for social work involvement have been developed in response to a succession of disasters, particularly since the Bradford fire in 1985 when 55 people were killed and hundreds more injured in a fire which swept through one end of a football stadium. Newburn (1996) described this as the turning point since which Social Service Departments have taken on board the responsibility to provide an organised and longer-term response to major emergencies. He also described three initial, practical responses which have become a standard feature of UK 'disaster work'. These are the production of a disaster leaflet, modelled on one produced after the Ash Wednesday bush fires in Australia; the provision of a telephone helpline, and the initiation of a newsletter subsequently run by survivors as part of the post-disaster work.

Newburn's research following a later emergency (the Hillsborough football stadium disaster in 1989, in which 96 people died and over 400 needed hospital treatment) suggested that most people (survivors, relatives, primary helpers) would not seek help from social workers without being prompted, and that a pro-active approach offering practical support, befriending and listening were as important as formal counselling (although this might be requested or offered later). The need for early and efficient *information* to minimise uncertainty and distress, and for flexibility in responses to individuals and groups was also noted (Newburn 1994).

The value of groups for survivors and relatives (which social workers might initiate but which may then become self-help groups) has also been noted, as well as creative approaches to helping people 'process' the experience, including encouraging the production of written or pictorial records or support in the use of news reports and video footage to help people 'make sense' of their own experience (Newburn 1996). Accompanying people to inquests or memorial services are practical acts which have been appreciated, and memorial services, in themselves, may offer opportunities such as the renewal of contacts between rescuers and survivors or relatives, which can sometimes be important in the recovery process.

Various accounts have also noted that, while some of the activity is concentrated in the immediate period following a disaster, people may still be suffering from the effects and seeking social work help for up to two years later and that although the intensity of distress may abate, this can recur with the advent of anniversaries or other occasions. The importance of marking the site of disasters and enabling relatives to visit has also been appreciated and was confirmed in interviews with people who lost relations in the 'Axminster' air disaster. Many had visited the Swiss mountainside soon after the crash and have returned for ceremonies to mark specific anniversaries subsequently, maintaining links with the place and the local people who also remembered the event.

The Axminster interviews (*Woman's Hour*, BBC Radio 4, 14 April 98) also confirmed the value of practical and emotional support from the local community (rather than professional help) in some circumstances; other literature has also stressed the importance of involving, and building on the strengths of, individuals and communities in the recovery/reconstruction phase. Gibson (1991) has identified the importance of stressing the abnormality of the event (and the normality of likely reactions to it) and that any help given must be aimed at reinforcing the coping mechanisms of individuals and communities. In this respect the development of specialist teams of peripatetic 'disaster workers' for instance, might lead to the marginalisation of the resources of local communities. Recent events in the US and UK have also led to criticisms that social professionals may be too quick to anticipate problematic responses and to offer counselling, for example, when it may not be needed or appropriate.

However, the provision of 'low-key', flexible support services in relation to small and medium-sized disasters, such as facilitating the establishment of the Lockerbie Family Support Group (which continued long after the withdrawal of formal services), have been described as cost-effective, non-stigmatising and empowering (Brook 1990). Newburn's research reiterated the importance of basic listening skills, acceptance and empathy in disaster work in the UK context (echoing much earlier findings about the qualities, as much as the skills, valued in social workers). Provision of an informal and accessible centre which can act as a focal point for advice, information and follow-up activities, perhaps with group or meeting room facilities, has also been appreciated (Newburn 1996).

The other area in which social professionals have demonstrated a useful role in disaster work in some advanced industrial countries is the *professional* support which can be offered to colleagues in the rescue services, who may themselves have experienced distress and shock as a result of disaster work. There has been increased recognition, not just of the need for various members of the rescue and relief services to work together in the period immediately following disasters, but also of the extent to which those engaged in this type of work need peer support or more specific supervision and debriefing. To this end, some services have developed in-house or inter-agency 'training' days which might afford such opportunities, and/or facilities such as helplines for professionals themselves, such as that established by BASW following the Hillsborough disaster (Newburn 1996). Gibson (1991) has suggested that helpers have sometimes become the 'secondary victims' of disasters, and a programme of Critical Incident Stress Debriefing (CISD) has been devised to prevent this.

Disasters which affect people from different areas or countries also pose particular challenges to social professionals faced with the immediate tasks of providing information and initial support to enquirers and longer-term support to survivors or the bereaved. In the Hillsborough disaster, a UK regional network was set up involving various agencies, social workers in different local authority departments and voluntary organisations (Newburn 1996), while in the case of the Zeebrugge ferry disaster, 'home' and 'away' teams were set up by Kent Social Services Department, to provide both locally based responses and to co-ordinate follow-up actions with people dispersed to other parts of the UK, or back to Belgium (Gibson 1991).

On a different level, the development and updating in the 1990s of IFSW policy papers about human rights, refugees, and peace and disarmament all suggest an internationally shared concern among social professionals about the conditions which may result from the particular disasters of war and civil conflict; Chetkow-Yanoov (1991) has advocated the teaching of peace studies and conflict resolution skills to social workers. There are certainly societies, such as Chile, the former Yugoslavia and South Africa, where these have been called into use at community or national levels in the recent past, following cessation of civil war or changes in regimes.

The need for greater understanding and lobbying about the links between poverty and the environment (and related chronic or potential disaster situations) have also been urged by Rogge and Darkwa. They suggest that 'the promotion of global sustainability represents the fullest realisation of the person in the environment perspective' (1996:406), traditionally advocated by important figures in the history of social work, although conceived more locally. It can also be recognised in the literature advocating more attention to social and community development approaches by the social professions, though there is rarely specific reference to disasters and emergencies, as such.

Conclusions

There are a range of potential roles and tasks for social professionals in relation to disasters, but this area of work has come onto agency and national agendas to variable degrees and relatively recently, and the international aspects of disaster work are, to date, little recognised. However, even this brief review of the varied causes, forms and scale of disasters suggests that some have cross-national or global implications which need to be better understood and addressed by social workers and the organisations which employ and represent them.

While it is in the nature of many disasters that they cannot be anticipated or prevented, it has been argued that some advance planning by social welfare agencies and training of personnel is appropriate (even on the basis of a 'what if' scenario), and that other disasters are of a more chronic or predictable nature and/or susceptible to prevention, control or reversal, given the political will and economic investment. While neither of these political and economic factors are directly the province of social professionals, there is a role in lobbying, for example, in relation to global aspects of environmental damage, or its localised effects, based on an informed understanding of the interconnections between political, military, commercial and technical decisions and consumption patterns in some parts of the world, and their likely impact on conditions and events elsewhere.

A UN Social Development Newsletter in 1993 (UN 1993a) referred to the existence of some states experiencing catastrophic environmental, economic or political situations, such that normal societal management strategies had broken down and been superseded by emergency programmes. It referred to the chronic semi-catastrophic conditions in many urban and rural areas of Africa, Asia and Latin America, particularly affecting indigenous or ethnic minority populations, and suggested that social policy had a contribution to make to the prevention of catastrophe and the rehabilitation of affected societies. It stated that social measures are needed to prevent conflict, for example between different ethnic groups, and to contribute to the prevention of 'natural' disasters and amelioration of their effects.

The Copenhagen Summit in 1995 confirmed that mass migration, collapsing states and environmental pollution take problems beyond national borders, and some disasters clearly also have wider repercussions. Just as the number and scale of disasters has increased in the latter part of the twentieth century, so the likelihood that other countries will be affected or that nationals from a number of countries will be involved in disasters has increased also. As suggested by the UN, multidimensional strategies, including technical, legal, economic and social measures are needed – of both the 'bottom-up' and 'top-down' variety – to address local and global problems leading to or resulting from disasters, and social professionals have a part to play in helping formulate and implement such policies.

8 Some conclusions and indications for the future

The preceding chapters have identified a range of themes and examples considered relevant to the development of social work knowledge which is more comparatively and globally informed. It has been argued that such perspectives can enrich social workers' understanding of the interrelated nature of the causes and effects of economic and political decisions which are apparently remote from their daily practice, and inform their interventions regarding the sometimes common issues which confront people across national boundaries.

It has also been suggested that the processes and consequences of globalisation increasingly apply to the development of welfare systems nationally and internationally, as to other areas of human organisation. Such systems provide the context within which social professionals operate, and the scope and need for social work activity which is cross-national or international in nature has correspondingly increased.

The chapters have aimed to demonstrate that the local organisation and practice of social professionals are substantially determined by national cultures (as well as being related to political decisions and economic resources), but that these are being affected by global forces. It has also been suggested that, notwithstanding some of the apparent differences in a comparative view of the settings, boundaries or activities of different branches of the social professions, there are recognisable core values and skills which are operationalised in varied forms of practice at local, national and international levels.

In the following sections, this chapter revisits some of the earlier themes, and reiterates some of the major concerns and perspectives. It does not provide a systematic summary as such, but draws on material from previous chapters and new examples to illustrate the interrelatedness of previously discussed phenomena and concepts to the development of international social work. It therefore firstly reviews the relationship between 'globalisation' and social problems and advances the concept of global citizenship. Secondly, it refocuses on the prevalence of poverty and the need to relate this to wider concerns about the environment and sustainable development, as well as identifying an emerging challenge to national and international welfare policies represented by the 'greying of the planet'. Lastly it considers the implications for social work of increased use of comparative perspectives and understanding of global processes and the local, regional and international experience of their effects.

Global problems and global citizenship

The nation states of the world have become increasingly interlinked through trade, financial arrangements, cultural exchange, information and communication technology and joint scientific endeavours. International organisations have increased in number and scope and are evident in all aspects of human activity, not least those concerned with economic and political transactions, but also in the fields of development and humanitarian aid. Significant proportions of populations around the globe have increased knowledge about other societies, and a growing awareness of the likely impact (at personal and local levels) of events and decisions outside the control of the governments which represent them.

The processes of globalisation have been evident in changing trade and employment patterns, instability of financial markets, environmental degradation, global warming, epidemics, a significant growth in intrastate conflict and mass migration, and an increase in international crime, including drug trafficking. These phenomena all reflect or result in problems which are not amenable to solution by individual states, but which require the concerted efforts of international and regional groupings, usually targeting a particular issue. However, the interrelated nature of many of these problem areas is also increasingly appreciated, with the concomitant need for multifaceted strategies to address them.

While globalisation is most apparent and usually discussed in the economic and (increasingly) environmental fields, the notion of the globalisation of culture is also important to a consideration of the development of societies, and particular aspects of them (for instance, assumptions about gender relationships and women's roles), which have a direct bearing on socioeconomic policies. Stockman et al. have suggested that *cultural* globalisation (promoted through business travel, tourism, the media and advanced technology) means that people experience 'cultural meanings originating outside their own cultures' (1995:212). Such exposure might reinforce cultural nationalism, or it might stimulate intercultural learning, based on an exchange of ideas and relativisation of self-identities. This can be linked to tendencies of populations to resist or accommodate minority groups and to the development of policies, including immigration and equal opportunities policies, which are aimed at discriminating against or respecting difference.

The recognition of the relevance of globalisation to welfare and the development of responses by social professionals has been relatively recent, and was rooted initially in comparative studies of social problems and trends in response to them, often between countries which were considered to be broadly similar, if only in belonging to such groupings as 'advanced industrial countries'. For example, in the European Union, political interest spread from concerns about economic goals to the wish to promote harmonisation in the area of social policies and resulted in the encouragement of such comparative study. This included funding for exchange schemes in higher education (and sometimes in the establishment of more formal research programmes), and also the funding of meetings of professionals to compare and report on specific concerns. For instance, meetings of European members of the IFSW to examine social work education in 1990, and policy and practice in relation to children and families in 1994, were partly funded by the EU.

But apart from comparative studies, which Stockman et al. (1995) have suggested tend to treat each society as self-contained entities, largely ignoring the interrelationships and influences between them, the past two decades have seen a growth in international initiatives, such as global summits which, Lister has suggested, have proved important in developing a 'global civil society' (Lister 1998:10). Some of the discussion in Chapter 3 referred to citizenship and rights, and mention was made in the introductory chapter of the notion of *global citizenship*. Lister, in discussing the exclusionary effects of much citizenship practice at national level, suggested that 'principles of distributive justice, combined with ecological imperatives, demand an internationalist interpretation of citizenship obligations' (1998:9). She argued that making a link between citizenship and human rights could encourage responsible behaviour of the economically affluent nations towards countries on the margins as well as more inclusionary practices in relation to migrants and refugees at national levels.

Oxfam, in proposing a curriculum for global citizenship, described the concept as requiring an understanding of how the world works (economically, politically, socially, culturally, technologically and environmentally), and suggested that global citizens would participate in the community at a range of levels from the global to the local and act to make the world a more equitable and sustainable place (1997:2). In this formulation, global citizenship encompasses such principles as antiracism, equal opportunities, multiculturalism and intercultural learning, and concerns about human rights and the environment (1997:6). Such goals would seem to fit well with the aspirations of many in the social professions, particularly if linked to increased understanding of global processes, and their implications for (international) social work.

While Oxfam's initiative followed from the educational element of Agenda 21 – a set of commitments on the environment and development signed by 178 governments at the Earth Summit in 1992 – it nevertheless promotes the idea, not just of economic growth, but of the establishment of the most basic of rights, to subsistence and security, as prerequisites for the development of other rights and improvement of the quality of life. Other aspects of the work of the UN have been important in the promotion of women's rights as human rights, although Stockman et al. (1995) suggested (as a result of their research in China, Japan, the UK and the US) that contrasting assumptions and patterns in the countries studied had implications for how societies adapted to changing economic conditions. Therefore, they could only speculate as to the likely longer-term effects of globalisation on women's roles in the context of particular societies, and it seems apparent that how societies interpret human (including women's and children's) rights will also vary.

1998 marked the fiftieth anniversary of the Declaration of Human Rights, but recent reports from Amnesty International suggest that these ideals are not realised in many places. Infringement of women's rights are under appeal in a number of countries (Croatia, India, Zimbabwe, Mexico, Pakistan and Saudi Arabia), although Egypt has announced a total ban on female genital mutilation (where until recently about 90 per cent of girls, usually between three and six years old, underwent this procedure). Nigerian political prisoners are being held under life-threatening conditions; people are being massacred or disappearing in Algeria, and the Grandmothers of Plaza del Mayo still lack information (or reparation) in respect of the hundreds of children who disappeared in the period of military government in Argentina between 1976 and 1983. But progress is being made in planning for a permanent International Criminal Court and the UN expects members to agree a Convention to establish this imminently (*Amnesty International*, Issue 98, 1998).

It is apparent therefore, that, in relation to global citizenship, rights are still very unevenly spread both within and between societies, presenting a direct challenge to workers in the social professions and people and organisations with related concerns. While the Universal Declaration of Human Rights suggests that there are common and inalienable rights of all human beings, nevertheless the contexts within which rights are to be exercised vary enormously, giving rise to a diversity of concerns, as reflected in the preceding chapters. The current linking of socio-economic rights to responsibilities in recent policy changes, for instance, in the UK and US, is of a different order to the concerns about the rights of people caught up in civil war, as in Algeria or Croatia, or of street children in Brazil, or of families barely surviving through varied efforts to 'earn' money in Bangladesh.

The latter reflect Oxfam's promotion of 'security and subsistence' rights, as matters of universal concern (not simply pertaining to less developed countries, or specific states engaged in conflict), both in the interests of the people affected and because of the 'knock-on' effects to other states. As UN and Worldwatch reports have demonstrated, poverty and war have led to increased migration with consequent debates about the actual or potential 'rights' of migrants, particularly of asylum seekers, in regional and international contexts, as well as at national levels (Kane 1995).

Social workers across the world have conventionally been involved in the protection or promotion of the rights of particular individuals or groups in given societies, but the adoption of the perspectives of global citizenship and international social work, suggest increased (or renewed) attention to (and more sophisticated understanding of) the causal factors of human rights abuses and the denial or diminution of other political, social, economic and civil rights. As was suggested in relation to the example of child labour in Chapter 5, simplistic or absolutist responses (or ones which are imposed from outside the society), may do more harm than good; and strategies are required which tackle problems at a number of levels and in association with the people affected and those who have power, including at international level.

Persistent and emerging social problems

Implicit or explicit in any discussion of rights are notions of justice, and questions about the distribution of power and resources. Fundamental to a range of individual, societal and global problems, and to the work of many social professionals, is the persistence of *poverty*, as an absolute or relative phenomenon, with evidence of increased inequalities within and between societies. The extent to which poverty is related to disease and disability, alienation, increased crime (including of international proportions), military conflict and environmental degradation are familiar to social professionals, usually in the national context, and have been illustrated or suggested at various points in the preceding chapters.

Oxfam has suggested that 'Poverty ... is the greatest challenge facing the world in the 21st century. It undermines our personal survival and quality of life, national security, the environment and sustainable development' (1997:1). This and other humanitarian organisations identify the moral imperative to combat poverty. There are also pragmatic arguments, for instance about risks to wealthier societies of increased drugs use or contaminated air, which can result from the 'spread' of problems associated with poverty to other sectors of society or states or continents. Irrespective of values poverty can be seen as a global concern, requiring international responses. The UN has stated that the elimination of *absolute* poverty is affordable and achievable; and has cited improvements in the conditions of 'the poor' in less developed countries over the last fifty years: the mortality rates of children have been cut by half; life expectancy rates have increased from 41 to 62 years; and the number of people with access to safe water has doubled (UNDP 1997).

Further progress requires continued commitment from the governments of advanced industrial countries, NGOs and international bodies such as the UN and World Bank, notwithstanding the critiques, for example, of aid agencies, or trading relationships, or the policies of the IMF, as advanced earlier. But, as examples of birth control policies in Indonesia, or the Grameen Bank in Bangladesh suggested, successful interventions are also related to attitudinal change and the efforts of governments and populations of the less developed countries themselves – international interventions must increasingly be negotiated with societies, rather than made on the terms of the 'donors'. Since the 1970s a critical alternative perspective on development, with development work rooted in the actions of the poor, supported by NGOs relative to the orthodox or mainstream perspective which has prevailed for nearly half a century has increased in importance. This has significant implications not only for the less developed countries but also for those in poverty (and their protagonists) in advanced industrial countries, and is reflected in the view that social professionals in the North have things to learn from those in the South, as advocated by some international social workers.

The economic interdependence of states has been illustrated in this book in a number of ways, and the interaction between economic conditions and social trends also indicated. These have included the effects of the policies of 'global companies' on labour market trends around the world (with concomitant implications for national welfare systems). So the 'restructuring' of companies to locate production where labour is cheap and relatively unorganised has led to increased employment opportunities, often in the newly industrialised countries at the expense of advanced industrial countries (AICs). This has sometimes been at the expense of poorer regions of

AICs, and impacted particularly on the people with least skills and/or least likelihood of alternative employment in the locality.

Jackson and Scally (1996) cited the case of the ex-mining communities in the valleys of South Wales, where the final collapse of heavy industry (coal mining) in the 1980s has been followed by considerable economic and social disintegration. Attempts to attract new employment opportunities in the form of light industry were often short-lived, with companies responding to incentives to set up locally, but relocating when time-limited tax and other advantages ran out. Similar occurrences have been apparent in Ireland and in other peripheral regions or states attempting to maintain or increase employment levels and to decrease costs of welfare or population migration. Implications of the changing nature of employment and the increase in unemployment for the role of social professionals are discussed further, later.

The changing nature of manufacturing production and the shift in AICs from employment in the primary and secondary sectors to the tertiary (service) sector of the economy have also led to an increasing *feminisation* of labour, around the world. Women more often provide a cheap and flexible labour force, whether as full-time workers in manufacturing plants in poorer parts of the world, or (more often) as part-timers in light industry or the service sector in the advanced industrial countries (Stockman et al. 1995). There have been related changes in the role relationships of men and women in many societies, impacting on family forms and resources, and contributing to the feminisation of *poverty* also evident in many parts of the world.

Mention of coal mining also echoes concerns identified in earlier chapters about the relationship between exploitation of resources (including the labour force itself) and the degradation of the environment evident in other extractive industries (for example, logging, or mining for gemstones and other minerals); the potential for disasters in relation to this area of activity can also be noted. Chapter 7 described an increase in the number of disasters, not least those resulting from human interference with, or impact upon, the natural environment. While the rapid increase of fluorocarbons in refrigerating equipment or the use of deodorant sprays would seem to have little to do with the poorest populations in the world, the damage to the ozone layer has resulted in climatic change which is impacting on rich and poor alike, is potentially disastrous for everyone, and must be tackled at a global level. This illustrates clearly the way in which the problem of poverty is also a problem of wealth, and concerns about economic distribution and social justice transcend national or even regional boundaries.

The earlier mentioned Oxfam report (1997) linked the concept of global citizenship to environment and development concerns, and saw these two as needing to be more closely integrated, rather than being separate strands in thinking and action. There is some indication that this view has also gained ground within the UN and, while there are clear distinctions between the roles and functions of the major NGOs (concerned primarily with the environment or development work), some development workers are now making connections between environmental concerns and the needs of local populations. Additionally, as noted in Chapter 7, there is an increasing awareness that social workers need to relate and address issues of poverty and the wider/global environment in their practice (Rogge and Darkwa 1996).

Turning now to a more recent concern, the UN Commission for Social Development has stated that the growth in the number of older people globally will be one of the most challenging demographic trends of the twenty-first century and 1999 has been designated the Year of Older People. Sixty million people cross the 60-year threshold each month, and 80 per cent of these are in the less developed countries. The population over 60 years is expected to reach 600 million by 2001 and 1.2 billion by 2025 (with 70 per cent in the LDCs) (IFSW Update 1/97). Obviously, this trend has different implications for different countries, not least related to existing age dependency ratios. These already vary in Asian countries from a very low percentage of the population being over 60 years (for instance about 5 per cent in the Philippines) to approaching 20 per cent in Japan, but as population control measures have reduced the birth rate in many Asian countries, so this region has the most rapidly growing proportion of older people (Graycar 1993).

Increasing life expectancy rates is one of the factors in the increasing proportion of older people in populations nationally and globally. For instance, the number of people aged over 60 years in European Union states grew by 50 per cent in the period 1960–90 (Hantrais 1995) and a similar pattern is occurring between 1990 and 2020 in Asia (Vasoo and Tiong 1993). Current variations in average life expectancy rates range from 49 years in Cambodia (Davis 1994) to a global maximum of 79 years in Japan (Graycar 1993), and any discussion about ageing immediately raises questions about perceptions of age. While many statistical measures take 60 years as the defining point other data use 65 years, coinciding with the likely age at which people in some advanced industrial countries become eligible for pension provisions, but there are clearly national and gender differences related to working/retirement patterns.

Additionally, many older people in advanced industrial countries remain healthy and active for a decade or more after retirement, and as Graycar (1993) noted in relation to Australia, a decreasing number are likely to find themselves in poverty (although Van Wormer (1997) suggested that 20 per cent of people over 65 in the US are on or below the poverty line and there is also an association between old age and poverty levels in other countries, including those of the FSU). In some societies (for instance, the US and the UK), older people have been active in social and political life, including lobbying for greater recognition and better provisions – which to some extent have followed as a result of the voting and purchasing power of this age group. So the extent to which old age is viewed as a dependency state and problematic depends on a range of considerations, including the existence of overt or implicit ageism in societies.

But as more people live into their eighties the likelihood of them needing care from informal or formal systems inevitably increases. Olsen (1994) examined the global implications of an ageing population and how various countries are accommodating these changes, including the different patterns of reliance on informal care (relative to formal domiciliary or residential services), and the relationship of social care to varying levels of health care. He suggested that respect for elders ensures that the family plays a major role in care giving in Israel, and that this is also the case in countries based on Confucian conceptions of filial piety. This, in part, accounts for a greater likelihood that families will support elders in the East, relative to the West (Graycar 1993) and is evidenced in countries such as Japan and Thailand (Buddhist traditions also support this tendency).

But given other changes in the family and society, not least the age dependency ratio and also the role of women, increased expectations of familial care may not be realistic in all societies or for all older people, particularly if ageing is accompanied by severe physical or psychological deterioration. Many countries have to consider urgently how to meet the health care and financial costs of ageing, including perhaps changes in policies in relation to retirement age, state pensions and private insurance systems. In Japan, for instance, 17 per cent of the population were over 60 years in 1990, and this figure is expected to rise to 30 per cent by 2025 (Graycar 1993), and Campbell (1995) has suggested that Japan is already facing up to this challenge, relative to the US where 10 per cent of the population will be over 80 years early in the twenty-first century (Van Wormer 1997).

The development of international social work

The aim of this book has been to illustrate the interconnections between issues discussed in different chapters and the extent to which occurrences and trends in one part of the world are mirrored by or interact with those elsewhere. It has also been suggested that a wide range of factors and issues – not always previously considered relevant to the social professions – have a bearing on their roles and tasks in different parts of the world; and that the effects of globalisation on societies around the world require all social workers to have some understanding of global influences. Comparative perspectives may assist in devising responses to common problems, and additionally, specific aspects of globalisation have increased the need for some social workers, not just to be globally aware, but to operate at cross-national, regional or international levels.

In relation to local problems but drawing on comparative and international perspectives to inform practice, Jackson and Scally (1996) suggested that these could help social workers in the development of effective responses to the social problems of people, for instance in the ex-mining communities of South Wales; and that these needed to be rooted in an analysis of the economic and social forces as well as of the personal psychology of the people affected. They cited the views of Abramovitz (1993) that, in the context of problems substantially related to poverty, social workers need to be educated for roles concerned with *social change*, and suggested that a preoccupation with care, control and 'individual helping' is inappropriate and ineffective in these circumstances.

With regard to a theoretical framework for developing social work practice, Jackson and Scally (1996) cited the work of Jansson, on policy practice developed in the US. This has similarities with the approach identified earlier as advanced by Elliott (1993) and others. It recognises the different 'levels' at which social workers need to intervene and does not dichotomise intervention with individuals and families, relative to social action and community development roles. This approach can be found in practice in the work of some locally based voluntary agencies in the UK, and is also evident in French responses to social exclusion. It is consistent with approaches developed by social professionals in other European countries, and in Latin America, and some other developing countries. It places human needs very clearly in their social context – which can now be seen to have local, national, regional and global aspects – and requires social workers to articulate the impact of policies on particular populations and to work with service users or communities and others to change them (Taylor Gooby 1991).

The tasks identified by Jansson have been summarised as agenda building (making problems visible), problem defining (analysing the definitions, causes, nature and prevalence of specific problems), proposal writing (promoting possible policy changes on the basis of evidence), policy enacting (using power resources in support of proposals or to resist alternatives), policy implementing (ensuring that enacted policies are implemented in ways which benefit people) and policy assessing (evaluating the impact of policies through research or evaluation programmes). Skills are required in analysis, value clarification, communication and interaction, and key concepts are empowerment, alliances (with clients and other professionals, including those with political power) and development. Participatory action research projects may have particular value in involving different sectors of demoralised and disempowered communities, in mobilising strengths and in developing new skills (Jackson and Scally 1996:149–50).

A comparative approach, therefore, can assist with the identification of common problems and provide encouragement for innovative approaches. While the direct transfer of ideas and practices from one society to another is rarely appropriate, the examples and experience of workers elsewhere can be drawn on to inform and refresh thinking and action at the local or national level. As suggested at earlier points, interaction of social professionals has increasingly been facilitated by policy and technological developments, as well as the existence of particular organisations and networks.

The effects of the European Union in this respect have already been referred to and Lorenz (1994) identified the development of a 'communicative community' (1994:182) in this region. He suggested that, despite the different languages (literally and metaphorically) in which social work is conducted, it is possible to come to terms with difference and to develop knowledge and practice through dialogue. He identified a core concern linking different traditions and forms of practice in Europe as 'citizenship' and social justice, and suggested that linking integration with differentiation is a crucial task facing European societies and social professionals (Lorenz 1994:183).

Examples have been provided throughout the preceding chapters of ways in which the operation of this professional community is facilitated by the existence of particular networks and organisations such as the IFSW, and of events which provide a focal point for interaction. These bodies and meetings enable sharing of information about new concerns and the formulation of agreed responses. They provide the basis for collective and regional or international representation of the social professions, including in dialogue with other organisations and professionals with related interests. The support (or otherwise) of regional and international professional bodies can impact on national practice and professional developments, as well as identifying targets and strategies for interstate activity.

The other major stimulus for the exchange of ideas and information has been the development of information and communication technology. The establishment of e-mail and Internet 'networks' open to or aimed at social professionals has become an important medium for information sharing and debate, as well as a potential tool for direct work. A survey in the mid-1990s suggested that the provision of direct services to social work clients via the Internet is not yet widespread but that there is increasing use of it by self-help groups (Wilson 1996); this is also the case in the field of social work education. Use of telephone and fax communications also have more potential and, together with electronic mail are important adjuncts to international work.

There are also disadvantages, in the sense that the use of such technology may (further) advantage some people relative to others. At the current stage of development, the English-language basis of many existing networks and the costs of equipment and line rentals are likely to discriminate against some countries or groups and individuals within them. However, the significant use of information technology in the newly industrialised countries of Asia, its availability, even if on a limited basis, in Africa and Latin America and small countries like Papua New Guinea, and its likely spread in countries like Bangladesh, promise new opportunities for the participation of social professionals in international dialogue and activity. Perusal of the communications on one list over a year have demonstrated the raising of questions and sharing of ideas and information over a broad range of topics, and from many corners of the globe.

It has also been suggested that global processes are likely to result in an increase of 'problems' which require negotiation at the inter-state, regional or global level. As discussed, disasters may have an international dimension and entail cross-national activities, but perhaps the most obvious phenomenon likely to result in increased international policy concerns and practice is *migration*. Mention was made in Chapter 6 of the need for increased understanding and flexibility of response of social professionals to asylum seekers or refugees as well as to established ethnic minorities in the national context (including initiatives which target host communities and state or regional policies).

A further aspect of migration touched on earlier is the extent to which mixed marriages are being arranged, sometimes assisted by e-mail, in many countries and between nationals from quite different societies. For instance a recent press report described the work of agencies arranging marriages between Brazilian women and German men (*Sunday Telegraph* 12 April 98) and population imbalances in other countries may increase this practice. Such relationships may afford new opportunities for individuals, including the prospect of children with a dual heritage and bilingual skills and may also assist in encouraging intercultural learning and developments in the wider society. But such families and children may also be more vulnerable to the prejudices and disadvantages faced by ethnic minority groups, and feel less able to turn to either family of origin if problems occur. Additionally, if partnerships break down and one parent returns to a different country of origin the common difficulties of enabling children to maintain contact with the absent parent are exacerbated by distance and cost. As in other cases of family problems, social work intervention may be indicated with the added dimension of cross-national communication.

At the other end of the life-cycle there is growing awareness of the plight of older migrants or long-established refugees, unemployed or retired and perhaps single or widowed, who feel 'stranded' in an alien country. A small minority have for some time come to the attention of the International Social Services and been assisted with repatriation (sometimes on mental health grounds), and there is anecdotal evidence to suggest that an increasing number are taking matters into their own hands and are returning, for instance, from England to Ireland. But many more feel trapped by the ties of adult children settled in the new country and/or lack of financial resources to secure their housing and health needs if they return, or the actual impossibility of returning to areas or societies which no longer exist in the remembered form. Their needs are not always highly visible or considered by social professionals, but in the context of 'global greying' they are likely to require differentiated responses in many societies.

Another 'group' which has been brought to attention of the IFSW at regional level are those more privileged migrants from northern Europe who have decided to spend their retirement years in the warmer southern European states, but who sometimes come to the attention of social professionals if problems arise (usually with finances and/or health). Responses to date have mainly been of a voluntary nature, and Spanish social workers, for instance, have suggested that they lack the resources (including of interpreters) to extend services to this group. Alternative approaches might be based on the further development of voluntary and self-help arrangements, perhaps facilitated by social professionals from relevant countries of origin, but questions arise about how such work might be funded, with the implication that it should not fall on the host country. While there are reciprocal arrangements for health care in the European Union, the situation with regard to the immediate crises or longer-term social care of such 'migrants' is less clear, and arguably the 'sending countries' are more able to meet the needs of their absent nationals than the receiving countries.

This example illustrates one way in which traditional assumptions about migration patterns and social needs, are being changed, in this case by the opportunities for choice and mobility open to more privileged sectors of the world's population. To date (and excluding earlier examples of people caught up in pre-war migration) there has been relatively little information about the extent to which social professionals themselves might be involved in such mobility. Within the European Union, free movement of labour has been established since 1992. While the concerns expressed about the comparability and recognition of British qualifications have been alluded to earlier, a small number of cases known to the author suggest that professionals from Europe seeking work in the UK have also had problems with recognition of qualifications, notwithstanding that they have taken longer courses and achieved higher awards than their British counterparts, and had experience that could be considered relevant.

The question of 'relevance' of qualifications and experience tends to lead back to a view of social work that is country specific, knowledgeable about policy, legislative and organisational matters and familiar with, if not part of, the indigenous culture (and certainly proficient in the language). This runs counter to a view of social work which suggests that specific knowledge can be learned and that a good grounding in the social sciences (which social work education in most places provides) and some understanding of global processes and comparative perspectives might be equally, if not more, valuable.

Additionally, it has been suggested that there are fundamental commonalities in skills and values which enable social professionals to 'transfer' their knowledge and to practice in ways which are relevant to new situations. Looked at from the other side, and on the basis of limited evidence of known cases of British social workers established in posts elsewhere (usually in English-speaking countries and often after a struggle for recognition of qualifications), it would seem that those who are motivated to settle and practice outside their country of origin are well able to adapt and indeed may bring particular knowledge and perspectives which can assist in the 'internationalising' of the social professions.

But internationalising social work is not simply about increased mobility of social professionals – though the learning and exchange afforded by such opportunities, even on a short-term basis, are important spurs to such an endeavour. It is more about a way of viewing and understanding individual societies and the global environment in order to develop practices which are responsive to identified and emerging needs, and which include comparative perspectives or cross-national activity, or which contribute to international policy change, as appropriate. It is also about recognising a wider solidarity and making connections between the disadvantages of disparate and geographically separate groups of people. White et al. (1997) suggested that global citizens can contribute to transforming processes aimed at reshaping the world and social professionals should be part of this endeavour.

Returning to the education of social workers, the multidisciplinary basis evident in many curricula, affords a necessary springboard to developing an understanding of social problems which are inevitably multifaceted and which often require inter-professional strategies aimed at prevention or amelioration as well as empowering others. Advocating for the development of comparative and international perspectives in social work does not aim to 'add another element' to the curriculum but rather to shift the focus of what is currently taught so that all social professionals are better equipped to face the dilemmas posed at various levels of society, and some may continue to develop particular skills in relation to areas of work which have a cross-national or international dimension.

The need for social professionals in many parts of the world to own, and 'reconnect' with, the moral basis and political aspects of social work have recently been urged in the literature (Lorenz 1994; Van Wormer 1997; Ramathan and Link forthcoming) and are specifically indicated in the UK context (Jackson and Scally 1996). An appreciation of global problems and trends, and of comparative perspectives on social work, can contribute to a refocusing on the core values of social work, as concerned with human rights and social justice, and assist in the development of theoretical frameworks for analysis and action at macro as well as mezzo and micro levels. In order to respond effectively to social needs in a world which is fast changing and interdependent in all its aspects, social workers, no less than other professionals, need to build on existing strengths and networks to develop further international perspectives, understanding and practice.

References

Note: IFSW and IASSW Updates and Newsletters have been cited in this book. Copies of these can be obtained from:

IFSW, Box 4649, Sofienburg, N-0506 Oslo, Norway

IASSW, Lena Dominelli, Department of Social Work Studies, University of Southampton, Highfield, Southampton SO17 1BJ.

Abrahamson, P. (1993) 'Welfare pluralism: Torwards a new consensus for a European Social Policy', *Cross-national research papers*, 2(6):5–22.
Abramovitz, M. (1993) 'Should all students be educated for social change?', *Journal of Social Work Education*, 29(1):6–11.
Agarwal, S., Attah, M., Apt, N., Grieco, E. A., Kwakye, E. A. and Turner, J. (1997) 'Bearing the weight: the Kayayoo, Ghana's working girl child', *International Social Work*, 40(3):245–63.
Allen, T. and Thomas, A. (eds) (1992) *Poverty and Development in the 1990s*, Milton Keynes: The Open University.
Angelou, M. (1969) *I Know Why the Caged Bird Sings*, New York: Random House.
Appleyard, R. T. (1992) 'Migration and Development: a Global Agenda for the Future', *International Migration*, xxx:17–32.
Artobolevskiy, S. (1991) 'Environmental Problems in the USSR', *Geography Review*, 4(4):12–16.
Axford, B. (1995) *The Global System: Economics, Politics and Culture*, Cambridge: Polity Press.

Bagley, C. (1993) 'Chinese adoptees in Britain: a twenty-year follow-up of adjustment and social identity', *International Social Work*, 36(2):143–57.

165

Bagley, C., Madrid, S. and Bolitho, F. (1997) 'Stress factors and mental health adjustment of Filipino domestic workers in Hong Kong', *International Social Work*, 40(4):373–82.

Bali, S. (1997) 'Migration and Refugees' in White et al. (1997).

Bamford, M. (1998) 'Children of the Dust: the Forgotten Legacy of Chernobyl', *Professional Social Work*, 4/98:8–10.

Barbaret, R., Barrett, D. and O'Neill (1995) 'Young People and Prostitution: no Respector of Boundaries in North Western Europe', *Social Work in Europe*, 2(2):44–5

Barr, H. (1990) *In Europe 1: Social Work Education and 1992*, London: CCETSW.

Becher, T. (ed.) (1994) *Governments and Professional Education*, Buckingham: SRHE/Open University Press.

Becker, S. (ed.) (1995) *Young Carers in Europe: an Exploratory Cross National Study in Britain, France, Sweden and Germany*, Loughborough: Young Carers Research Group.

Berren, J., Beigel, C. and Ghertner, N. (1989) 'A Typology for the Classification of Disaster: Implications for Intervention', *Community Mental Health Journal*, 18(2).

Berridge, G. (1992) *International Politics, States, Power and Conflict since 1945* (2nd edition), Hemel Hempstead/New York: Harvester Wheatsheaf.

Boehm, W. W. (1980) 'Teaching and learning international social welfare', *International Social Work*, 23(2):17–24.

Boh, K., Sgritta, G. and Sussman, M. (eds) (1989) *Changing Patterns of European Family Life: a Comparative Analysis of 14 European Countries*, London: Routledge and Kegan Paul.

Bose, A. B. (1992) 'Social Work in India: Developmental Roles for a Helping Profession' in Hokenstad et al. (1992).

Brannen, J. and O'Brien, M. (eds) (1996) *Children and Families: Research and Policy*, London/Washington: Falmer Press.

Brauns, H. J. and Kramer, D. (1986) *Social Work Education in Europe: A Comprehensive Description of Social Work Education in 21 Countries*, Frankfurt-on-Main: Eigenverlag des Deutschen Vereins für Öffentliche und Privat Fürsorge.

Brittain, V. (1994) 'Troops Given Tools to Fight Battle for Survival', *The Guardian*, 19 July: 6.

Brody, E. (1990) 'Mental Health and World Citizenship: Socio-Cultural Bases for Advocacy' in Holzman, W. and Bornemann, T. (1990).

Brook, R. (1990) *An Introduction to Disaster Theory for Social Workers*, UEA/SWT Monograph no. 85, Norwich: University of East Anglia.

Brooks, E. E. (1996) 'The care of AIDS patients in rural Zambia: a case study in the North Western Province', *International Social Work*, 3(7):265–74.

Brown, P. (1996) 'Weather Forecast: Drought and Floods', *Observer*, 29 September.

Browne, A. (1998) 'Most Poor Stuck in Poverty Trap', *Observer*, 8 February.

Burt, W. (1994) 'The Social Components of Foreign Policy: Implications for Social Work Involvement', paper presentation at 27th Congress of IASSW, Amsterdam, 11–15 July.

Campbell, J. (1995) 'Is there a Japanese-style welfare state?', *Social Science Japan*, 4(August):22.

Campfens, H. (1996) 'Partnerships in International Social Development: Evolution in Practice and Concept', *International Social Work*, 39(2):201–23.

Cannan, C., Berry, L. and Lyons, K. (1992) *Social Work and Europe*, Basingstoke: BASW/Macmillan.

Caplan, G. (1968) *Crisis Intervention: an Approach to Community Mental Health*, New York: Grunne Statton.

Castles, S. and Miller, M. (1993) *The Age of Migration: Population Movements in the Modern World*, London: Macmillan.

Cemlyn, S. and Vdovenko, T. (1995) 'Working with Street Children in St. Petersburg', *Social Work in Europe*, 2(2):15–22.

Cemlyn, S. (1995) 'Social Work in Russia and the UK: what are we exchanging?', *Social Work Education*, 14(1):77–92.

Centre for Human Rights (1994) *Human Rights and Social Work: a Manual for Schools of Social Work and the Social Work Profession*, Geneva/New York: United Nations.

Cetingok, M. and Hirayama, H. (1990) 'Foreign Students in Social Work Schools: their characteristics and assessment of programmes in the US', *International Social Work*, 33(3):243–53.

Chalker, L. (1994) 'Liberty, Equality and Maternity', *Observer Supplement*, 16 October:8.

Chetkow-Yanoov, B. (1991) 'Teaching Conflict Resolution in Schools of Social Work: a Proposal', *International Social Work*, 34(1):57–68.

Chi, I. and Cheung, S. K. (eds) (1996) *Social Work in Hong Kong*, Hong Kong: Hong Kong Social Workers Association.

Chipaka, S. (1998) 'City Squatters Emerge from the Bridge's Shadows', *The Nation*, 5 January:A2.

Cho, G. (1997) *Trade, Aid & Global Interdependence*, London: Sage.

Chomsky, N. (1996) *Class Warfare: Interviews with David Barsamian*, London: Pluto Press.

Chow, N. and Ho, K. M. (1996) 'Social Work with New Arrivals' in Chi, I. and Cheung, S. K. (1996).

Clarkson, E. (1990) 'Teaching Overseas Students in Great Britain', *International Social Work*, 33(4):353–64.

Cochrane, A. and Clarke, J. (eds) (1993) *Comparing Welfare States: Britain in International Context*, London: Sage.

Cocozza, L. (ed.) (1990) 'Social Workers and the EC: Training and Employment Perspectives 1992', *Report of La Hulpe Seminar*, Brussels: IFSW.

Coleman, R. (1996) 'Exchanges between British and overseas social work and social work education' in Jackson and Preston Shoot (1996).

Colton, M. and Hellinckx, W. (1994) 'Residential and Foster Care in the European Community: Current Trends in Policy and Practice', *British Journal of Social Work*, 24(5):559–76.

Colton, M. and Williams, M. (1997) *The World of Foster Care*, Aldershot: Ashgate.

Connelly, N. and Stubbs, P. (1997) *Trends in Social Work and Social Work Education across Europe: Report on a Joint NISW/CCETSW Workshop (November 1995)*, London: NISW.

Consumer's Association (1997) 'Giving to Charity', *Which? Report*, December.

Cox, D. (1986) 'Intercountry Casework', *International Social Work*, 29(3):247–56.

Council of Europe (1995) *The Initial and Further Training of Social Workers Taking into Account Their Changing Roles*, Strasbourg: Steering Committee on Social Policy.

CRE (1990) 'Refugees and Asylum Seekers' Factsheet, London: CRE.

Currey, L., Wergin, J. F. and Associates (1993) *Educating Professionals: Responding to New Expectations for Competence and Accountability*, San Francisco: Jossey-Bass.

Danaher, K. (1997) 'How to take away the World Bank's money', *Peace and Justice News* (Washington DC: NASW), Spring:6.

Darvil, E. (1975) *Bargain or Barricade*, Beckhampstead: The Volunteer Centre.

Davis, L. (1989) *Revolutionary Struggle in the Philippines*, Basingstoke: Macmillan.

Davis, L. (1994) *Children of the East*, London: Janus Publishing.

Deacon, B. (1993) 'Developments in East European Social Policy' in Jones, C. (ed.), *New Perspectives on the Welfare State in Europe*, London: Routledge.

Devore, W. and Seale, A. (1993) 'An International Social Work Curriculum for Children and Families: UK and US Perspectives', *Social Work Education*, 12(2):67–89.

De Waal, A. (1996) 'Sorry St. Bob but it is time we banned aid', *Observer*, 20 October:24.

Dobash, R. E. and Dobash, R. P. (1992) *Women, Violence and Social Change*, London/New York: Routledge, Chapman Hall.

Doel, M. and Shardlow, S. (eds) (1996) *Social Work in a Changing World: an International Perspective on Practice Learning*, Aldershot: Arena.

Donnellan, C. (ed.) (1998) *Poverty*, Cambridge: Independence Educational Publishers.

Durham, M. (1994a) 'Humana's Rags to Riches Cash Trial', *Observer*, 28 January:10.

Durham, M. (1994b) 'A deal too far in trade and aid', *Observer Supplement*, 16 October:8.

Edelson, J. L., Eisikovits, Z. C. and Peled, E. (1992) 'A Model for Analysing Societal Responses to Woman Battering: Israel as a case in point', *International Social Work*, 35(1):19–33.

Edwards, M. (1994) 'Chernobyl: Living with the Monster', *National Geographic*, 186(2):100–115.

EEC (1989) *Directive on a General System for the Recognition of Higher Education Diplomas*, Council Directive 89/48/EEC.

Ehteshami, A. (1997) 'Islamic Fundamentalism and Political Islam' in White et al. (1997).

Elliott, D. (1993) 'Social Work and Social Development: Towards an Integrative Model for Social Work Practice', *International Social Work*, 36(1):21–36.

Elliot, D., Watts, T. D. and Mayadas, N. S. (eds) (1994) *International Handbook on Social Work Theory and Practice*, Westport CT: Greenwood Press.

Esping-Anderson, G. (1990) *The Three Worlds of Welfare Capitalism*, Oxford: Polity Press.

Esping-Anderson, G. (1996) *Welfare States in Transition*, London: Sage.

Esposito, J. L. (1992) *The Islamic Threat: Myth or Reality?*, Oxford: Oxford University Press.

Estes, Richard J. (ed.) (1992) *Internationalising Social Work Education: a Guide to Resources for a New Century*, Philadelphia PA: University of Pennsylvania School for Social Work.

Estes, R. (1997) 'Social Work, Social Development and Community Welfare Centres in International Perspective', *International Social Work*, 40(1):43–55.

Etzione, A. (1993) *The Spirit of Community: the Reinvention of America*, New York: Touchstone Books.

Ewalt, P. (1994) 'Poverty Matters', *Social Work*, 39(2):149–51.

Falk, D. and Nagy, G. (1997) 'Teaching International and Cross-Cultural Social Work', IASSW Newsletter, Issue 5.

Ferea, W. (1995) 'A Commentary on Child Abuse in Papua New Guinea', *South Pacific Journal of Psychology*, 8:36–9.

FRCD (1994) *Special Education Manual*, Chicago: Family Resource Centre on Disabilities.

Friere, P. (1972) *Pedagogy of the Oppressed*, Middlesex: Penguin Books.

Frost, M. (1991) 'What ought to be done about the condition of states?' in Navain, C. (ed.), *The Condition of States: a Study of International Political Theory*, Milton Keynes: Open University Press.

Gammon, E. H. and Dziegielewska, J. (1995) 'The Butterflies of ARKA: grassroots initiatives for child welfare in Poland', *International Social Work*, 38(2):133–7.

Gammon, E. H. and Dziegielewska, J. (1997) 'Polish Social Services to Families of Children with Disabilities: practice in an emerging setting', *International Social Work*, 40(4):393–406.

Gergen, J. K. (1991) 'The Saturated Family', *Networker*, September/October:27–35.

Ghazi, P. (1994) 'World on Her Shoulders', *Observer (Concern Supplement)*, 16 October.

Gibson, M. (1991) *Order from Chaos: Responding to Traumatic Events*, Birmingham: Venture Press.

Gilbert, N. (1998) 'From Service to Social Control: Implications of Welfare Reform for Professional Practice in the US', *European Journal of Social Work*, 1(1):101–108.

Ginsberg, B. E. (1994) 'Migration and Welfare', *Scandinavian Journal of Social Welfare*, 3(3):102–108.

Ginsberg, L. (1995) *Social Work Almanac* (2nd edition), Washington DC: NASW.

Ginsburg, N. (1992) *Divisions of Welfare: a Critical Introduction to Comparative Welfare*, London: Sage.

Glennerster, H. (1995) *British Social Policy since 1945*, Oxford: Blackwell.

Goldenburg, S. (1995) 'Where Baby Girls Must Die', *Observer*, 22 October:21.

Graycar, A. (1993) 'Ageing in Asia and Australia: Prospects and Policies', *Asia Pacific Journal of Social Work*, 3(2):6–27.

Grebel, H. and Steyaert, J. (1995) 'Social Informatics: Beyond Technology', *International Social Work*, 38(2):151–64.

Green, D. (1991) *Faces of Latin America*, London: Latin America Bureau.

Greenfield, J. (1994) 'A Journey into the Unknown', *Social Work in Europe*, 1(1):54–8.

Grieve Smith, J. (1994) 'Time for a New Global Vision', *Observer*, 3 July, Business Section: 5.

Grossman, B. and Perry, R. (1996) 'Re-engaging Social Work Education with the Public and Social Services: the California Experience and its Relevance in Russia' in Doel and Shardlow (1996).

Guibernau, M. (1995) *Nationalisms: the Nation-State and Nationalism in the Twentieth Century*, Cambridge: Polity Press.

Guzzetta, Charles (1996) 'The Decline of the North American Model of Social Work Education', *International Social Work*, 39(3):301–15.

Hall, A. (1996) 'Social Work or Working for Change? Action for Grass Roots Sustainable Development in Amazonia', *International Social Work*, 39(1):27–40.

Halloran Lumsdaine, D. (1993) *Moral Vision in International Politics: the Foreign Aid Regime*, Princeton NJ: Princeton University Press.

Hanson, A. (1998) 'Jakarta to merge 4 State Banks', *The Nation*, 8 January: A3.

Hanstock, S. (1991) 'Global Warming: Accepting the Implications', *Geography Review*, 4(4):30–36.

Hantrais, L. (1995) *Social Policy in the European Union*, Basingstoke: Macmillan.

Harris, R. and Lavan, A. (1992) 'Professional Mobility in the New Europe: the Case of Social Work', *Journal of European Social Policy*, 2(1):1–15.

Harrison, P. (1994) 'It's Time We Put Population Control in Women's Hands', *Observer (Concern Supplement)*, 16 October: 5.

Harrison, W. (1987) *The Bradford City Fire Disaster: Social Services Response Information Pack*, Bradford: City of Bradford Metropolitan Council.

Hartman, K. M. (1989) 'Professional versus academic values: cultural ambivalence in university professional schools in Australia', *Higher Education*, 18:491–509.

Harvey, B. (1992) *Networking in Europe: a Guide to European Voluntary Organisations*, London: NCVO Publications and Community Development Foundation.

Hazenkamp, J. L. and Popple, K. (eds) (1996) *Racism in Europe: the Challenge for Youth Policy and Youth Work*, London: University College London Press.

Healy, L. M. (1986) 'The International Dimension in Social Work Education: Current Efforts, Future Challenges', *International Social Work*, 29(2):135–47.

Healy, L. M. (1992) *Introducing International Development Content in the Social Work Curriculum*, Washington DC: NASW Press.

Healy, L. M. (ed.) (1996) 'Realities of Global Interdependence: Challenges for Social Work Education', Plenary Papers and Abstracts for 1992 International Congress of Schools of Social Work, Alexandria VA: Council on Social Work Education.

Heatherington, R., Cooper, A., Smith, P. and Wilford, G. (1997) *Protecting Children: Messages from Europe*, Lyme Regis: Russell House Publishing.

Hegar, R. L. and Greif, G. L. (1991) 'Parental Kidnapping Across International Borders', *International Social Work*, 34(4):353–63.
Held, D. (1995) *Democracy and the Global Order: from the Modern State to Cosmopolitan Governance*, Cambridge: Polity Press.
Hewitt, T. (1992) 'Developing Countries – 1945 to 1990' in Allen, T. and Thomas, A. (1992).
Hewlett, S. (1993) *Child Neglect in Rich Societies*, Geneva: UNICEF.
Hill, M. (1996) *Social Policy: a Comparative Analysis*, Hemel Hempstead: Prentice Hall/Harvester Wheatsheaf.
Hill, M. and Tisdall, K. (1997) *Children and Society*, London/New York: Addison Wesley Longman.
Hirayama, K. K., Hirayama, H. and Kuroki, Y. (1995) 'Southeast Asian Refugee Settlement in Japan and the USA', *International Social Work*, 38(2):165–76.
Hoff, M. and McNutt, J. (eds) (1994) *The Global Environment Crisis: Implications for Social Welfare and Social Work*, Aldershot: Avebury.
Hokenstad, M., Khinduka, S. and Midgley, J. (eds) (1992) *Profiles in International Social Work*, Washington DC: NASW Press.
Horncastle, J. and Brøbeck, H. (1995) 'An International Perspective on Practice Teaching for Foreign Students', *Social Work in Europe*, 2(3):48–52.
Hugman, R. (1994) *Ageing and the Care of Older People in Europe*, Basingstoke: Macmillan.
Hugman, R. (1996) 'Professionalisation in Social Work: the Challenge of Diversity', *International Social Work*, 39(2):131–47.
Hunt, I. (1996) 'Double Standards' *Guardian Education*, 12 November: 8–9.

IASSW (1995) *Directory*, Sheffield: IASSW.
IFSW (1997) *Policy Paper: Human Rights*, Oslo: IFSW.
IFSW (1994) *The Ethics of Social Work: Principles and Standards* (revised 1997), Oslo: IFSW.
ILO (1996) *International Labour Review Special Edition: Perspectives on the Nature and Future of Work*, 135(6).

Jackson, S. and Scally, M. (1996) 'Casualties of the Market: Social Work Education in Deindustrialised Communities' in Jackson and Preston Shoot (1996).
Jackson, S. and Preston Shoot, M. (eds) (1996) *Educating Social Workers in a Changing Policy Context*, London: Whiting & Birch.
Jiminez, M. and Aylwin, N. (1992) 'Social Work in Chile: Support for the Struggle for Justice in Latin America' in Hokenstad et al. (1992).
Johnston, C. (1997) 'Lending a Helping Hand', *Times Higher Education Supplement*, 31 January.

Jones, L. (1996) 'Regulating Social Work: a review of the review' in Jackson and Preston Shoot (1996).

Jordon, B. (1996) *A Theory of Poverty and Social Exclusion*, Cambridge: Polity Press.

Julia, M. (1994) 'The Changing Status of Women: Social Development in a Repopulated Village', *International Social Work*, 37(1):61–73.

Julia, M. (1995) 'Revisiting a Repopulated Village: a Step Backwards in the Changing Status of Women', *International Social Work*, 38(3):229–42.

Kahn, A. and Kamerman, S. (1994) *Social Policy and the Under Threes: Six Country Case Studies*, New York: Columbia University School of Social Work (NISW Library).

Kane, H. (1995) *The Hour of Departure: Forces that Create Refugees and Migrants*, Paper 125, Washington DC: World Watch.

Kelsey, J. (1995) *The New Zealand Experiment – a World Model for Structural Adjustment*, Auckland: Auckland University Press.

Kemp, A. (1996) 'Migration Fears Divert EU Aid Flows', *Observer*, 20 October.

Kemp, C. H., Silverman, F. N., Steele, B. T., Droegemuetter, W. and Silver, H. K. (1962) 'The Battered Child Syndrome', *Journal of American Medical Association*, 181:17–22.

Kennedy, S., Whiteford, P. and Bradshaw, J. (1996) 'The Economic Circumstances of Children in Ten Countries' in Brannen and O'Brien (1996).

Kettschau, I., Methfessel, B. and Schmidt-Waldherr, H. (eds) (1993) *Youth, Family and Household: Global Perspectives on Development and Quality of Life*, Baltmanasweiler: Schneider Verlag Höhengehren GmbH.

Kilmister, A. (1992) 'Socialist Models of Development' in Allen and Thomas (1992).

Lane, D. (1998) 'Same Problems, Different Answers', *Child Care Forum*, 33(February):15.

Lazar, A. and Erera, R. (1997) 'The Telephone Helpline as a Social Support', *International Social Work*, 41(1):89–101.

Leung, V. W. K., Lay, B. Y. P., Ketchwell, A., Clark, C. and Harris, A. (1995) 'Hong Kong Social Work Students at the University of Hull', *Social Work Education*, 14(3):44–60.

Lewis, J. (ed.) (1993) *Women and Social Policies in Europe: Work, Family and the State*, Aldershot: Edward Elgar.

Link, R. (1998) 'Infusing Global Perspectives into Social Work Values and Ethics' in Ramathan and Link (1998).

Lippa, H. V. (1983) 'Interplay of Public and Private Welfare in the Federal Republic of Germany', *International Social Work*, 26(2):1–8.

Lister, R. (1998) 'Citizenship, Social Work and Social Action', *European Journal of Social Work*, 1(1):5–18.

Lorenz, W. (1994) *Social Work in a Changing Europe*, London: Routledge.

Lorenz, W. (1998) 'Project Report (ECSPRESS)', *European Journal of Social Work*, 1(1):113–14.

Lowenberg, F. (1992) 'Notes on Ethical Dilemmas in Wartime: Experiences of Israeli Social Workers During Operation Desert Shield', *International Social Work*, 35(4):429–39.

Lusk, M. W. (1992) 'Street Children of Rio de Janeiro', *International Social Work*, 35(3):293–305.

Lyons, K. (1996a), 'Education for International Social Work', *IASSW/IFSW Proceedings*, Hong Kong.

Lyons, K. (1996b) *ERASMUS and the Social Professions in the UK: an Evaluation*, Country Report for the European Union, Koblenz: ECCE.

Lyons, K. (1997) 'Educating for Social Work in a Multicultural Society', Paper to EASSW/IFSW Conference, Dublin.

Lyons, K., Lavalle, I. and Grimwood, C. (1995) 'Career Patterns of Qualified Social Workers: Discussion of a Recent Survey', *British Journal of Social Work*, 25:173–90.

Lyons, K. and Ramanathan, C. (1998) 'Models of Field Practice in Global Settings' in Ramathan and Link (forthcoming).

MacPherson, S. (1996) 'Social Work and Economic Development in Papua New Guinea', *International Social Work*, 39(1):55–68.

Madge, N. (1994) *Children and Residential Care in Europe*, London: NCB.

Matsubara, Y. (1992) 'Social Work in Japan: Responding to Demographic Dilemmas' in Hokenstad et al. (1992).

Matthews, R. (1998) 'See Naples and die?', *Sunday Telegraph*, 12 April: 21.

Mazibuko, F., McKendrick, B. and Patel, L. (1992) 'Social Work in South Africa: Coping with Apartheid and Change' in Hokenstad et al. (1992).

McGlone, F. (1997) *Families*, Surrey: Community Care/Research Matters International.

McGrath, C. (1998) 'Voluntary and Statutory Sector Roles in Child Care in Romania', unpublished: University of East London.

McGrew, A. (1992) 'The Third World in the New Global Order' in Allen and Thomas (1992).

Mensendiek, M. (1997) 'Women, Migration and Prostitution in Thailand', *International Social Work*, 40(2):145–62.

Midgley, J. (1983) *Professional Imperialism: Social Work and the Third World*, London: Heinemann.

Midgley, J. (1995) *Social Development: the Developmental Perspective in Social Welfare*, London: Sage; New Delhi: Thousand Oaks.

Midgley, J. (1996) 'Social Work in Economic Development', *International Social Work*, 39(1):5–25.

Miles, I. (1996) 'The Future of Working Life in an Information Society', *Issues Paper for European Social Policy Forum*, University of Manchester.

Milner, M. (1994) 'Change Brings Money with Strings Attached', *The Guardian*, 19 July: 15.

Mosek, A. (1993) 'Well-being and Parental Contact of Foster Children in Israel: a Different Situation from the USA', *International Social Work*, 36(3):261–75.

Mumin, Abu (1998) 'Child Labour in Rural Bangladesh', unpublished: University of East London.

Munday, B. (ed.) (1989) *The Crisis in Welfare: an International Perspective on Social Services and Social Work*, Hemel Hempstead: Harvester Wheatsheaf.

Newburn, T. (1994) 'Social Work After Disasters', *National Institute of Social Work Policy Briefing*, No.7, London: NISW.

Newburn, T. (1996) 'Social Work After Major Emergencies' in Jackson and Preston Shoot (1996).

Newland, K. (1994) 'Refugees: the Rising Flood', *Worldwatch*, May/June, 7(3):10–20.

Ngai, Ngan-Pun (1996) 'Revival of Social Work Education in China', *International Social Work*, 39(3):289–300.

O'Connor, K. (1994) 'Juvenile Justice System in Queensland', *International Social Work*, 37(3):197–212.

O'Gorman, F. (1992) *Charity and Change: from Band-Aid to Beacon*, Melbourne: World Vision Australia.

Olsen, L. (ed.) (1994) *The Graying of the World: Who Will Care for the Elderly?*, New York: Haworth Press.

Otto, H. U. and Lorenz, W. (1998) 'The New Journal for the Social Professions in Europe', *European Journal of Social Work*, 1(1):1–4.

Oxfam (1997) *A Curriculum for Global Citizenship*, Oxford: Oxfam, UK and Ireland.

Page, A. (1997) 'Celebrating Diversity: Ethnic Minorities in European Cities', Conference Report, London: London Research Centre.

Papadopoulos, T. (1996) 'Family, State and Social Policy for Children in Greece' in Brannen and O'Brien (1996).

Payne, M. (1991) *Modern Social Work Theory: a Critical Introduction*, Basingstoke: Macmillan.

Peach, C. (1996) 'A Question of Collar', *Times Higher Education Supplement*, 23 August.

Pearson, R. (1992) 'Gender Matters in Development' in Allen and Thomas (1992).

Powell, J. and Lovelock, R. (1997) 'Participants and Recipients – Disabled People's Involvement in a Euro-Programme', *British Journal of Social Work*, 27(4):565–83.

Prigoff, A. (1997) 'Latino Concerns about "Welfare Reform": How US Policy Creates, then Compounds, a Problem', *Peace and Justice News* (Washington: NASW), Fall 97:2–3.

Pugh, M. (1997) 'Peacekeeping and Humanitarian Intervention' in White et al. (1997).

Raffaelli, M. (1997) 'The Family Situation of Street Youth in Latin America: a Cross National Review', *International Social Work*, 40(1):89–100.

Raheim, S. (1996) 'Micro-enterprise as an approach for promoting economic development in social work: lessons from the self-employment investment demonstration', *International Social Work*, 39(1):69–82.

Ramathan, C. and Link, R. (eds) (1998) *All Our Futures: Principles and Resources for Social Work Practice in a Global Era*, Carmel CA: Brookes Cole.

Rapaport, R. (1989) 'Ideologies about Family Forms' in Boh et al. (1989).

Raphael, B. (1986) *When Disaster Strikes*, London: Hutchinson.

Ratcliffe, P. (ed.) (1996) *Race, Ethnicity and Nation: International Perspectives on Social Conflict*, London: University College London Press.

Rees, S. (1996) 'Humanity, Peace and International Citizenship', *IASSW/IFSW Proceedings*, Hong Kong.

Rees, S. (1991) *Achieving Power: Practice and Policy in Social Welfare*, Sydney: Allen & Unwin.

Reunite (undated) *Home and Away: Child Abduction in the Nineties*, London: Reunite.

Richan, W. C. (1997) 'Social Works Historic Stake in the Plight of Immigrants', *Peace and Justice News* (Washington: NASW), Fall 97:5–6.

Richards, H. (1996) 'Warrior on Want', *Times Higher Education Supplement*, 30 August:13.

Richards, H. (1997) 'Global Theatre', *Times Higher Education Supplement*, 7 February.

Robertson, R. (1992) *Globalisation: Social Theory and Global Culture*, London: Sage.

Rogers, G. (1996) 'Comparative Approaches to Practice Learning' in Doel and Shardlow (1996).

Rogge, M. and Darkwa, O. (1996) 'Poverty and the Environment: an International Perspective for Social Work', *International Social Work*, 39(4):395–409.

Rosenthal, B. S. (1990) 'US Social Workers Interest in Working in the Developing World', *International Social Work*, 33(3):227–32.

Runnymede Trust (1998) *Citizenship*, London: Runnymede Trust Briefing Paper.

Russell, A. (1997) 'Trade, Money and Markets' in White et al. (1997).

Ruxton (1996) *Children in Europe*, London: NCH Action for Children.

Ryan, S. (1997) 'Nationalism and Ethnic Conflict' in White et al. (1997).

Sacco, T. (1996) 'Towards an Inclusive Paradigm for Social Work' in Doel and Shardlow (1996).

Sachs, J. (1998) 'Out of the Frying Pan into the IMF Fire', *Observer (Business Section)*, 8 February: 8.

Sanders, J. S. and Pederson, P. (1984) *Education for International Social Welfare*, Manoa: University of Hawaii.

Schindler, R. (1993) 'Emigration and the Black Jews of Ethiopia: Dealing with Bereavement and Loss', *International Social Work*, 36(1):7–19.

Schneider, G. (1993) 'Women Between Subsistence Economy and Market Economy: the Effects of Modernisation on the Role of Women in Papua New Guinea' in Kettschau, et al. (1993).

Seacombe, M. (1996) 'Bullyboy Croat Regime Swaggers through Doors of European Club', *Observer*, 20 October.

Seager, J. and Olsen, A. (1986) *Women in the World: an International Atlas*, London/Sydney: Pan Books.

Seidl, F. W. (1997) 'Welcome from the New Chair', *Peace and Justice News* (Washington: NASW), Fall 97:1.

Sen, A. (1991) *On Ethics and Economics*, Oxford: Blackwell.

Shahid, A. (1998) 'Net Gains', *Child Care Forum*, (Magazine of the Institute of Child Care and Social Work Education), 33 (February): 6.

Sheppard, M. (1995) 'Social Work, Social Sciences and Practice', *British Journal of Social Work*, 25(3):265–93.

Sherraden, M. S. and Martin, J. J. (1994) 'Social Work with Immigrants: International Issues in Service Delivery', *International Social Work*, 37(4):369–84.

Slavin, T. (1998) 'Where Business Begins with the Three Ps', *Observer (Business Section)*, 8 February: 8.

Smith, A. D. (1991) *National Identity*, Harmondsworth: Penguin.

Smith, M. (1997) 'Regions and Regionalism' in White et al. (1997).

Snow, J. and Collee, J. (1996) 'The Rape of an Island Paradise', *Observer (Forests of Life Supplement)*, 29 September.

Sperling, L. and Bretherton, C. (1996) 'Women's Policy Networks and the European Union', *Women's Studies International Forum*, 19(3):303–314.

Standing Committee on Community Affairs (1995) *Report on Aspects of Youth Homelessness*, Canberra: Australian Government Publishing Service.

Stockman, N., Bonney, N. and Xuewen, S. (1995) *Women's Work in East and West: the Dual Burden of Employment and Family Life*, London: University College London Press.

Suin de Boutemard, B. (1990) 'Reflections on the Creation of a Science of Social Work', *International Social Work*, 33(3):255–67.

Sunesson, S., Blomberg, S., Edebalk, P. G., Harryson, L., Magnusson, J., Meeuwisse, A., Petersson, J. and Salonen, T. (1998) 'The Flight from Universalism', *European Journal of Social Work*, 1(1):19–29.

Swift, A. (1998) *Children for Social Change: Education for Citizenship of Street and Working Children in Brazil*, Nottingham: Educational Heretics Press.

Tam, T. S. K. and Yeung, S. (1994) 'Community Perception of Social Welfare and its Relations to Familism, Political Alienation, and Individual Rights: the Case of Hong Kong', *International Social Work*, 37(1):47–60.

Taylor Gooby, P. (1991) *Social Change, Social Welfare and Social Science*, London: Harvester Wheatsheaf.

Thomas, R. (1996) 'Body Count is Excluded from World Leaders Profit and Loss Account', *The Guardian*, 30 October: 15.

Titmus, R. M. (1974) *Social Policy*, London: GAU.

Townsend, P. (1978) *Poverty in the UK: a Survey of Household Resources and Standards of Living*, Berkeley: University of California Press.

Townsend, P. (1993) *The International Analysis of Poverty*, London: Harvester Wheatsheaf.

Trevillion, S. (1997) 'The Globalisation of European Social Work', *Social Work in Europe*, 4(1):1–9.

Tunbridge, L. (1998) 'Spectre of Famine Creeps Up on Sudan', *Sunday Telegraph*, 12 April: 25.

Tutvedt, O. and Young, L. (eds) (1995) *Social Work and the Norwegian Welfare State*, Oslo: Nota Bene.

UN (1964) *Training for Social Work, Fourth International Survey*, New York: United Nations Department of Economic and Social Affairs.

UN (1993a) *Social Development Newsletter*, 31 (January), New York: UN.

UN (1993b) *Social Development Newsletter*, 32 (February), New York: UN.

UN (1994) *Outcome of the World Summit for Social Development: Draft Declaration and Programme of Action*, New York: United Nations.

UN (1996) *Impact of Armed Conflict on Children*, Geneva: United Nations.

UNDP (1995), *UN Development Programme Annual Report*, New York: UNDP.

UNDP (1997), *Human Development Report*, New York: United Nations.

UNHCR (1997) *UNHCR at a Glance*, UNHCR Public Information Sheet, 25 July.

Van der Laan, G. (1998) 'The Professional Role of Social Work in a Market Environment', *European Journal of Social Work*, 1(1):31–40.
Van Wormer, Katherine (1997) *Social Welfare: a World View*, Chicago: Nelson Hall Publications.
Vasoo, S. and Tiong, T. N. (1993) 'Strengthening Service Delivery and Programmes for Senior Citizens', *Asia Pacific Journal of Social Work*, 3(2):1–5.
Vogler, J. (1997) 'Environment and Natural Resources' in White et al. (1997).

Wallis Jones, M. and Lyons, K. (1997) *1996 Employment Survey of Newly Qualified Social Workers*, London: CCETSW.
Wallerstein, I. (1974) *The Modern World System*, New York: Academic Press.
Walton, R. (1975) *Women in Social Work*, London: Routledge.
Webber, M. (1997) 'States and Statehood' in White et al. (1997).
White, B., Little, R. and Smith, M. (eds) (1997) *Issues in World Politics*, Basingstoke: Macmillan Press.
White, K. (1998) 'Indian Summary', *Child Care Forum*, 33 (February): 13.
Williams, F. (1989) *Social Policy: a Critical Introduction*, Oxford: Polity Press.
Wilson, C. (1996) 'Distant Communication in the Caring Sector', unpublished: University of East London.
Wilson, T. and Wilson, D. (eds) (1991) *The State and Social Welfare: the Objectives of Policy*, Harlow: Longman.
Wong, J. (1997) 'Welfare Reform: the New Immigrant Exclusion Act', *Peace and Justice News* (Washington: NASW), Fall: 3.
Woolf, M. (1997) 'Toy firms boycott help for child "slaves"', *The Guardian*, 12 July: 7.
Wright Mills, C. (1959) *The Sociological Imagination*, Oxford: Oxford University Press.

Yadama, G. (1997) 'Tales from the Field: Observations on the Impact of Non-Governmental Organisations', *International Social Work*, 40(2):145–62.
Young, A. (1997) *The Harmony of Illusions: Inventing Post Traumatic Stress Disorder*, Princeton University Press.

General index

abduction of children 85
Aborigines 83, 111
accountability 63
Accra 103
action research 159
active citizenship 52
active labour market policies 98
Adair, Red 139
Addams, Jane 7
adoption of children 85
advanced industrial countries (AICs) 33, 151, 154–5
Afghanistan 39, 70, 114–15, 117
Afro-Caribbeans 112, 126
age dependency ratios 70, 156–7
ageing population 156–7
agenda building 158
Agenda 21 152
aid programmes 4, 97–8, 141
    compared with trade 93–5, 122
AIDS 38, 43, 84, 95, 128
    children affected by 79
Algeria 119, 152–3
alliances 159
America see United States
American Council for Social Work Education 20
'American model' of social work
Amnesty International 39, 43, 127, 152
Argentina 114, 152
arms trade 95

Asia-Pacific Economic Co-operation (APEC) forum 35
assessment of policy 158
assimilation of immigrants 124–7
associations see international social work associations
Asylum and Immigration Appeals Act (1993), UK 119
asylum seekers 51–2, 109, 112–28 passim, 153, 160
    children amongst 115
    Dublin Convention on 121
atrocities 51
austerity measures 35–6
Australia 19, 22, 57, 61–2, 74, 76, 82–3, 100, 111, 115, 117, 134, 145, 156
Austria 55
auxiliary workers 17
'Axminster' air crash 137, 146

Band Aid 97, 141
Bangladesh 58, 60, 70–1, 90–1, 93, 98–9, 102–3, 112, 126, 135, 140, 153–4, 160
Belarus 42
Belgium 117, 142
Beveridgian welfare 55
Bhopal disaster 136
bi-culturalism 125
birth control 70–2, 76, 90, 154
birth rates 90, 156
Bismark, Otto von 55
Body Shop 96

cultural nationalism and cultural
    globalisation 150–1
cultural rights 52
cultural values 69–70
cyclones 134
Czech Republic 42

debt repayments 95
deforestation 26, 96, 134–5
demographic trends 69, 156
Denmark 20, 41–2, 51, 57, 72, 74, 78, 82,
    84, 92, 94, 126
dependency
    of countries 94
    of individuals 56, 105, 126–7
    of older people 157
'Desert Shield' 137
Dhakar 91
difference and diversity, valuing of 3,
    13, 121, 125, 151
disablement 20, 47, 77
disasters 14, 112, 128, 131–48
    advance planning for 148
    classification of 132–8
    natural and man-made 132–3
    nature of 131
    problems and needs associated with
        138–42
    role of the social professions in
        dealing with 142–8
disease 135
distance learning 22
'distorted development' 106
distribution of income and wealth 89–
    90
    between nations 92, 155
divorce 74
domestic violence 77, 79–80
drought 134–5
drug use 83
Dublin Convention on asylum seekers
    121
Dutch experience *see* Netherlands

Earth Summit (1992) 152; *see also*
    Environment and Development
earthquakes 132–3, 138
ecosystems approach to development
    11, 46
education *see* school attendance;

training for social work; vocational
    education
Education for All, UN Declaration on
    90
Egypt 152
El Salvador 136–7, 141
elderly people 38, 69–70, 128
emotional support 145–6
employment-related welfare provision
    8
employment of social workers 60–6
empowerment 7, 46, 77, 106, 125, 159
End Child Prostitution, Pornography
    and Trafficking in Children
    (ECPAT) 102
English Language Empowerment Act
    (1996), US 118
entry qualifications *see* qualifications
Environment and Development, UN
    World Conference on 37; *see also*
    Earth Summit
environmental damage 4, 9, 38, 96, 135–
    6, 138, 148, 155
environmental health services 62
equal opportunities 20, 57, 72, 152
ERASMUS exchange programme 24,
    27–8, 64
ethical business 96, 104
ethics, codes of 23, 43, 66
Ethiopia 123, 135, 141
ethnic cleansing 136–7
ethnic minorities 20, 83, 111, 116, 118,
    121–2, 128, 160
'Europe II' 34
European Association of Schools of
    Social Work (EASSW) 34
European Centre for Community
    Education (ECCE) 27
European Coal and Steel Community
    34
European Court of Justice 121
European Economic Community 34
European Observatory on Homeless-
    ness 91
European Single Market 120
European Union 3, 10, 13, 17, 23, 27, 34–
    5, 43, 45–6, 51–2, 57, 63, 72, 75–82
    passim, 89, 92, 94, 97, 119–22, 151,
    156, 159, 161
    Court of Auditors 122

Uganda 95
unemployment 91, 126; definition of 33
Union Carbide 136
United Kingdom 19, 51–2, 55–8, 61–2,
    73, 76, 80, 82–3, 85, 92, 99, 104, 111–
    12, 115, 117, 126, 145, 157
United Nations 7, 9, 16, 35–8, 51, 74, 84,
    92, 96, 98, 152, 154, 156
  Centre for Human Rights 9, 24, 43
  Centre for Human Settlement 100
  Commission for Social Development
    156
  Declaration on Education for All
    (1990) 90
  Declaration on Primary Health Care
    (1978) 90
  Development Programme (UNDP)
    37–8, 91, 93, 98, 104, 106
  Economic and Social Council 43
  Educational, Scientific and Cultural
    Organisation (UNESCO) 37, 44
  Environment Programme 37
  Global Strategy for Shelter 91
  High Commission for Refugees
    (UNHCR) 37, 110, 113–19, 128,
    141
  International Children's Fund
    (UNICEF) 37–8, 43–4, 76, 90, 94,
    136
  Protection Force (UNPROFOR) 140
  role in dealing with disasters 139–42
  surveys of training for social work 17
  see also International Labour Office;
    Rights of the Child; World
    Health Organisation
United Nations Association 37
United States 3, 7–8, 10–11, 18–20, 37,
    52, 55–6, 58–9, 61–3, 73–4, 76, 78,
    80, 82–3, 90, 99, 114, 117, 119, 126,
    137, 142–3, 156–8
universities 18–19
University of Papua New Guinea 25
University of the Transkei 25
Uruguay Round 35

Vesuvius 134
Vietnam 117
Vietnam War 143
vocational education 105
volcanic eruptions 132–4

voluntary organisations, definition of 8
voluntary sector 58–9, 61, 64, 78, 80
Voluntary Service Overseas (VSO) 38
voting systems of international organi-
    sations 35

war crimes 142, 152
warfare, effects of 9, 110, 113–16, 128,
    136–7
  civilian casualties 136
  vulnerable position of children *see*
    children
  vulnerable position of women 136,
    143
welfare
  definition of 54–5
  different models of 55–6
  global 36
  role of the state 54; *see also* welfare
    state
  'welfare mix' 56
welfare state, the 55–6, 60, 66
women
  advancement and emancipation of
    38, 71
  role and status of 7, 20, 71–4, 93, 99,
    152, 155, 157
  UN Decade for 72
  UN World Conference on (1995) 37,
    72, 99
  see also equal opportunities;
    feminisation; poverty
women's rights 152
women's studies 46
working mothers 73
World Bank 4, 32, 34–6, 51, 94, 154
world building 11
World Census Project 44
World Health Organisation (WHO) 37–
    8, 43, 90
World Psychiatric Association 38
World Trade Organisation (WTO) 35, 96
Worldwatch 110, 113, 122, 153

xenophobia 127

Y Care 38
Yanomami Indians 96
Young Women's Christian Association
    39

Index of authors cited

Abrahamson, P. 56
Abramovitz, M. 158
Agarwal, S. *et al* 73, 103
Angelou, Maya 80
Appleyard, R.T. 112
Apt, N. *see* Agarwal, S. *et al*
Artobolevskiy, S. 135
Asia Pacific Journal of Social Work 70
Attah, M. *see* Agarwal, S. *et al*
Axford, B. 3, 5, 32, 35, 37, 51
Aylwin, N. 59, 61, 64, 144

Bagley, C. 85; *et al* 73, 124
Bali, S. 110–12, 115–17, 119, 128
Bamford, M. 135
Barbaret, R. *et al* 102
Barr, H. 19
Barrett, D. *see* Barbaret, R. *et al*
Barsamian, David 76
Becher, T. 20
Becker, S. 79
Beigel, C. *see* Berren, J. *et al*
Berren, J. *et al* 132
Berridge, G. 51
Berry, L. *see* Cannan, C. *et al*
Blomberg, S. *see* Sunesson, S. *et al*
Boehm, W.W. 25
Bonney, N. *see* Stockman, N. *et al*
Bose, A.B. 22
Bradshaw, J. *see* Kennedy, S. *et al*
Brauns, H.J. 16
Bretherton, C. 46

Brittain, V. 36
Brobeck, H. 28
Brody, E. 125
Brook, R. 146
Brooks, E.E. 79
Brown, P. 135
Browne, A. 92
Burt, W. 9–10

Campbell, J. 157
Campfens, H. 34, 39
Cannan, C. *et al* 17, 23, 34, 41, 57, 59, 76
Caplan, G. 142–3
Castles, S. 110, 118
Cemlyn, S. 17, 24, 100–1
Cetingok, M. 28
Chetkow-Yanoov, B. 147
Cheung, S.K. 59
Chi, I. 59
Chipaka, S. 120
Cho, G. 32
Chomsky, N. 76
Chow, N. 40, 124
Clark, C. *see* Leung, V.W.K. *et al*
Clarke, J. 10, 33, 54
Clarkson, E. 28
Cochrane, A. 10, 33, 54
Cocozza, L. 17
Coleman, R. 27
Collee, J. 96
Colton, M. 82, 83
Connelly, N. 18